高职高专"十三五"规划教材
辽宁省职业教育改革发展示范校建设成果

职场实用英语教程

贾琳琳　王晶晶　于　莹　主编

化学工业出版社
·北京·

《职场实用英语教程》设计了 8 个场景的主题：人际沟通、职业生涯规划、求职应聘、入职培训、办公自动化、会议、出差、外事接待。全书以李欣同学的大学生活以及工作经历为主线，将各个主题连接在一起。每个主题设计若干学习情境，每个学习情境设置多个任务，每个任务后附有相关的知识帮助学生理解并完成任务。每个学习情境之后各设置一组相关会话或实用文体写作范例，将项目教学法、情境教学法与体验式教学法融合到英语教学中，以增强学生英语语言应用能力。

《职场实用英语教程》可供高职高专各专业学生作为英语教材使用，还可供社会各界人士作为学习实用英语的教材使用。

图书在版编目（CIP）数据

职场实用英语教程/贾琳琳，王晶晶，于莹主编. —北京：化学工业出版社，2018.9（2023.1 重印）
高职高专"十三五"规划教材
ISBN 978-7-122-32806-9

Ⅰ.①职… Ⅱ.①贾… ②王… ③于… Ⅲ.①英语-高等职业教育-教材 Ⅳ.①H319.39

中国版本图书馆 CIP 数据核字（2018）第 180739 号

责任编辑：满悦芝　石　磊　　　　　　　文字编辑：李　曦
责任校对：王素芹　　　　　　　　　　　装帧设计：张　辉

出版发行：化学工业出版社（北京市东城区青年湖南街 13 号　邮政编码 100011）
印　　装：北京科印技术咨询服务有限公司数码印刷分部
787mm×1092mm　1/16　印张 18　字数 441 千字　2023 年 1 月北京第 1 版第 5 次印刷

购书咨询：010-64518888　　售后服务：010-64518899
网　　址：http://www.cip.com.cn
凡购买本书，如有缺损质量问题，本社销售中心负责调换。

定　　价：49.00 元

《职场实用英语教程》编写人员名单

主　编　贾琳琳　王晶晶　于　莹

副主编　杜彬彬　陈　越　刘　涛　井　镭

参　编　高　嵩　姜　莹　李赫男　张丽娜

　　　　赵　新　王　婧　张晓星　郑黎明

主　审　李　娟

序 FOREWORD

世界职业教育发展的经验和我国职业教育的历程都表明，职业教育是提高国家核心竞争力的要素之一。近年来，我国高等职业教育发展迅猛，成为我国高等教育的重要组成部分。《国务院关于加快发展现代职业教育的决定》、教育部《关于全面提高高等职业教育教学质量的若干意见》中都明确要大力发展职业教育，并指出职业教育要以服务发展为宗旨，以促进就业为导向，积极推进教育教学改革，通过课程、教材、教学模式和评价方式的创新，促进人才培养质量的提高。

盘锦职业技术学院依托于省示范校建设，近几年大力推进以能力为本位的项目化课程改革，教学中以学生为主体，以教师为主导，以典型工作任务为载体，对接德国双元制职业教育培训的国际轨道，教学内容和教学方法以及课程建设的思路都发生了很大的变化。因此开发一套满足现代职业教育教学改革需要、适应现代高职院校学生特点的项目化课程教材迫在眉睫。

为此学院成立专门机构，组成课程教材开发小组。教材开发小组实行项目管理，经过企业走访与市场调研、校企合作制定人才培养方案及课程计划、校企合作制定课程标准、自编讲义、试运行、后期修改完善等一系列环节，通过两年多的努力，顺利完成了四个专业类别20本教材的编写工作。其中，职业文化与创新类教材4本，化工类教材5本，石油类教材6本，财经类教材5本。本套教材内容涵盖较广，充分体现了现代高职院校的教学改革思路，充分考虑了高职院校现有教学资源、企业需求和学生的实际情况。

职业文化类教材突出职业文化实践育人建设项目成果；旨在推动校园文化与企业文化的有机结合，实现产教深度融合、校企紧密合作。教师在深入企业调研的基础上，与合作企业专家共同围绕工作过程系统化的理论原则，按照项目化课程设计教材内容，力图满足学生职业核心能力和职业迁移能力提升的需要。

化工类教材在项目化教学改革背景下，采用德国双元培育的教学理念，通过对化工企业的工作岗位及典型工作任务的调研、分析，将真实的工作任务转化为学习任务，建立基于工作过程系统化的项目化课程内容，以"工学结合"为出发点，根据实训环境模拟工作情境，尽量采用图表、图片等形式展示，对技能和技术理论做全面分析，力图体现实用性、综合性、典型性和先进性的特色。

石油类教材涵盖了石油钻探、油气层评价、油气井生产、维修和石油设备操作使用等领域，拓展发展项目化教学与情境教学，以利于提高学生学习的积极性、改善课堂教学效果，对高职石油类特色教材的建设做出积极探索。

财经类教材采用理实一体的教学设计模式，具有实战性；融合了国家全新的财经法律法规，具有前瞻性；注重了与其他课程之间的联系与区别，具有逻辑性；内容精准、图文并茂、通俗易懂，具有可读性。

在此，衷心感谢为本套教材策划、编写、出版付出辛勤劳动的广大教师、相关企业人员以及化学工业出版社的编辑们。尽管我们对教材的编写怀抱敬畏之心，坚持一丝不苟的专业态度，但囿于自己的水平和能力，错误和疏漏之处在所难免。敬请学界同仁和读者不吝指正。

盘锦职业技术学院　院长

2018 年 9 月

前言 PREFACE

本教程依据教育部颁布的《高等职业教育英语课程教学基本要求（试行）》，并贯彻"实用为主、够用为度、与时俱进"的编写原则，结合项目化教学理念，紧扣"高等学校英语应用能力考试（A、B级）"大纲要求，融入国内外职业英语教育最新的教学理念，在反复探讨、研究的基础上编写而成。项目化教学是师生通过共同实施一个完整的项目工作而进行的教学活动。其实施的流程如下。①明确项目任务：教师提出任务，学生讨论。②制订计划：学生制订，教师审查并给予指导。③实施计划：学生分组及明确分工，合作完成。④检查评估：学生自我评估，教师评价。⑤归档或应用：记录归档，应用实践。

本书遵循语言学习的一般规律，在整体设计上，摒弃了学科本位的学术理论中心设计，广泛收集了与日常生活和职业生涯息息相关的话题，选取了大量相互联系的、符合实际需求的语言材料，充分考虑了课程材料的生活性、前沿性、趣味性以及科学性，涵盖了全球化背景下实用英语基本方向的内容。

为了配合高职高专各专业有效课堂的开展以及项目化教学的需求，本教材以"工学结合、能力为本"的教育理念为指导，以提高学生的英语交际能力与综合职业素质为目标，设计了8个场景的主题：人际沟通、职业生涯规划、求职应聘、入职培训、办公自动化、会议、出差、外事接待。全书以李欣同学的大学生活以及工作经历为主线，将各个主题联系在一起。每个主题设计若干学习情境（Situations），每个学习情境设置多个任务（Tasks），每个任务后附有相关的知识帮助学生理解并完成任务。每个学习情境之后各设置一组相关会话或实用文体写作范例，将项目教学法、情境教学法与体验式教学法融合到英语课堂教学中，以增强学生的英语语言应用能力。

本书的框架由贾琳琳、王晶晶提出，全书内容由李娟主审。第一单元由于莹撰写；第

二、三单元由王晶晶撰写；第四单元由杜彬彬撰写；第五单元由陈越撰写；第六单元由井镭撰写；第七单元由贾琳琳撰写；第八单元由刘涛撰写。

王婧参与了第一单元的审稿工作；赵新参与了第二单元的审稿工作；张晓星参与了第三单元的审稿工作；李赫男参与了第四单元的审稿工作；姜莹参与了第五单元的审稿工作；张丽娜参与了第六单元内容的审稿工作；高嵩参与了第七单元的审稿工作，并为此章提供了相关图片；郑黎明为第一、三单元提供了相关图片；本书在编写过程中还得到盘锦职业技术学院基础部李朝阳主任的大力支持，在此一并表示衷心感谢。

由于编者水平有限，时间紧张，教材的编写难免存在不妥或疏漏之处，诚挚地希望广大专家及读者批评指正。我们真诚地期待您的每一条宝贵意见和建议，联系邮箱：46316830@qq.com。

编　者

2019 年 7 月

目录 CONTENTS

Unit One Interpersonal Communication

1.1 Establish Friendship

Section One: Tasks

Situation 1: *Liu Xu is a freshman and Wang Qin is a sophomore. They meet on the first day of a new semester and they are greeting each other on campus. Make a conversation, and then act with your partner.*

Situation 2: *Liu Xu is going to register with the help of Wang Qin and they are talking about the registration procedure. Make a conversation, and then act with your partner.*

Situation 3: *After registration, Liu Xu goes to his dormitory and he greets his new roommates. Make a conversation, and then act with your partners.*

Section Two: Related Information

How to Establish Friendship

Friends have a huge impact on your happiness. Good friends relieve stress, provide comfort and joy, prevent loneliness and isolation, and even strengthen your health.

We tend to make friends with people we cross paths with regularly: people we go to school with, work with, or live close to. The more we see someone, the more chances we have to develop friendship. [1]Another big factor in friendship is common interests. We tend to be drawn by people we share things with: a hobby, the same cultural background, and the same career path.

When you are going to meet some new people, try to open new experiences. Not everything you try will be successful but you can always learn from the experience and hopefully have some fun.

Volunteering can be a great way to help others while also meeting new people.

Volunteering also gives you the opportunity to practice and develop your social skills regularly.

Take a class or join a club to meet people with common interests，such as a book group，dinner club，or sports team can help you find local groups and connect with others who share similar interests. Attend clubs，book readings，lectures，or other community events where you can meet people with similar interests. [2]

Behave like someone new to the area. Even if you've lived in the same area for years，take the time to re-explore your neighborhood's attractions. New arrivals tend to visit these places first，and they're often keen to meet new people and establish friendships，too.

Unplug. It's difficult to meet new people in any social situation if you're more interested in your phone than the people around you. [3] Remove your headphones and your smart phone while you're in the campus or waiting for a bus，for example. Making eye contact and exchanging small talks with strangers are great practice for making connections[4] —and you never know where it may lead！

Vocabulary

establish [ɪˈstæblɪʃ] *vt.* 建立，创建

relieve [rɪˈliːv] *v.* 救济；减轻；解除

prevent [prɪˈvent] *v.* 预防；防止，阻止；挡住

isolation [aɪsəˈleɪʃ(ə)n] *n.* 隔离；孤立

strengthen [ˈstreŋθ(ə)n] *vt.* 加强；巩固

career [kəˈrɪə] *n.* 生涯；职业；事业

volunteer [ˌvɒlənˈtɪə] *vi.* 志愿 *n.* 志愿者

opportunity [ˌɒpəˈtjuːnəti] *n.* 时机，机会

behave [bɪˈheɪv] *v.* 表现；举止端正

keen [kiːn] *adj.* 敏锐的，渴望的；热心的

unplug [ʌnˈplʌg] *vt.* 去掉……的障碍物；拔去

remove [rɪˈmuːv] *v.* 移动，开除

headphone [ˈhedfəun] *n.* 双耳式耳机，头戴式耳机

exchange [ɪksˈtʃeɪndʒ] *v.* 交换；兑换

cross paths with   不期而遇

have an impact on   对……产生影响，对……造成冲击

close to   接近于；在附近

care about   担心，关心

connect with   连接；与……联系

exchange…with   与……交换

Notes

1. The more we see someone，the more chances we have to develop friendship. 我们见面的

次数越多，发展友谊的可能性就越大。The more…the more…越……越……此结构为"the＋比较级，the＋比较级"结构，意为"越……，（就）越……"。

2. Attend clubs，book readings，lectures，or other community events where you can meet people with similar interests. 参加俱乐部，读书会，听讲座或者参与其他社区活动，在那里你会遇到与你有相似兴趣爱好的伙伴。where you can meet people with similar interests 为定语从句，where 在从句中作地点状语，修饰先行词 community events。

3. It's difficult to meet new people in any social situation if you're more interested in your phone than the people around you. 如果你对你的手机比周围的人更感兴趣，那么在任何社交场合都很难结识新朋友。It's difficult to meet new people in any social situation 为"it＋系动词＋形容词＋不定式"结构，其中 it 为形式主语，真正的主语为 to meet new people in any social situation，if you're more interested in your phone than the people around you 为 if 引导的条件状语从句，be more interested in…than…为比较结构，意为"对前者比后者更感兴趣"。

4. Making eye contact and exchanging small talks with strangers are great practice for making connections. 你会发现与陌生人进行眼神交流并进行短暂交谈是一种很好的交际方式。此句中 making eye contact and exchanging small talks with strangers 为两个并列的动名词短语作主语，意为"进行眼神交流和与陌生人短暂交谈"。

Section Three：Situational Task Samples

Situation 1：Li Xin is a freshman and Wang Lin is a sophomore of the college. They are talking with each other on the playground.（A：Wang Lin；B：Li Xin）

A：Nice to meet you! Welcome to our college. My name is Wang Lin.

B：Nice to meet you，too! My name is Li Xin. I'm a freshman and this is my first time to come to this city. Everything on campus is new to me.

A：Oh，that's what I felt when I first came to the college. By the way，what is your major?

B：I major in[1] accounting. How about you?

A：I major in nursing.

B：That's a hot major[2]. I want to go to the registration office[3]. Would you like to show me the way?

A：Of course，please follow me. I will show you around the campus later.

B：Thank you very much.

A：It's my pleasure.

Situation 2：Li Xin is a freshman and Wang Lin is a sophomore of the college. Li Xin is going to register with the help of Wang Lin and they are talking about the registration procedure.（A：Li Xin；B：Wang Lin）

A：Good morning!

B：Good morning，which department have you been admitted to?

A：Financial Department. I major in accounting.

B：That's a hot major. Have you got registered?

A：Not yet. I don't know what I shall do.

B: You should get registered at the reception desk.

A: Is the registration procedure complicated?

B: Not really, first, there will be a level test[4]. Please don't forget to bring your ID card and Letter of Admission[5], then you should fill in some forms.

A: Sounds easy, what else?

B: You will get your room number and then get registered in the dormitory. After getting the key, you can put your luggage there.

A: What should I do then?

B: Finally, You can go to the financial office[6] to pay the tuition[7] or get the receipt if you have paid by bank transfer.

A: OK, I got it. Thank you very much.

B: You are welcome. If you need any help, please don't hesitate to ask me.

A: Yes, I will.

Situation 3: *Li Xin and Wang Qi are both freshmen. Li Xin goes to the dormitory and talks with his new roommate Wang Qi in Room 304.*（*A*: *Li Xin*; *B*: *Wang Qi*）

A: Hello, everyone. My name is Li Xin.

B: Nice to meet you, Li Xin. My name is Wang Qi. Oh, here is your bed.

A: Thank you. It's interesting to live with roommates. I'm very excited.

B: So am I. Is this the first time you leave your home?

A: Yeah, I think most of us will be homesick.

B: Well, it's a new beginning. Where is your hometown?

A: I'm from Dandong.

B: Oh, it's a beautiful city with popular seaside and delicious food.

A: Yes, welcome to Dandong during the summer vocation. Where are you from?

B: I'm a local person[8].

A: Great, would you like to show me around the city on weekends?

B: With pleasure!

A: Thank you.

B: You're welcome.

Notes

1. major in 主修
2. hot major 热门专业
3. registration office 登记处
4. level test 水平测试
5. Letter of Admission 录取通知书
6. financial office 财务办公室
7. pay the tuition 付学费
8. local person 当地人

Section Four：Functional Expression Bank

Greetings（打招呼）

1. Nice to meet you! /I am delighted to meet you! 见到您很高兴。

2. How is everything? 一切如何？

3. How have you been? 您近来可好？

4. What brings you here? 什么风把您吹来了？

5. Long time no see! 好久不见!

Responding to Greetings（回复打招呼）

1. Nice/Pleased/Delighted to meet you，too. 我也很高兴认识您。

2. Couldn't be better/worse. 很好/糟。

3. Just fine. 还好。

4. As usual. 老样子。

5. Not too good，I'm afraid. 我觉得情况不是很妙。

Introducing Yourself（介绍自己）

1. Hello，my name is… 您好，我叫……

2. Hi，I am… 您好，我叫……

3. How do you do? My name is… 您好，我叫……

4. Allow me to introduce myself. 请允许我做自我介绍。

Introducing Somebody（介绍他人）

1. Let me introduce her to you. 让我介绍她给您认识。

2. I'd like to introduce…to you. 我想给您介绍一下……

3. This is… 这位是……

4. Allow me to introduce… 请允许我为大家介绍……

Responding to an Introduction（回复自我介绍）

1. Pleased/Glad/Nice to see you. 很高兴认识您。

2. How do you do? 您好!

3. It's a pleasure to meet you. 很荣幸认识您。

4. I've long heard of you. 久仰，久仰。

Greeting for Long Time No See（好久未见面人之间的问候）

1. How are you，Mrs. Li? I haven't seen you for about half a year. Have you moved or something else?
   您好，李太太，大概有半年没见到您了，您是搬家了，还是有其他什么事了？

2. Hello，John. I'm glad to see you. What have you been doing since I saw you last time?
   您好，约翰，很高兴见到您，自从上次见面后您怎么样？

3. Good heavens，John! Haven't seen you for ages. 天啊，约翰！好几年没看到您了。

4. Hello，John! I haven't seen you for a long time. How have you been? /How is everything? 您好，约翰，好久不见! 过得怎么样? /一切都好吗?

Greeting for Coincidence（巧遇时打招呼）

1. What a surprise to see you here! 在这里见到您太巧了！

2. How nice to bump into you. 碰见您太好了。

3. Fancy seeing you here! 真想不到在这儿见到您。

4. Hello，Tom，where did you spring from? 您好，汤姆，您从哪儿冒出来的？

5. Hello there，what a coincidence! 您好，真凑巧！

Greeting on Behalf of Others （请代为问候）

1. Kindly send my regards to your parents.【正式】请代我向您父母问好。

2. Please remember me to all your colleagues.【正式】请代我向您所有的同事问好。

3. Please present my compliments/respects to your manager.

   【正式】请代我向您们经理致意。

4. Say hello to John.【非正式】代我向约翰问好。

5. Give my love to Mary.【非正式】向玛丽问好。

回答可用：

1. Thank you，I shan't fail to do so. 谢谢，我会这样去做的。

2. Thank you，I will. 谢谢，我会的。

3. Certainly，I will. 当然，会的。

Expressing Others' Greetings （转达他人的问候）

1. My managing director asks to be remembered to your board of directors.

   【正式】我的常务董事让我替他向你们董事会的董事们问好。

2. Please give your manager my director's warmest greetings.

   【正式】请向你们经理转达我们主任的最热烈的问候。

3. Mary sends her love to your wife. 玛丽向您的妻子问好。

4. Please remember Mr. Black to Mr. Smith. 请代布莱克先生向史密斯先生问好。

5. John asked me to say hello to you. 约翰叫我代他向您问好。

Asking Personal Information （询问个人信息）

1. May/Could I have your name，please? 请问您叫什么名字？

2. Where do you come from? 您从哪儿来？

3. What do you think of the college life? 您觉得大学生活怎样？

4. How do you like your roommates? 您的室友们怎样？

Responding to Personal Questions （回复个人信息）

1. My name is…/I'm…我叫……

2. I come from…/I'm from…我来自……

3. I think the college life is colorful. 我认为大学生活是丰富多彩的。

4. My roommates are nice/easygoing. 我的室友们都很友好/很好相处。

Section Five：Culture Tips

中西方问候方式的差异

英语和汉语的问候方式有很大差异。在中国，我们熟悉的朋友见面时常会问候："上哪儿去?""吃饭了吗?"。如果把这些问候翻译成英语就是"Where are you going?""Have you eaten yet?"。英美国家的人听到诸如此类话可能会引起误解,他们会认为"Have you eaten yet?"的意思是您在向他发出进餐邀请。而"Where are you going?"这样的问候会让对方认为你的问候不得体,因为去哪儿这不关你的事。英美国家的人在见面问候时一般会用"Good morning/afternoon/evening!"("早上好/下午好/晚上好!"),"Nice to meet you!"("见到你很高兴!"),"How are you doing?"("近来好吗?")。关系亲密的朋友可以直接用"Hi!"或"Hello!"。中西方告别中使用的语言也不相同。在中国,我们送别客人时常用"慢走!""再来啊!"等。这也不符合英美人的习惯,他们送别客人时常用"Goodbye!"("再见!"),"See you later!"("回头见!")。

译　文

第二部分:相关信息

如何建立友谊

朋友对你的幸福有巨大的影响。好朋友可以帮你减压,带给你安慰和快乐,让你远离孤独和寂寞,甚至还会改善你的健康。

我们倾向于与我们经常见面的人交朋友:比如和我们一起上学、工作或比邻居住的人。我们见面的次数越多,发展友谊的可能性就越大。建立友谊的另一个重要因素是共同的兴趣爱好。与我们有共同之处的人更容易吸引我们:相同的爱好,共同的文化背景,共同的职业道路。

当你想结交一些新朋友时,尝试去接受新的经历。不是你每次尝试都会成功,但你总是可以从这些经历中有所收获并可能得到乐趣。

志愿服务是个帮助别人的好方法,同时也能结交新朋友。志愿服务也让你经常有机会锻炼和提高自己的社交技巧。

参加课程或加入俱乐部可以遇到和你有相同兴趣的人,例如一个阅读小组,晚餐俱乐部或运动队,都可以帮助你找到当地的团体并与你有相似兴趣爱好的人相互联系。参加俱乐部,读书会,听讲座或者参与其他社区活动,在那里你会遇到与你有相似兴趣爱好的伙伴。

行为举止表现得像个新人。即使你已经在同一个地区住了多年,还是要花时间去你附近吸引人的地方逛逛。新来的人们往往先去这些地方,他们通常渴望结识新朋友并建立友谊。

去除障碍。如果你对你的手机比周围的人更感兴趣,那么在任何社交场合都很难结识新朋友。例如,当你在校园里散步或是等公共汽车的时候,收起耳机和手机。你会发现与陌生人进行眼神交流并进行短暂交谈是一种很好的交往方式,而且你永远不知道它会把你带向何方!

第三部分:情境任务范例

情境1:李欣是大一新生,王林是这所学院的大二学生。他们正在操场上交谈。(*A*:王林;*B*:李欣)

A：很高兴见到你，欢迎到我们学院就读，我叫王林。

B：见到你也很高兴，我叫李欣，是名大一新生。我第一次到这个城市，校园里的一切对我来说都很新鲜。

A：我第一次到这所学院时跟你的感受是一样的。顺便问一下，你是学什么专业的？

B：我主修会计。你学什么专业？

A：我主修护理。

B：护理是个热门专业。我想去注册，你能告诉我在哪儿吗？

A：当然，请跟我走，过一会儿，我会带你在校园里转转。

B：非常感谢。

A：不客气。

情境2：李欣是大一新生，王林是这所学院的大二学生。李欣在王林的帮助下将去注册，他们两个人正在谈论有关注册的流程。（A：李欣；B：王林）

A：早上好！

B：早上好，你被哪个系录取了？

A：财经系，我主修会计。

B：那是个热门的专业。你注册了吗？

A：还没有。我不知道该做些什么。

B：你应该去接待处注册。

A：注册的流程复杂吗？

B：不是很复杂。首先，他们会进行水平测试，别忘了带上身份证和录取通知书，然后你需要填一些表格。

A：听起来挺容易的，还需要做什么？

B：你会拿到你的寝室门牌号，然后去寝室登记。拿到钥匙后，你就可以把行李放寝室了。

A：然后我还应该做什么？

B：最后，你可以去财务办公室交学费，如果你已经通过银行转账，你就可以领取缴费单据。

A：好的，我明白了，非常感谢你。

B：不客气。如果还有什么需要帮助的地方，可以尽管问我。

A：好的，我会的。

情境3：李欣和王奇都是大一新生，李欣来到他的宿舍304和他的新室友王奇交谈。（A：李欣；B：王奇）

A：大家好，我叫李欣。

B：很高兴认识你，我叫王奇。噢，这是你的床位。

A：谢谢你。和室友们一起住很有趣，我非常兴奋。

B：我也是，这是你第一次离开家吗？

A：是的。我认为大部分大一新生都会想家的。

B：大学是一个新的开始。你的家乡在哪儿？

A：我来自丹东。

B：噢，丹东是个美丽的海滨城市，而且还有很多美食。

A：是的，欢迎你暑假到丹东玩。你的家乡在哪里？

B：我是本地人。

A：太好了，周末你愿意带我逛逛这座城市吗？

B：非常乐意。

A：谢谢。

B：不客气。

1.2 Take an Outward Bound

Section One: Tasks

Situation 1: *Liu Xu and his classmate Yang Wei who are both freshmen are talking about the military training on the playground during the rest time. Make a conversation, and then act with your partner.*

Situation 2: *A week later, Liu Xu and Wang Lin meets on campus and they are talking about the feeling of military training. Make a conversation, and then act with your partner.*

Situation 3: *A month later, the college organizes an outward bound, Liu Xu who participates in it talks about the activity with his classmate Yang Wei. Make a conversation, and then act with your partner.*

Section Two: Related Information

How to Build a Successful Work Team

Teamwork is the actions of individuals, brought together for a common purpose or goal, which subordinates the needs of the individual to the needs of the group.[1] In essence, each person in the team puts aside his or her individual needs to work towards the larger group objective. The interactions among the members and the work they complete are called teamwork.

People in every workplace talk about building the team, working as a team and my team, but few understand how to gain the experience of team work or how to develop an effective team. Here are some tips for building a successful work team.

Determine the purpose and goals of the team. You may write a business plan that covers the mission of the team. All team members must have a copy of this document.[2]

Help employees understand what goals need to be met and how they can be met by creating a yearlong plan that provides structure and clarity.[3] Help employees understand the prioritization of the goals and focus on short-term goals.

Choose the members of the team. After describing the team's goals, plug in collaborators that can execute each goal. Team members must not be limited to employees. They can include consultants or freelancers with special expertise. Assign a team leader who is an experienced and ethical role model. He/She must challenge the team members while providing respect and support.[4]

Define each team member's duties. Lay out the roles of each member clearly in a document for members to sign. Connect the team with the company's vision and mission.

Conduct team meetings at the end of each term to reassess what goals have been met, what priorities need to change and whether implemented strategies need adjustment. Conduct teambuilding exercises can create a cohesive team. Successful teams stem from good relationships, so business teams must create these relationships quickly.

Vocabulary

subordinate [sə'bɔːdɪnet] *vt*. 使……居下位，使从属，使服从

yearlong ['jɪəlɒɪ] *adj*. 整整一年的

prioritization [praɪɔɪretaɪ'zeɪʃn] *n*. 优先次序；优化

plug [plʌg] *vi*. 塞住，插入

collaborator [kə'læbəreɪtə] *n*. 合作者

execute ['eksɪkjuːt] *vt*. 实行；执行

freelancer ['friːlɑːnsə(r)] *n*. 自由职业者；自由记者

expertise [ˌekspɜː'tiːz] *n*. 专门知识；专门技术

assign [ə'saɪn] *vt*. 分配；指派

ethical ['eθɪk(ə)l] *adj*. 伦理的；道德的

conduct ['kɒndʌkt] *v*. 组织；引导；表现

reassess [ˌriːə'ses] *v*. 再估价；再评价

implement ['ɪmplɪment] *vt*. 实施，执行

adjustment [ə'dʒʌstmənt] *n*. 调解，调整

cohesive [kəʊ'hiːsɪv] *adj*. 凝聚的；有结合力的

stem [stem] *v*. 阻止，遏制

in essence　本质上，大体上，其实

put aside　搁；撇开，储备

lay out　安排；列出

stem from　基于；出于；由……造成的

Notes

1. Teamwork is the actions of individuals，brought together for a common purpose or goal，which subordinates the needs of the individual to the needs of the group. 团队合作是指为了实现共同的目的或目标将个人的行为汇集在一起的行为，团队合作使个人的需求服从于团队的需求。brought together 过去分词短语作定语，修饰 the actions of individuals，which subordinates the needs of the individual to the needs of the group 为非限定性定语从句，which 是关系代词，在从句中作主语，修饰先行词 teamwork。

2. copy of this document 此文件的副本

3. Help employees understand what goals need to be met and how they can be met by creating a yearlong plan that provides structure and clarity. 帮助员工了解需要达到什么目标，以及通过制订一个结构清晰的年度计划帮助他们了解如何实现这些目标。what goals need to be met and how they can be met 是宾语从句，作 understand 的宾语，意为"需要达到什么目标和如何实现这些目标"。that provides structure and clarity 为定语从句，that 是关系代词，修饰先行词 a yearlong plan，在从句中作主语。

4. He/She must challenge the team members while providing respect and support. 他或她在给予团队成员尊重和支持的同时必须能对他们提出挑战。while providing respect and support 是时间状语从句，从句的主语与主句主语一致可省略从句的主语＋谓语的一部分（一般是 be）。

Section Three：Situational Task Samples

Situation 1：*Li Xin and Wang Qi who are freshmen in the same class are walking on the playground and they are talking about the military training.*（*A*：*Li Xin*；*B*：*Wang Qi*）

A：Our campus is big and beautiful，right?

B：Yes，it's much bigger than I have expected. And we have the military training here.

A：You look much stronger than I first met you here.

B：Really? And my face was tanned，right?

A：So am I. Sometimes I feel tired，but it is good for our health.

B：I do agree with you，some of our classmates have complained about it，but I think military training can build our strong will and good discipline[1].

A：That's right，by the way，have you got this kind of training before?

B：I attended an outward bound[2] in the last summer vocation.

A：I heard of that. Is that interesting?

B：Yes，very interesting.

A：I'll have a try if it is possible. Look，the training starts. Let's go.

B：OK，let's go.

Situation 2：*Li Xin is a freshman and Li Lin is a sophomore. They are talking about the feeling of military training on the playground.*（*A*：*Li Lin*；*B*：*Li Xin*）

A：Glad to see you again. Do you adapt yourself to the college life?

B：Yes，better than before，we just finished our military training.

A：What do you think of military training life?

B：Oh, I felt almost fatigued to death[3] after the first day of the military training.

A：Is there anything difficult for you?

B：Yes, It's difficult for me to shoot accurately. I can't shoot well.

A：Is there anyone giving up half way?

B：Oh, no, everyone did his part in earnest[4]. Our instructor said that they had training every day.

A：Being a soldier is not easy.

B：Yes, soldiers are often our role models, I think it's quite a different experience for me.

A：The military training gave us the importance of good discipline and teamwork.

B：Yes, I got a kick out of[5] military training.

Situation 3：*Li Xin and Wang Lin are both freshmen. They are talking about an outward bound on campus.*（*A*：*Wang Lin*；*B*：*Li Xin*）

A：What did you do last Sunday?

B：I had an outward bound training.

A：Oh, fantastic, it was very stimulated and terrible, right?

B：Yes, and some programs were very interesting.

A：What programs did you have?

B：Hand In Hand, Entrapment, Trolley Bus, Trinity, Descending[6] and so on.

A：Sounds interesting, did you finish them all?

B：Yes, I took part in all the programs.

A：Which program was the most difficult?

B：Descending, this training required players to descend from the height of 30 meters. Since I was a little fear of heights, descending was very difficult for me.

A：Yes, when I went to that height for the first time, I was trembled in my legs. But I think you must enjoy the happiness after overcoming that difficulty.

B：Oh, really. Action is the best method to conquer the fear[7]. And I got a lot from this outward bound training.

A：Of course. You are so brave.

Notes

1. build our strong will and good discipline 锻炼我们坚强的意志力，养成我们自律的好习惯

2. outward bound 拓展训练，户外训练项目，其目的是为了培养合作精神和进取意识。

3. feel/be fatigued to death 累坏了。fatigue *v*. 使疲劳

4. everyone did his part in earnest 每个人都尽自己最大的努力。earnest *n*. 认真

5. get a kick out of…从某事中得到乐趣

6. Hand In Hand, Entrapment, Trolley Bus, Trinity, Descending（拓展训练项目）牵手、偷天陷阱、有轨电车、三人行和下降

7. Action is the best method to conquer the fear. 行动是克服恐惧的最好方法。

Section Four: Functional Expression Bank

Military Training Condition（军训条件）

1. We must get up bright and early every morning. 我们必须每天一大早起床。

2. We drilled more than six hours a day, though it was hot at the time.
   尽管那时天气炎热，我们每天都要训练6个多小时。

3. It is hot and humid, we are sweaty and sticky all the time.
   天气闷热潮湿，我们一直流汗，身上黏黏的。

4. Three days later, our faces were tanned. 三天后，我们的脸都晒黑了。

Military Training Procedure（军训过程）

1. What do you think of your military training life here? 你觉得这儿的军训生活怎么样？

2. I was almost fatigued to death after the first day of military training.
   第一天军训后我都快要累死了。

3. Come on! It's not easy to get started. 坚持！万事开头难。

4. I've just trying to catch up with others. 我正努力赶上其他人。

5. During training, each of us did his part in earnest.
   在训练中，我们每个人都认真地完成了自己的任务。

6. The unique principle of military training lies in obedience. 军训唯一的原则就是服从。

Military Training Results（军训结果）

1. Our team went all out to win in shooting performance.
   我们队竭尽全力在射击表演中获得胜利。

2. That's the result of exercise in military training. 这是在军训中锻炼的结果。

3. I've no doubt of your ability all along. 我一直确信你有这个能力。

4. He hits the center of a target to a hair. 他射中靶心毫厘不差。

Military Training Experience（军训经验）

1. I get a kick out of military training. 我从军训中得到了很大乐趣。

2. Military training is more interesting than I expected. 军训比我期望的更加有趣。

3. It's quite a different experience for me. 对我来说它是一段截然不同的经历。

4. Although military training was very tiring, it benefited me greatly, and I began to enjoy
   the life like this. 军训虽然很累，却让我受益匪浅，我开始喜欢上这种生活了。

Usual Events of Outward Bound Training（拓展训练常见训练项目）

Can Shoe 罐头鞋	Combined Fleet 联合舰队
The Darkness 黑暗	Trinity 三人行
Egg-craft 鸡蛋飞行器	Suspended Ladder 天梯
Spider Web with Negotiation 交易电网	Descending 下降
Landmine Cleaning In the Bush 荆棘排雷	Blind House-outline 盲人绳房

Blind Square 盲阵

Blind Drawing 盲屋

Magic Carpet 魔毯

Shepherd 牧羊

Close Shave 千钧一发

Hand in Hand 牵手

Clear up Nuclear Waste 清除核废料

Speed 生死时速

Body Chess 十面埋伏

Space-time Tunnel 时空隧道

Broken Bridge 断桥

Rock Climbing 攀岩

Trust Fall 背摔

Final Wall 求生

Get Over Barrier 越障

Mining for Gold 挖金矿

The Ultimate Cube 终极魔方

Tower Building 筑塔

Crocodiles Lake 鳄鱼潭

Lonely Island 孤岛

Aim for Outward Bound（拓展训练目的）

1. In outward bound activities，we can know one's own advantages and shortcomings.
在拓展训练活动中，我们可以了解自己的优势和不足。

2. We can understand and help each other，reach the goal by harmonious cooperation.
我们可以相互理解并互相帮助取长补短，团结协作达成目标。

3. Combined Fleet can make team members have fun to cooperate with the team.
联合舰队可以让队员们感受团队合作的快乐。

4. Landmine Cleaning In the Bush can foster the ability of planning, organizing and carefully cooperation. 荆棘排雷这项活动可以培养队员计划、组织和精细合作的能力。

5. Blind Square is to test the importance of trust in building team and achieving goals.
盲阵这个项目是为了测试信任在团队建设和目标达成中的重要性。

6. The goal of Lonely Island is to understand the importance of sharing information and cooperating across functions. 孤岛项目的目的是理解在跨部门间分享信息和合作的重要性。

7. Descending tells us adjusting plans according to the necessity of objectives is the best method to conquer the fear.
下降这个项目告诉我们根据目标需要调整行动计划是克服恐惧的最好办法。

8. Egg-craft is to test the ability of how to make prompt and efficient decision in short time. 鸡蛋飞行器这个项目是为了测试如何在短时间内进行有效可行的团队决策。

9. The goal of The Darkness is to foster efficient decision mechanism and executive ability.
黑暗这个项目的目的是为了培养团队形成高效的决策机制和执行能力。

10. The aim of Spider Web with Negotiation is to improve communicative skills and overcome obstacles in communication.
交易电网项目的目的是为了提高沟通技巧，克服沟通障碍。

11. The Darkness can inspire team moral and enhance team cohesiveness.
黑暗这个项目能激发团队士气，增强团队凝聚力。

12. The aim of Tower Building is to make team members understand the importance of the willpower when they do tasks.
筑塔项目的目的是让队员们理解在完成任务时意志力的重要性。

Section Five: Cultural Tips

拓展训练的发展历程及价值观

拓展训练的发展历程

拓展训练的概念源于英国，英文名为 Outward Bound，意为"投向外界未知世界，迎接挑战"。后来拓展的独特创意和训练方式逐渐被推广开来。1970 年，中国香港成立了香港外展训练学校。这是中国第一个加入 Outward Bound 国际组织的专业培训机构，1999 年，该组织在广东肇庆建立了拓展训练基地，是国内第一个该组织下属的培训基地。

拓展训练是以体育技术为原理，充分整合各种资源，融入科技手段，运用独特的情境设计，通过创意独特的专业户外项目体验，帮助参与者改变态度及心智模式的训练方式。它是一种全新的体验式学习方法和训练方式。大多数拓展训练的项目是以培养合作意识和进取精神为宗旨，帮助企业和组织激发成员的潜力，增强团队活力、创造力和凝聚力，以达到提升团队合作力和竞争力的目的。

拓展训练的价值观

积极主动：积极的工作态度和人生态度是拓展精神的核心。乐观自信，从我做起，环境因我而变。

开拓创新：以开放的心态，应对变化，积极进取。

认真负责：人和事因认真而完美，注重细节是专业化的表现。坚守承诺，积累信用。

独立协作：独立自主，各司其职，独当一面。个人和公司的竞争力来自个人不可替代的价值。高水平的独立，才有可能带来高水平的协作。局部利益服从整体利益；以双赢的心态创造最大动力。

共享成功：成功来自每个人的努力和贡献，成功是协作的结晶；共享成功的经验，共享成功的好处。

译 文

第二部分：相关信息

如何创建一个优秀的团队

团队合作是指为了实现共同的目的或目标将个人的行为汇集在一起的行为，团队合作使个人的需求服从于团队的需求。实质上，团队中的每个人都将个人的需求放置一边，朝着更大的团队目标努力。成员间的互动和他们共同完成的工作称为团队合作。

每个工作场所的人都在谈论团队建设，团队工作和自己的团队，但很少有人懂得如何获得团队工作的经验，或者如何培养一支高效的团队。下面是一些帮助建立一个成功的工作团队的技巧。

确定团队的目的和目标。撰写一份涵盖团队任务的业务计划书。所有团队成员必须拥有此文件的副本。

帮助员工了解需要达到什么目标，以及通过制订一个结构清晰的年度计划帮助他们了解如何实现这些目标。帮助员工了解这些目标的优先级，并将重点放在短期目标上。

选择团队成员。描述团队的目标后，安排可以执行每个目标的协作者。团队成员不能仅限于员工，还可以包括具有特殊专长的顾问或自由职业者。指派一个经验丰富、具有道德模范作用的团队领导。他或她在给予团队成员尊重和支持的同时必须能对他们提出挑战。

确定每个团队成员的职责。在给成员签署的文件中明确列出每个成员的职责。把团队与公司的前景和使命联系起来。

在每个期限结束时召开团队会议，重新评估哪些目标已经达到，哪些事项的优先级需要改变，以及已经实施的战略是否需要调整。进行团队建设训练能够创建一个有凝聚力的团队。成功的团队源于良好的关系，因此，业务团队必须快速建立这些关系。

第三部分：情境任务范例

情境 1：李欣和王奇是大一新生，并且两人是同班同学，他们俩正在操场上散步并谈论有关军训的事。（A：李欣；B：王奇）

A：我们的校园很大并且很漂亮，是吧？

B：是的，它比我预想的大很多，而且我们现在在这里军训。

A：你看起来比我第一次在这里见到你时更强壮了。

B：真的吗，我的脸都晒黑了，是吧？

A：我现在也晒黑了，有时候我觉得军训很累，但是它对我们的健康有好处。

B：我十分赞同你的观点，一些同学已经在抱怨军训的苦与累，但是我认为军训可以锻炼我们坚强的意志力，让我们养成自律的好习惯。

A：是的，顺便问一下，你之前参加过这类的训练吗？

B：去年暑假我参加过一次拓展训练项目。

A：我听说过这种训练项目。有意思吗？

B：是的，非常有趣。

A：有机会我也要尝试一下。看，训练要开始了。我们过去吧！

B：好的，走吧。

情境 2：李欣是大一新生，李林是大二学生。他们俩正在操场上谈论军训的感受。（A：李林；B：李欣）

A：很高兴再见到你，你适应大学生活了吗？

B：是的，比之前好多了，我们刚刚结束了军训。

A：你觉得军训生活怎么样？

B：第一天结束的时候，我感觉累极了。

A：军训对你来说有什么困难吗？

B：准确射击对我来说太难了，我总是射不准。

A：有没有人中途退下来啊？

B：噢，没有，每个人都认真地完成了训练。我们的教官说，他们每天都训练。

A：当兵很不容易。

B：是的，军人常常是我们的榜样，我认为军训对我来说是一段不寻常的经历。

A：军训教会我们遵守纪律和团队合作的重要性。

B：是的，我从军训中得到了乐趣。

情境 3： 李欣和王林都是大一新生，他们俩正在校园里谈论有关拓展训练的事。（A：王林；B：李欣）

A：上周日你干什么了？

B：我参加了一个拓展训练项目。

A：噢，太棒了，是不是又刺激又吓人啊？

B：是的，但有些项目很有意思。

A：你都参加什么项目了？

B：牵手，偷天陷阱，有轨电车，三人行还有下降项目，等等。

A：听起来不错，你都完成了吗？

B：是的，我参加了所有项目。

A：哪个项目最难？

B：下降项目。这个项目要求参赛者从 30 米的高度下降。因为我有些恐高，所以这个项目对我来说非常困难。

A：是的，我第一次从那个高度下来时，我的双腿都在颤抖，但是我想你现在一定很享受战胜困难的喜悦。

B：噢，确实如此。行动是克服恐惧的最好办法。我从这次的拓展训练中收获很多。

A：当然了，你很勇敢。

1. 3 Association Activities

1. 3. 1 Join an Association

Section One: Tasks

Situation 1: *Liu Xu and Zhang Jing are both freshmen. Liu Xu is looking at a notice about club recruitment at the notice board where she meets Zhang Jing. They are talking about joining a club. Make a conversation, and then act with your partner.*

Situation 2: *Liu Xu meets Zhang Jing again, and they are talking about their club activities. Make a conversation, and then act with your partner.*

Situation 3: *Liu Xu invites his friend David to attend their English club activity, and they talk about western festivals in the club. Make a conversation, and then act with our partner.*

Section Two: Related Information

Student Association

A student association or student society is an organization or a society, operated by students in a university, whose membership typically consists only of students or alumni. [1] Aims may involve practice of a certain professional hobby, or to promote professional development. Examples of common associations found in most universities are debate association, international student association and rock association, etc.

Student associations typically have open membership, thus differing from honor societies[2] that admit members by invitation only. Students typically join associations at the beginning of the school year when many societies present themselves in a societies fair to attract new members. The students may pay a membership fee to the association, since the associations are non-profit organizations. This fee is often nominal and purely exists to cover insurance or to fund association events.

In Australia, student associations play an important role in university life by bringing together like-minded students to engage in activities the association seeks to promote. [3] An example of a large student association in Australia is the Caulfield Business & Commerce Students' Society in Monash University[4]. The Alma Mater Society in Queen's University[5] is the oldest organization in Canada, and currently the most extensive in regard to student involvement. It is currently a corporation employing over 500 students. Student associations are widespread in Ireland's universities, with a wide range of activities catered for, including debating, performing arts, role-play, faculty-based activities, political activities etc. The range of support for associations varies from university to university, though all universities provide funding and facilities to some extent for associations.

Joining a university association is a great way to exercise your brain and body, learn new things, practice your leadership, skills and make friends who share your interests. It can also give you valuable skills for gaining future employment.

Vocabulary

alumni [ə'lʌmnaɪ] *n.*校友，毕业生

propagation [ˌprɒpə'geɪʃən] *n.*传播；繁殖

professional [prə'feʃ(ə)n(ə)l] *adj.*专业的；职业的；职业性的

admit [əd'mɪt] *v.*承认；准许进入

nominal ['nɒmɪn(ə)l] *adj.*名义上的；有名无实的

fund [fʌnd] *vt.*投资；资助

promote [prə'məʊt] *vt.*促进；提升

extensive [ɪk'stensɪv] *adj.*广泛的；大量的

involvement [ɪn'vɒlv(ə)nt] *n.*牵连；包含

currently ['kʌrəntlɪ] *adv.*当前；一般地

range [reɪn(d)ʒ] *n.*范围；幅度

cater ['keɪtə] *vt.*投合，迎合；满足需要

faculty ['fæk(ə)ltɪ] *n.*系；全体教员

employment [ɪm'plɔɪm(ə)nt] *n.*职业；雇用

consist of 由……组成；由……构成；包括

differ from 与……不同；区别于……

play an important role 起着重要作用

cater for 迎合；为……提供所需

to some extent 在一定程度上；在某种程度上

Notes

1. A student association or student society is an organization or a society，operated by students in a university，whose membership typically consists only of students or alumni. 学生社团，又称学生协会或学生组织，是由大学生组织操办的社团或组织，其成员通常仅由学生或校友组成。operated by students at a university 意为"由大学生组织操办"，过去分词短语作后置定语，whose membership typically consists only of students or alumni 为定语从句，whose 为关系代词，先行词为 an organization or a society，whose 在从句中作定语。

2. Honor Society 荣誉协会，美国大学里的全国性社团之一，根据学生成绩而定；另外两个全国性社团分别是：Professional Honor Society，根据学生毕业的主修和成绩决定；Fraternity/Sonority（兄弟/姐妹会），通常入会需要会员举荐，当然与课业表现无关。这三种都是全国性的社团。

3. In Australia，student associations play an important role in university life by bringing together like-minded students to engage in activities the association seeks to promote. 在澳大利亚，学生社团在大学生活中起着重要作用。学生社团通过聚集志同道合的学生参与社团寻求促进的活动。like-minded students "有共同志向的学生"；the association seeks

to promote 是省略关系代词 that 的定语从句，先行词是 activities，在从句中作 seeks 的宾语，"社团寻求促进的活动"。

4. Caulfield Business & Commerce Students' Society in Monash University 莫纳什大学的考尔菲尔德商学会

5. The Alma Mater Society in Queen's University 皇后大学的母校协会

Section Three：Situational Task Samples

Situation 1：*Li Xin and Wang Qi meet on campus. They are talking about joining the club.* （*A*：*Li Xin*；*B*：*Wang Qi*）

A：Hi，Wang Qi，what are you doing?

B：I'm looking at these club notices. I'm thinking of joining one.

A：Which club do you want to join?

B：I have no idea，which club are you interested in?

A：I like English. I want to join the English Club.

B：Sounds great! But my English is not very good.

A：It doesn't matter. I think it will be interesting and it can also improve your oral English.

B：OK，I will join it with you. Do we need to pay membership dues[1]?

A：No，it's free. Our school public performance[2] is just round the corner[3]，I heard that there would be an English drama performance.

B：It should be fun. Let's see it together.

A：Great! I'm looking forward to it.

Situation 2：*Li Xin and Wang Ning who are both freshmen are talking about their club activities during the class interval.* （*A*：*Wang Ning*；*B*：*Li Xin*）

A：How did you like the English Club?

B：I enjoyed it very much.

A：What did you do in the English Club?

B：We had English games, short plays and three-minute speeches. And I met several foreign friends here.

A：Sounds interesting. Did you talk to foreigners?

B：Yes, at first, I was very nervous and couldn't speak complete sentences in English. But they were very friendly and listened to me carefully, and I felt better later.

A：I am glad to hear that. Well begun is half done[4]. I think you will improve your oral English soon.

B：Thank you for encouraging me. What about the Basketball Club?

A：Great. We have matches every week.

B：Sports can keep us healthy and get away from pressure.

A：That's right. Nice talking to you. See you next time.

B：See you. Goodbye!

Situation 3：Li Xin invites his friend Frank to join their club activity, and they talk about Christmas Day at the club.（A：Li Xin；B：Wang Qi；C：Frank）

A：Hello, everyone! Long time no see. Let me introduce my friend, Frank. He is from England.

B：Hi, Frank. Nice to meet you.

C：Nice to meet you, too.

B：We've just talked about Christmas Day[5]. Can you give us some information about Christmas, Frank?

C：Of course. Christmas is a religious holiday of Christians to celebrate as the anniversary of the birth of Jesus Christ[6].

A：Christmas is a time for families and fun of westerners, right?

C：Yeah, it is a time of family gatherings and holiday meals.

B：How do you celebrate Christmas?

C：We often exchange gifts and people attend the church, share meals with families and friends. Children are happy because they will receive presents which they want in their stockings or pillowcases.

A：Great, just like our Chinese Spring Festival.

B：What do you often eat on Christmas Day? Anything special?

C：Turkey[7] or chicken is the most popular food. We often eat Christmas puddings[8] on Christmas Day.

B：Thank you for telling us so much.

A：Let's sing a Christmas song together.

Notes

1. membership dues 会员费
2. school public performance 学校公演，学校大型演出节目

3. round/around the corner 即将到来，近在咫尺

4. Well begun is half done. 好的开始是成功的一半。

5. Christmas Day 圣诞节，西方传统节日，在每年的 12 月 25 日。

6. Jesus Christ 耶稣

7. turkey 火鸡，西方国家感恩节、圣诞节餐桌上的常见食物。

8. Christmas puddings 圣诞布丁。西方圣诞节的常见食物，类似一种大蛋糕。

Section Four：Functional Expression Bank

College Clubs/Associations（大学社团）

Invite to Join a Club（邀请加入社团）

1. Which club do you want to join? /Would you like to join the English Club/Guitar Club/ Basketball Club? 你想参加哪个社团？/你愿意加入英语社团/吉他社/篮球社团吗？

2. I'm going to join the Geology Club. 我要加入地质俱乐部。

3. I'm dying to join the Music Association. /I'm really longing to join the Music Club. 我很想加入音乐社团。

4. I'm thinking of joining a club. 我正想加入一个社团。

5. You can join the Guitar Club if you like. 如果你愿意，可以加入吉他社。

6. Are you interested in joining the Guitar Club? 你有兴趣加入吉他社吗？

7. I think I'll sign up for the Photography Association. 我想我会参加摄影协会。

Apply to Join a Club（申请加入社团）

1. How do I join this club? 我怎么才能加入这个社团？

2. You should fill out an application form. 你需要填写一张申请表。

3. Do I have to fill out an application form? 我必须要填写一张申请表吗？

4. Are you a member of any clubs? 你加入社团了吗？

5. I am in the Movie Club. 我在电影社团。

6. I am not interested in joining any clubs. 我没有兴趣加入任何社团。

7. I'm afraid joining a club will take up much of my time. 我担心参加社团会占用我很多时间。

8. Do we need to pay membership dues? 我们需要交会员费吗？

9. Yes，we do. /No，it's free of charge. 是的，需要。/不需要，加入是免费的。

Club Introduction（社团介绍）

1. The Drama Club is one of our major clubs. 话剧社是我们主要的社团之一。

2. There are a variety of activities in our club. 我们社团组织各种各样的活动。

3. In our club, you can make friends and get more fun. 在我们社团，你可以交朋友并且得到更多乐趣。

4. In English Club, you can enjoy a variety of activities including staging musical dramas, holding English speeches and watching Oscar-winning movies. 参加英语社团，你可以尽情享受各种舞台音乐剧表演，英语演讲比赛，并且观看奥斯卡获奖影片。

Clubs and Activities（社团与活动）

Names of the Associations/Clubs（社团名称）

Oral English Club 英语口语社团

Speech and Eloquence Association 演讲与口才协会

Drama Association/Club 话剧社

Dancing Association/Club 舞蹈协会/社团

Music Club/Society 音乐社团/协会

Film Society/Association/Club 电影协会/社团

Football Association/Club 足球协会/社团

Basketball Association/Club 篮球协会/社团

Association of Table Tennis Contest 乒乓球协会

Shuttlecock Association 毽球协会

Photography Association 摄影协会

Stamp Collecting Association 集邮协会

Calligraphy Association 书法协会

Association of Advancement of Mental Health 心理健康促进协会

Accounting Association 会计协会

Debating Society 辩论社

Science Fiction Society 科幻小说协会

Hiking Club 远足俱乐部

International Student Society 国际留学生协会

Law Promotion Association 法律促进协会

Moot Court Competition 模拟法庭竞赛

Activities（具体活动）

1. I'm getting together with members from the Drama Association. 我正和话剧社的会员们在一起活动。

2. The Drama Club is teaming up with the Filmmakers Club. 戏剧社将和电影制片人俱乐部合作。

3. The Oral English Association is meeting tomorrow. 英语口语协会明天要会面了。

4. You can tell a Dancing Club member right off. 你能够立即分辨出舞蹈社团的成员。

5. I met several foreigners in the English Club. 我在英语社团遇见几个外国人。

Section Five：Culture Tips

美国大学里的社团

国外的社团起步比中国早，发展历史悠久，种类比较繁多。参加社团活动也是大学生活的重要组成部分。下面介绍美国大学里的社团，主要有以下几类：各类艺术社团，学术/专业社团，联谊会生活，国际文化俱乐部和运动俱乐部等。

各类艺术社团　美国大学里有各类艺术社团供学生施展才华。如果学生在音乐方面有才华，可以加入合唱团或各类乐器俱乐部；如果学生有各类舞蹈天赋，可以加入各类舞蹈社团；如果学生擅长表演，则可以加入戏剧社等。在这里学生们可以尽情展示自己的才华。

学术/专业社团　这些社团更倾向于为未来职业道路做准备，在这里学生可以更深入地研究自己的专业和发展自己的兴趣爱好。通常此类社团包括数学、物理、法学俱乐部等，喜欢政治和商业的学生在这里可以成立他们自己的组织，这些社团为他们毕业后的职业发展提供舞台。

联谊会生活　联谊会生活主要是指美国大学里的兄弟会和姐妹会。它们是校园生活的组成部分。顾名思义，兄弟会只招收男生，姐妹会只招收女生。每个社团都有自己的规章制度，参加兄弟会或姐妹会可以帮助学生快速建立自己的人际关系。慈善也是联谊会生活的重要内容，它可以通过不同的方式为学校或社区服务。

国际文化俱乐部　国际文化俱乐部主要是为各国留学生提供文化交流的地方，在这里来自不同国家的学生们可以一起参与活动并分享自己国家的文化。如果你对日本文化感兴趣，可以加入日本文化俱乐部，在这里你可以感受日本文化的诸多方面，从传统的茶道到日本的动画等。对中国儒、道、佛教文化感兴趣的学生可以加入中国传统文化俱乐部等。

运动俱乐部　运动俱乐部主要是为一些高中时比较出色的运动员开设的。运动员在进入大学后决定专心学习而不再进行校队中的职业训练，他们会选择某些喜欢的运动项目和同学们一起娱乐。运动俱乐部里的项目不像校队里的训练强度那样高，任何级别的学生都可以加入。如果想参与到更激烈的比赛中去，你可以去大学里的专业训练队，与其他队友一比高下。在这里如果自己喜欢的项目不是那么普及的话，学生们也可以自己召集成员成立自己感兴趣的俱乐部。

译　文

第二部分：相关信息

学生社团

学生社团，又称学生协会是由大学生组织成立的社团或组织，其成员通常仅由学生或校友组成。社团成立的目的是对某种职业兴趣的实践，或者是为了促进其职业发展。大学里常见的社团通常有辩论社，国际留学生交流社，摇滚乐社团，等等。

学生社团通常有开放的会员资格，因此不同于仅通过邀请接纳成员的荣誉社团。学生们通常在学年初时加入社团，届时许多社团会在社团展示会上推介自己的社团以吸引新成员加入。社团成员须向社团支付会员费，因为社团是非营利组织。这种会费通常是名义上的，并且纯粹是为了支付保费或为社团活动提供资金。

在澳大利亚，学生社团在大学生活中起着重要作用。学生社团通过聚集志趣相投的学生参与社团寻求促进的活动。莫纳什大学的考尔菲尔德商学会是澳大利亚大型学生社团的一个典型。加拿大皇后大学的母校协会是加拿大历史最悠久的社团，目前在学生参与方面是最广泛的。它目前是一个拥有超过 500 名学生的社团。学生社团在爱尔兰各大学中很普遍，其中包含很多种类的社团活动，包括辩论、表演艺术、角色扮演、学院活动、政治活动等。尽管所有大学在一定程度上为社团提供资金和设施，但不同大学对社团的支持程度各不相同。

加入大学里的社团可以锻炼身心，学习新知识，实践领导才能，掌握新技能，结交志趣相投的朋友。加入社团还可以教会我们一些未来职业所需的宝贵技能。

第三部分：情境任务范例

情境1： 李欣和王奇在校园里相遇，他们正在谈论加入社团的事。（A：李欣；B：王奇）

A：你好，王奇，你在干什么呢？

B：我正看这些社团通知呢，我正想加入一个社团。

A：你想参加什么社团？

B：我不知道，你对哪个社团感兴趣？

A：我喜欢英语，我想加入英语社团。

B：听起来不错。但是我的英语不太好。

A：没关系。我认为英语社团会很有趣，而且能提高你的英语口语水平。

B：好的，我跟你一起加入。需要付会员费吗？

A：不需要，免费的。咱们学校公演就要开始了。我听说会有英语戏剧表演。

B：一定很有趣，咱们一起去看吧。

A：太好了！我一直期待着呢。

情境2： 李欣和王宁都是大一新生，他们在课间时间正谈论他们所参加的社团活动。（A：王宁；B：李欣）

A：英语社团怎么样？

B：我很喜欢。

A：你们英语社团都做些什么？

B：我们用英语做游戏，演短剧，还有三分钟演讲。我还认识了几个外国朋友。

A：听起来很有趣。你跟外国朋友交谈了吗？

B：是的，交谈了。起初，我跟他们说话时非常紧张，都不能说完整的英语句子。但是他们都很友好，非常认真听我说话，后来我感觉好多了。

A：听你那么说我真为你高兴。好的开始是成功的一半。我想你的英语口语将很快得到提高。

B：谢谢你的鼓励。篮球社团怎么样？

A：好极了。我们每周都有比赛。

B：运动可以使我们保持健康，远离压力。

A：说得对。跟你聊天很开心，下次见。

B：下次见，拜拜！

情境3： 李欣邀请他的好友弗兰克参加他们的社团活动，而且他们在社团活动中谈论关于圣诞节的事。（A：李欣；B：王奇；C：弗兰克）

A：大家好，好久不见，让我介绍我的好朋友弗兰克，他来自英格兰。

B：你好，弗兰克，很高兴认识你。

C：我也很高兴认识你们大家。

B：我们正讨论圣诞节呢，你能给我们讲讲圣诞节吗，弗兰克？

C：当然可以。圣诞节是个宗教节日，它是基督教徒为了纪念耶稣的诞生而设立的节日。

A：圣诞节是西方人家人欢聚的日子，对吗？

C：是的，圣诞节是家人欢聚聚餐庆祝的日子。

B：你们都怎么庆祝圣诞节？

C：我们经常交换礼物，人们参加教堂活动并和家人朋友一起共享晚餐。孩子们很开心，因为他们会在长筒袜或枕套里收到他们想要的礼物。

A：太好了，圣诞节就像我们中国的春节。

B：你们在圣诞节当天吃些什么食物，有什么特别的吗？

C：火鸡或鸡肉是最受欢迎的食物，我们在圣诞节还经常吃圣诞布丁。

B：感谢你给我们讲这么多圣诞节的事。

A：让我们一起唱一首圣诞歌吧。

1. 3. 2 Write a Notice

Section One: Tasks

Situation 1: *There is going to be a lecture on Career Planning given by Professor Liu in the lecture hall this Friday afternoon. Suppose you were a member of Students' Union, please write a notice according to the situation.*

Situation 2: *English Association is going to have a Christmas party this Friday evening. All freshmen who want to attend the party should come on time. Suppose you were a member of the English Club, please write a notice according to the situation.*

Section Two: Related Information

How to Write a Notice of a Meeting

Whether you run a small business, a club or a civic organization, writing a notice of a meeting will allow interested members of your community to participate and learn more about your organization. [1] A successful notice of a meeting will clearly and succinctly inform the public and other interested parties of the location, date and time of your meeting. It will also draw attention to the meeting itself and give readers contact information pertaining to the meeting.

Write the name of your organization at the top of the page in a relatively large font size. Type "Notice of Meeting" a few lines down in a larger font. Write "Notice of Public Meeting" if your meeting will be open to the public.

Type the date and time of the meeting a few lines down in a smaller font. Write the location of the meeting on the next line in the same font size.

Write a brief, one-to-two sentence description of the purpose of the meeting further down the page. For example, if you are holding an information session, you would simply write, "This meeting will be a brief information session to answer any questions members of the community might have about our organization. "

Add beneath the description of the meeting's purpose any other pertinent information, such as whether an RSVP[2] is required or if light refreshments will be served. Type this information in the same font size as the description of the meeting's purpose.

Write the organizer's contact information at the bottom of the page, so that people interested in attending can get in touch with the group or business. [3] A phone number or an e-mail should be sufficient.

Print as many copies as you need and post them in public spaces or in local publications. [4] All information in the notice should be relevant to the meeting. Avoid including information that relates to any company-related issues that will not be discussed at the meeting. [5]

Vocabulary

civic ['sɪvɪk] *adj*. 市的；公民的

succinctly ［sək'sɪŋktli］ *adv.* 简洁地；简便地

font ［fɒnt］ *n.* 字体；字形

brief ［briːf］ *adj.* 简短的，简洁的

roughly ［'rʌflɪ］ *adv.* 粗糙地；概略地

session ［'seʃ(ə)n］ *n.* 会议；开会

beneath ［bɪ'niːθ］ *adv.* 在下方；*prep.* 在……之下

pertinent ［'pɜːtɪnənt］ *adj.* 相关的，切题的

refreshments ［rɪ'freʃm(ə)nts］ *n.* 点心；茶点；小吃

publication ［ˌpʌblɪ'keɪʃ(ə)n］ *n.* 出版；出版物

sufficient ［sə'fɪʃ(ə)nt］ *adj.* 足够的；充分的

avoid ［ə'vɔɪd］ *vt.* 避免；避开

draw attention to　吸引……的注意力

at the top of　在……的顶端；在首位

at the bottom of　在……的底部

get in touch with　与……联系；和……接触

Notes

1. Whether you run a small business，a club or a civic organization，writing a notice of a meeting will allow interested members of your community to participate and learn more about your organization. 无论您是经营小型企业，俱乐部还是民间组织，撰写会议通知都将让您团体中感兴趣的成员参与并了解更多有关您的组织的信息。Whether you run a small business，a club or a civic organization 中，whether…or 引导让步状语从句，意为"不论……还是……"。

2. RSVP 这个词语来自法语，意思是"请回复"。

3. Write the organizer's contact information at the bottom of the page，so that people interested in attending can get in touch with the group or business. 在页面底部写上主办单位的联系信息，以便让感兴趣参加会议的人可以与举办团体或商务组织取得联系。so that people interested in attending can get in touch with the group or business 中，so that 引导目的状语从句，意为"目的是，以便"。

4. Print as many copies as you need and post them in public spaces or in local publications. 打印你所需要的尽可能多的副本，并将其贴在公共场所或当地出版物中。Print as many copies as you need… 中 as…as 引导比较状语从句，意为"和……一样"。

5. Avoid including information that relates to any company-related issues that will not be discussed at the meeting. 至于一些不需要在此次会议上讨论的公司问题，应避免出现在会议中。company-related issues "与公司有关的问题"，这个句子里两个 that 分别引导两个定语从句，第一个 that 在从句中作主语，先行词是 information；第二个 that 在从句中作主语，先行词是 issues。

Section Three：Situational Task Samples

Situation 1：*Li Xin is a member of Students' Union and he is required to write a notice on the Career Planning Lecture this Thursday afternoon.*

NOTICE

Please be informed that a lecture about Career Planning[1] for College Students will be given from 2：00 to 4：00 this Thursday afternoon in the Conference Room 301. All freshmen are required to be there on time. Everybody should take notes[2]. Handouts[3] will be distributed before the meeting.

The Students' Union

Oct. 16，2020

Situation 2：*Li Xin is a member of the English Association and he is required to write a notice about holding a Christmas party this Friday evening.*

NOTICE

There will be a Christmas party organized by English Association in the auditorium[4] this Friday evening. Food and drinks are supplied free there. The party will begin at 6：30 p. m. ，and there will be splendid at that time. You are welcome to come on time！

The English Association

Dec. 21，2020

Notes

1. career planning 职业规划。也叫职业生涯规划，是对职业生涯进行系统计划的过程。
2. take notes = make notes 记笔记
3. handout 讲义；文字资料
4. auditorium = assembly hall 礼堂

Section Four：Functional Expression Bank

Opening Sentences（通知开头常用句型）

1. The Students' Union has made a decision that…学生会已决定……
2. We will have a lecture on…我们将听一个关于……的讲座。
3. Now please let me inform something important to you.
   现在请让我通知你们一些重要的事情。
4. There will be a report this afternoon. 今天下午将有一个报告。
5. Notice is hereby given that…兹通知……
6. This is to announce…通知……
7. Please be informed that 请告知……
8. We are pleased to inform…很高兴通知大家……
9. Our college is going to hold…我校将举办……

10. I beg to inform you that…特此奉告/通知你们大家……

11. We inform you that we shall move to a new address on June 15.
我们将于 6 月 15 日搬入新址，特此通知。

12. A lecture on…will be given by…at 3：00 p. m. this afternoon in the lecture hall of…University.
今天下午三点在……大学报告厅将由……就……（内容/话题）做一个报告。

Content Sentences（通知正文常用句型）

1. A welcoming ceremony for our new CEO，Mr. Wilson，will be held in Los Angeles Grand Hotel on May 10.
我们的新任首席执行官威尔森先生的就职典礼将在 5 月 10 日在洛杉矶大酒店举行。

2. All professors and related professors will be required to attend the meeting.
所有本专业的教授和相关专业的教授务必参加会议。

3. Whoever has found or knows…is requested to phone. 无论谁找到或知道……请致电。

4. Please take your pen and notebook with you. 请随身携带笔和笔记本。

5. On and after July 5，the address of…will be changed to…
自七月五日起，……的地址将改变为……

6. Our store will close on Jan. 20，and we will reopen after Lantern Festival.
我们店将于 1 月 20 日关店，并将在元宵节后重新开店。

7. To mark this special occasion，customers will be offered with an opening discount.
为庆祝这个特殊的日子，所有顾客将享受开业打折优惠。

8. Effective from Sep. 1，2017. 自 2017 年 9 月 1 日起生效。

9. Effective immediately，the following items are applicable. 下列条款即时生效。

Closing Sentences（通知结尾常用句型）

1. Please contact…for any more information. 想要得到更多相关信息，请联系……。

2. Everyone is expected to attend it. 欢迎所有人加入。

3. Be sure to attend it on time. 请准时出席。

4. Please be present on time. 请按时到场。

5. You are welcome to join in it. 欢迎踊跃参加。

Common Formats for Notice of Meeting（常用会议通知的格式）

Notice for Official/Non-official Meeting（正式/非正式会议通知）

NOTICE（通知）
Date 日期
Time 时间
Venue 地点
Agenda/Purpose 议程/目的
Who is to attend 与会人
Specific instructions 具体说明
Contact person/Address 联系人/地址

```
                          NOTICE （通知）

    Name 名称

    Objective/Purpose 目标/目的

    Date 日期

    Time/Duration 时间/持续时间

    Place/Venue 地点/场所

    Essential qualifications/Conditions 基本资格/条件

    Contact information 联系方式

    Specific instructions 具体说明
```

```
                          NOTICE （通知）

    Name and Nature 名称和性质

    Occasion 场合

    Venue 地点

    Objective-information，awareness，invitation etc. 目标信息，注意事项，邀请等

    Date/Time 日期/时间

    Expenditure/Entry fee etc. 开支/入场费等

    Beginning/Conclusion 开始/总结

    Duration：from…to… 持续时间：从……到……

    Contact information 联系方式

    Specific instructions 具体说明
```

Section Five: Cultural tips

撰写通知时的注意事项

通知的标志：书面通知是书面的正式公告或布告，常常用 notice 作标志，有时为了引起注意，每个字母也可用大写 NOTICE。常写在正文上方的正中位置。通知也可用内容的核心部分作标题。

发通知的人或单位名称：一般写在标志的左上方或正文后面的右下角，发出通知的时间要写在正文的左下角，也可写在正文的右上角。

通知的正文：正文要写明所通知事情的具体时间、地点及内容，出席对象和相关注意事项。通知的正文一般采用文章式，也可采用广告式。

通知的对象：被通知的单位或个人一般采用第三人称，但如果带有称呼语，则用第二人称表述被通知的对象。

通知的文体：书面通知用语要贴切，语句要简明扼要。

译　文

第二部分：相关信息

如何撰写会议通知

无论你是经营小型企业，俱乐部还是民间组织，撰写会议通知都将让你团体中感兴趣的成员参与并了解更多有关你的组织的信息。一个成功的会议通知将清楚和简洁地通知公众和其他有关方会议的地点、日期和时间。同时，它还会提醒注意会议本身，并向读者提供与会议有关的联系信息。

将组织的名称用相对较大的字号写在页面顶部。"会议通知"用较大号字打在向下几行的位置。如果你的会议向公众开放，请写"公开会议通知"。

将会议的日期和时间用较小字体键入几行。在下一行以相同的字体大小写下召开会议的地点。

撰写简短的通知，用一到两句话的内容为描述会议的目的。例如，如果你即将举办信息交流会议，你只需写道："本次会议将是一个简短的信息交流会议，以回答组织成员对我们组织提出的任何问题。"

在会议目的描述的下面添加其他相关信息，例如是否需要回复或是否会提供点心。用与描述会议目的相同字号的字键入这些信息。

在页面底部写上主办单位的联系信息，以便让感兴趣参加会议的人可以与举办团体或商业组织取得联系。留下一个电话号码或一个电子邮件地址即可。

打印你所需要的尽可能多的副本，并将其贴在公共场所或当地出版物中。通知中的所有信息应与会议相关。至于一些不需要在会议上讨论的公司问题，应避免出现在会议中。

第三部分：情境任务范例

情境1： 李欣是学生会的成员，学生会让他撰写一则关于这周四下午举办职业规划讲座的通知。

通　知

请告知如下内容：本周四下午2点到4点在会议室301召开关于大学生职业生涯规划的讲座。要求所有大一新生准时参加。每名同学要求记笔记，会前会给大家分发讲义。

学生会
2020 年 10 月 16 日

情境2： 李欣是英语社团的成员，英语社团让他撰写一则关于这周五晚上举办一场圣诞联欢晚会的通知。

通　知

本周五晚英语社团将在校礼堂举办一场圣诞联欢晚会。会上食物和饮料免费发放。晚会将在晚上6:30开始，并且会有精彩的演出。欢迎同学们准时到来！

英语社团
2020 年 12 月 21 日

Unit Two　My Future Career

2.1　Determine Career Goals

Section One: Tasks

Situation: *Suppose you were a freshman named Li Xin. On the third day of your college life, a career development plan is lectured with a heated discussion on "Determine Career Goals". Make a conversation with your team members on "Career Goals" and act it out.*

Section Two: Related Information

Basic Career Goals

Every now and then we come across people who are unhappy with their jobs. The reasons of their unhappiness may vary—some do not like their work schedule, or some do not like a particular colleague in their office, or some do not like their bosses. However, these vague reasons actually serve as a cover for the underlying reasons of all dissatisfaction with jobs—the employee is unaware of or has not given thought to his/her career goals and objectives. It is only when a person has a clear thought about his/her career goals and objectives that he/she gets ultimate satisfaction from his/her job and therefore progresses faster. [1] Here is an example list of some basic career goals that an employee should think about and keep in mind:

Growth in Resources

Change is the only constant, and be it in everyday life or in a profession. With the change and growth in business, it is only natural that one would have to constantly upgrade and enhance their knowledge and resources that he/she offers to the business or to the client. [2] Therefore, upgrading one's knowledge and resources is an important career goal to pursue.

Financial Aspect

The financial aspect is one of the most important ones. If a person is underpaid, he or she will become bitter and frustrated and this will be manifested in his or her work ethics and work method. If a person is overpaid, he/she may become lethargic and may not be as productive to the company as they were when they were hired and may soon be given the pink slip. Therefore, another important career goal is to be paid only as much as the worth of the job position for the company.

Satisfaction

No activity in this world is carried out without a certain level of satisfaction being one of a person's requirements. One important career goal should be to be satisfied with whatever you are doing. Of course, that does not mean that you should stop experimenting or impede your enhancement process. You should make sure that you are completely satisfied with whatever job you are doing.

New Experience

We spend almost three-fourths of our life in the professional world. Therefore, it is logical that we look into our professional lives not only to progress and get ahead in life, but also to learn new things and gain new experience. [3] An added experience can add to a person's richness in terms of thought and knowledge. Therefore, another important career goal to keep in mind is to accumulate experience such as learning about the cultures of different countries, meeting new people and basically becoming familiarized with customs and traditions worldwide. This will enable us to increase our tolerance levels and change our perspectives.

Stability

Another important career goal that a person should look for is stability. Once a person gets into a stable company, he or she does not bother about his/her daily needs and can concentrate on growing as an individual and a professional, which will also add to the growth of the company. [4]

Vocabulary

determine [dɪ'tɜ:mɪn] v. (使) 做出决定

vary ['veərɪ] vi. 变化

schedule ['ʃedju:l] vt. 安排，计划   n. 时间表，计划表

colleague ['kɒli:g] n. 同事

vague [veɪg] adj. 模糊的

ultimate ['ʌltɪmət] adj. 最终的

upgrade [ʌp'greɪd] vt. 提升

enhance [ɪn'ha:ns] vt. 提高

manifest ['mænɪfest] vt. 表明

lethargic [lɪ'θɑ:dʒɪk] adj. 昏睡的，无生气的

client ['klaɪənt] *n*. 客户

accumulate [ə'kjuːmjuleɪt] *vi*. 累积，积聚

stability [stə'bɪlɪtɪ] *n*. 稳定性；恒心

familiarize [fə'mɪlɪəraɪz] *vt*. 使熟悉

tolerance ['tɒl(ə)r(ə)ns] *n*. 宽容，容忍

every now and then 每时每刻

come across 遇到

Notes

1. It is only when a person has a clear thought about his/her career goals and objectives that he/she gets ultimate satisfaction from his/her job and therefore progresses faster. 只有当一个人清楚地认识到自己的职业目标时才能从工作中获得最大的满足，从而进步更快。此句是 "It is…that…" 强调句，被强调内容为 "only when a person has a clear thought about his/her career goals and objectives，…he/she gets ultimate satisfaction from his/her job and therefore progress faster."

2. … it is only natural that one would have to constantly upgrade and enhance their knowledge and resources that he or she offers to the business or to the client. 很自然，人们必须不断地提升他们为企业或客户提供的知识和资源。此句中 it 作为形式主语，真正的主语是 that one would have to constantly upgrade and enhance their knowledge and resources that he or she offers to the business or to the client，句中第二个 that 引导定语从句，修饰先行词 knowledge and resources。

3. …it is logical that we look into our professional lives not only to progress and get ahead in life，but also to learn new things and gain new experiences. ……我们的职业生涯不仅要追求在生活中取得进步和成功，而且要学习新事物并获得新的经验。"it is logical that…" 中 it 是形式主语，that 引导的从句为真正的主语，"it is logical that…" 意为 "……是合理的"；"not only to…but also to…" 为并列结构作目的状语。

4. Once a person gets into a stable company，he or she does not bother about his/her daily needs and can concentrate on growing as an individual and a professional，which will also add to the growth of the company. 一旦进入了一家稳定的公司，就不用担心日常所需，可以专注于个人的成长以及专业的提升，这同时也促进了公司的发展。"Once" 引导条件状语从句，"he or she does not bother about his/her daily needs and can concentrate on growing as an individual and a professional，which will only add to the growth of the company" 为主句部分，其中 "which" 引导非限定性定语从句，对前句进行补充说明。

Section Three: Situational Task Samples

Situation：*Li Xin，a freshman[1] who majors in accounting，is studying in Financial Division of Panjin Vocational & Technical College. The main topic of the first week of his college life is Entrance Education[2]. Now the course of Career Development Plan is being lectured on the topic "Determine the Career Goals" with a heated discussion. Li Xin is having a conversation on*

"Career Goals" with his classmate Wu Rui.（A：Li Xin；B：Wu Rui）

B：Where do you want to be in 5 years?

A：I don't want to have a specific title[3]. I just want to enjoy what I like to do.

B：That sounds very reasonable.

A：It's the most important thing to me. I want to put my knowledge and experience into a challenging position. In order to achieve my goal，I just want to work step by step[4].

B：What is your long-range objective?

A：As I have some administrative experience from my last job，I hope I may use my organizational and planning skills in the future.

B：How do you plan to accomplish this?

A：By doing everything necessary and through further study. I do believe the industry I take up will develop rapidly. Generally it is possible to move from the position to a management position with enough experience in a company.

Notes

1. freshman，翻译为"大一新生"，大二学生一般称为 sophomore，大三学生称为 junior，大四学生称为 senior。

2. Entrance Education 译为"入学教育"，中国大学新生入学一般都要进行为期一周的入学教育，其中包括军事训练、户外拓展、职业生涯教育等。

3. title 此处译为"头衔""职务"。

4. step by step 逐渐地，一步一步地

Section Four: Functional Expression Bank

Describe Career Goals（描述职业目标）

1. To get a job in my field is most important to me.
   对我来说，能在我的专业领域找到一份工作是最重要的。

2. I feel that learning how to motivate people and to work together as a team will be the major goal of my leadership.
   我觉得学习如何把人们的积极性调动起来，以及如何作为一个团队一起工作，将是我领导工作的主要目标。

3. I expect to have a good opportunity to put all of my knowledge into practice. I am a doer and I can contribute a great deal to the company. I hope that within five years，I could lead an energetic and productive marketing team.
   我希望得到一个好的机会把我全部的知识应用到工作实践中。我是个实干者，我能为公司贡献很多。我希望在五年内，我能够领导一支有活力且高效的市场团队。

4. Now I start with an entry-level secretarial position and hope to become an administrative assistant in a few years.
   我现在从初级秘书职位开始工作，希望几年以后能成为一名行政助理。

5. I hope to be the best I can be at my job，because many in this line of work are promoted

to area manager，I am planning on that，too. 我希望能在我的职位上尽力做到最好，由于在这一领域工作的许多人都被提升为区域经理，所以我也有此打算。

6. I would devote to the medical research，because I want to do something to help others.
我想要致力于医药研究，因为我想做些事帮助他人。

7. As I have some administrative experience in my last job，I may use my organizational and planning skills in the future.
因为我在上一份工作中积累了一些管理经验，我将来可以运用我的组织和计划才能。

8. I hope to demonstrate my ability and talents in this field adequately.
我希望能充分展示我在这个领域的才能和天赋。

Section Five: Cultural Tips

霍兰德职业兴趣测验（HLD）

您愿意从事下列活动吗？（是？否？在相应的□里打"√"）（选择"是"计1分；选择"否"计0分）

	是	否
1. 装配修理电器或玩具。	□	□
2. 修理自行车。	□	□
3. 用木头做东西。	□	□
4. 开汽车或摩托车。	□	□
5. 用机器做东西。	□	□
6. 参加木工技术学习班。	□	□
7. 参加制图、描图学习班。	□	□
8. 驾驶卡车或拖拉机。	□	□
9. 参加机械和电气学习。	□	□
10. 装配修理电器。	□	□
11. 素描，制图或绘画。	□	□
12. 参加话剧或戏曲表演。	□	□
13. 设计家具，布置室内。	□	□
14. 练习乐器，参加乐队。	□	□
15. 欣赏音乐或戏剧。	□	□
16. 看小说，读剧本。	□	□
17. 从事摄影创作。	□	□
18. 写诗或吟诗。	□	□
19. 进艺术（美/音）培训班。	□	□
20. 练习书法。	□	□
21. 读科技图书和杂志。	□	□
22. 在试验室工作。	□	□
23. 改良品种，培育新水果。	□	□
24. 分析土和金属等的成分。	□	□
25. 研究自己选择的问题。	□	□
26. 解算式或数学游戏。	□	□

27. 上物理课。　　　　　　　　　　　　　　　　　　　是□　否□

28. 上化学课。　　　　　　　　　　　　　　　　　　　是□　否□

29. 上几何课。　　　　　　　　　　　　　　　　　　　是□　否□

30. 上生物课。　　　　　　　　　　　　　　　　　　　是□　否□

31. 参加学校或单位的正式活动。　　　　　　　　　　　是□　否□

32. 参加社会团体或俱乐部。　　　　　　　　　　　　　是□　否□

33. 帮助别人解决困难。　　　　　　　　　　　　　　　是□　否□

34. 照顾儿童。　　　　　　　　　　　　　　　　　　　是□　否□

35. 参加晚会、联欢会、茶话会。　　　　　　　　　　　是□　否□

36. 和大家一起出去郊游。　　　　　　　　　　　　　　是□　否□

37. 获得心理方面的知识。　　　　　　　　　　　　　　是□　否□

38. 参加讲座会或辩论会。　　　　　　　　　　　　　　是□　否□

39. 观看或参加体育比赛。　　　　　　　　　　　　　　是□　否□

40. 结交新朋友。　　　　　　　　　　　　　　　　　　是□　否□

41. 说服鼓动他人。　　　　　　　　　　　　　　　　　是□　否□

42. 卖东西。　　　　　　　　　　　　　　　　　　　　是□　否□

43. 谈论政治。　　　　　　　　　　　　　　　　　　　是□　否□

44. 制订计划、参加会议。　　　　　　　　　　　　　　是□　否□

45. 影响别人的行为。　　　　　　　　　　　　　　　　是□　否□

46. 在社会团体中任职。　　　　　　　　　　　　　　　是□　否□

47. 检查、评价别人的工作。　　　　　　　　　　　　　是□　否□

48. 结识名流。　　　　　　　　　　　　　　　　　　　是□　否□

49. 指导项目小组。　　　　　　　　　　　　　　　　　是□　否□

50. 参与政治活动。　　　　　　　　　　　　　　　　　是□　否□

51. 整理好桌面和房间。　　　　　　　　　　　　　　　是□　否□

52. 抄写文件和信件。　　　　　　　　　　　　　　　　是□　否□

53. 为领导写报告或公函。　　　　　　　　　　　　　　是□　否□

54. 检查个人收支情况。　　　　　　　　　　　　　　　是□　否□

55. 参加打字培训班。　　　　　　　　　　　　　　　　是□　否□

56. 参加算盘、文秘等培训。　　　　　　　　　　　　　是□　否□

57. 参加商业会计培训班。　　　　　　　　　　　　　　是□　否□

58. 参加情报处理培训班。　　　　　　　　　　　　　　是□　否□

59. 整理信件、报告、记录等。　　　　　　　　　　　　是□　否□

60. 写商业贸易信。　　　　　　　　　　　　　　　　　是□　否□

您具有擅长或胜任下列活动的能力吗？（是？否？在相应的□里打"√"）（选择"是"计1分；选择"否"计 0 分）

61. 能使用电锯、电钻和锉刀等木工工具。　　　　　　　是□　否□

62. 知道万用表的使用方法。　　　　　　　　　　　　　是□　否□

63. 能够修理自行车或其他机械。　　　　　　　　　　　是□　否□

64. 能够使用电钻床、磨床或缝纫机。　　　　　　　　　是□　否□

65. 能给家具和木制品刷漆。　　　　　　　　是□　否□

66. 能看建筑等设计图。　　　　　　　　　　是□　否□

67. 能够修理简单的电器用品。　　　　　　　是□　否□

68. 能够修理家具。　　　　　　　　　　　　是□　否□

69. 能修收录机。　　　　　　　　　　　　　是□　否□

70. 能简单地修理水管。　　　　　　　　　　是□　否□

71. 能演奏乐器。　　　　　　　　　　　　　是□　否□

72. 能参加二部或四部合唱。　　　　　　　　是□　否□

73. 独唱或独奏。　　　　　　　　　　　　　是□　否□

74. 扮演剧中角色。　　　　　　　　　　　　是□　否□

75. 能创作简单的乐曲。　　　　　　　　　　是□　否□

76. 会跳舞。　　　　　　　　　　　　　　　是□　否□

77. 能绘画、素描或书法。　　　　　　　　　是□　否□

78. 能雕刻、剪纸或泥塑。　　　　　　　　　是□　否□

79. 能设计海报、服装或家具。　　　　　　　是□　否□

80. 写得一手好文章。　　　　　　　　　　　是□　否□

81. 懂得真空管或晶体管的作用。　　　　　　是□　否□

82. 能列举三种含蛋白质多的食品。　　　　　是□　否□

83. 理解铀的裂变。　　　　　　　　　　　　是□　否□

84. 能用计算尺、计算器、对数表。　　　　　是□　否□

85. 会使用显微镜。　　　　　　　　　　　　是□　否□

86. 能找到三个星座。　　　　　　　　　　　是□　否□

87. 能独立进行调查研究。　　　　　　　　　是□　否□

88. 能解释简单的化学式。　　　　　　　　　是□　否□

89. 理解人造卫星为什么不落地。　　　　　　是□　否□

90. 经常参加学术会议。　　　　　　　　　　是□　否□

91. 有向各种人解释说明的能力。　　　　　　是□　否□

92. 常参加社会福利活动。　　　　　　　　　是□　否□

93. 能和大家一起友好相处地工作。　　　　　是□　否□

94. 善于与年长者相处。　　　　　　　　　　是□　否□

95. 会邀请和招待别人。　　　　　　　　　　是□　否□

96. 能简单有效地教育儿童。　　　　　　　　是□　否□

97. 能安排会议等活动的顺序。　　　　　　　是□　否□

98. 善于体察人心和帮助他人。　　　　　　　是□　否□

99. 帮助护理病人或伤员。　　　　　　　　　是□　否□

100. 安排社团组织的各种事务。　　　　　　　是□　否□

101. 担任过学生干部并且干得不错。　　　　　是□　否□

102. 工作上能指导和监督他人。　　　　　　　是□　否□

103. 做事充满活力和热情。　　　　　　　　　是□　否□

104. 有效地用自身的行为调动他人。　　　　　是□　否□

105. 销售能力强。	是□	否□
106. 曾作为俱乐部或社团的负责人。	是□	否□
107. 向领导提出建议或反映意见。	是□	否□
108. 有开创事业的能力。	是□	否□
109. 知道怎样做能成为一个优秀的领导者。	是□	否□
110. 健谈善辩。	是□	否□
111. 会熟练地打印中文。	是□	否□
112. 会用外文打字机或复印机。	是□	否□
113. 能快速记笔记和抄写文章。	是□	否□
114. 善于整理保管文件和资料。	是□	否□
115. 善于从事事务性的工作。	是□	否□
116. 会用算盘。	是□	否□
117. 能在短时间内分类和处理大量文件。	是□	否□
118. 能使用计算机。	是□	否□
119. 能搜集数据。	是□	否□
120. 善于为自己或集体做财务预算表。	是□	否□

评分提示：

R 实物型（与物打交道）1～10；61～70

A 艺术型（创造性思维和情感表达）：11～20；71～80

I 探究型（思考和解决问题，以得出结论或概念）：21～30；81～90

S 社会型（理解他人需要并提供帮助）：31～40；91～100

E 经营型/进取型（影响和控制他人）：41～50；101～110

C 事务型（与信息、规则打交道）：51～60；111～120

按得分从高到低的顺序，选择得分最高的三项，并记下相应的字母，就是你的测试结果。

译　文

第二部分：相关信息

基本职业目标

我们每时每刻都会遇到对工作不满意的人，他们不满意的原因各有不同。有些人是因为不喜欢他们的工作时间表，有些人是因为不喜欢他们办公室里的某位同事，甚至有些人是因为不喜欢他们的老板。然而，这些模糊的理由实际上是为对所有工作不满的根本潜在原因提供了掩护。事实上，这些员工是因为不知道或没有考虑过自身的职业目标。只有当一个人清楚地认识到自己的职业目标时才能从工作中获得最大的满足，从而进步更快。以下是一名员工应该思考并记住的一些基本职业目标的示例清单：

资源增长

无论是在日常生活还是工作中，变化都是无时无刻的。随着业务的变化和增长，很自然人们必须不断地提升他们为企业或客户提供的知识和资源。因此，提升自己的知识和资源是一名员工应该追求的一个重要的职业目标。

财务方面

财务方面是需要考虑的最重要的方面之一。如果一个人的薪酬不足，就会变得痛苦和沮丧，这将会体现在他或她的工作标准和工作方法上。如果一个人的薪酬过高，他或她可能变得精神萎靡，或许不如刚被雇佣时那么高效，很快在工作岗位上走下坡路。因此，另一个重要的职业目标是实现薪酬与所在岗位对公司的价值相当，这也是一名员工应追求的职业目标。

满意度

世界上没有哪种活动能够在没有一定程度上让一个人的某个要求达到满意而可以进行的。一个重要的职业目标应该是对正在从事的任何工作都满意。当然，这并不意味着你应该停止尝试或放缓你的提升进程。你应该确保你完全满足于你正从事的工作。

新经验

我们一生大约四分之三的时间几乎都花在工作上。因此，我们的职业生涯不仅要追求在生活中取得进步和成功，而且要学习新事物并获得新经验。经验增加可以丰富一个人的思想和知识。因此，要记住的另一个重要职业目标是积累经验，比如了解不同国家的文化，认识新朋友，基本熟悉全世界的习俗和传统。这将会增强我们的包容性并改变我们的观念。

稳定性

一个人应该寻求的另一个重要的职业目标是稳定性。一旦进入了一家稳定的公司，就不用担心日常所需，可以专注于个人的成长以及专业的提升，这同时也促进了公司的发展。

第三部分：情景任务范例

情境：会计专业大一新生李欣正就读于盘锦职业技术学院财经分院。他大学生活第一周的主题是入学教育。在职业发展规划课堂上，大家正在热烈地讨论，李欣正在与同学吴瑞就"职业目标"进行交谈。（A：李欣；B：吴瑞）

B：在五年后你希望做到什么位置？

A：我并不想要什么特别的头衔，我只想做我喜欢做的事情。

B：听起来非常有道理。

A：这对我来说是最重要的。我想把我的知识和经验运用到一份具有挑战性的工作中，为了达到这个目标，我只想一步一步地踏实工作。

B：你的长远目标是什么？

A：因为我从以前的工作中获得了一些管理经验，我希望将来我可以运用我的组织和计划才能。

B：你计划怎样实现呢？

A：做任何需要做的事情并且继续深入学习，我确信我所从事的这个行业将迅猛发展。通常情况下在一家公司具有了足够的工作经验后是有可能从现在的职位升到一个管理层职位的。

2.2   Make a Career Plan

Section One: Task

Situation: *Sun Rui*, *a freshman who majors in nursing of Panjin Vocational & Technical College*, *dreams of being an excellent nurse after graduation. Suppose you were Sun Rui*, *please fill in the Career Development Plan Form.*

Section Two: Related Information

The Career Planning

A career plan helps you determine your skills and interests, what career best suits your talents, and what skills and training you need for your chosen career. [1] The Career planning is the continuous process of thinking about your interests, values, skills and preferences, exploring the life, work and learning options available to you, ensuring that your work fits with your personal circumstances and fine-tuning your work and learning plans to help you manage the changes in your life and work, which has four steps:

Step 1: Knowing Yourself

Begin by thinking about where you are now, where you want to be and how you're going to get there. Once you have thought about where you are at now and where you want to be, you can work on getting to know your skills, interests and values.

Step 2: Finding Out

This step is about exploring the occupations and learning areas that interest you. Once you have some idea of your occupational preferences, you can research the specific skills and qualifications required for those occupations. Explore occupations that interest you and ask yourself how the skills and interests match up with these occupations. [2]

Step 3: Making Decisions

This step involves comparing your options, narrowing down your choices and thinking about what suits you best. After this step you will have narrowed down your options and have more of an idea of what you need to do next to help you achieve your goals.

Step 4: Taking Action

Here you plan the steps you need to take to put your plan into action. Use all you have learnt about your skills, interests and values together with the information you have gathered about the world of work to create your plan. [3] At the end of this step you will have a plan which sets out the steps to help you achieve your next learning or work goal.

Vocabulary

talent　['tælənt]　*n.* 才能
option　['ɒpʃ(ə)n]　*n.* 选项
occupation　[ˌɒkjuˈpeʃən]　*n.* 职业

specific [spə'sɪfɪk] *adj.* 特殊的

qualify ['kwɒlɪfaɪ] *vt.* 使具有资格

match up with 和……相配

narrow down 缩小

sets out the steps to 着手制订……的步骤

Notes

1. A career plan helps you determine your skills and interests，what career best suits your talents，and what skills and training you need for your chosen career. 职业规划帮助你确定自己的技能和兴趣，确定什么职业最适合你的才能，和对于你所选择的职业需要什么技能和培训。"what career best suits your talents，and what skills and training you need for your chosen career" 是 what 引导的名词性从句，在句中作动词 determine 的宾语。

2. Explore occupations that interest you and ask yourself how the skills and interests match up with these occupations. 探索你感兴趣的职业，并问问自己如何将技能和兴趣与这些职业相匹配。"that interest you" 为 that 引导的定语从句修饰先行词 occupations，"how the skills and interests match up with these occupations" 为 how 引导的名词性从句作动词 ask 的宾语。

3. Use all you have learnt about your skills，interests and values together with the information you have gathered about the world of work to create your plan. 运用你所学到的所有技能，结合你的兴趣、价值观以及收集的关于工作的信息创建你的计划。此句主体结构为 "Use all you have learnt about … to create your plan"，其中 "your skills，interests and values together with the information you have gathered about the world of work" 为并列结构作介词 about 的宾语，"you have gathered about the world of work" 为省略了关系代词的定语从句，修饰并列结构中的 information。

Section Three: Situational Task Samples

Situation：*Li Xin，a freshman whose major is accounting，has had a basic vision of his profession after one-week Freshman Entrance Education. He writes a Career Plan for himself so as to perfect his college life and future career.*

My Career Plan		
Name：Li Xin	Period of Plan：	
Major：Accountant	Current Position：College freshman	
Long Term Goal：Senior Accountant		
Current Skills and Interests：		
1.	Mastering basic accounting skills	
2.	Setting certain knowledge of mathematics and science	
3.	Experience of working as a team leader	
4.	Skilled in using Office Software and Internet	
5.	Served as class monitor for 3 years	

Continued

Career Requirements：		
	1.	College diploma
	2.	Presentation and writing skills
	3.	Knowledge of physical science and mathematics
	4.	Job/Professional certificates
	5.	Analytic and creative mind
	6.	Computer operation and English skills

Educational Activities：		
Training or Courses：	Date Scheduled	Date Completed
Basic accounting	9/2017	3/2018
Financial accounting	3/2018	9/2018
Accounting practice	9/2018	3/2019

Section Four: Functional Expression Bank

Positions（职业）

accountant 会计

bank teller 银行出纳员

manager 经理

assistant 助理

secretary 秘书

supervisor 主管

consultant 顾问

clerk 职员

agent 房地产经纪人

instructor 教师

chemist 药剂师

nurse 护士

builder 建筑工人

architect 建筑师

civil engineer 土木工程师

electrician 电工

maintenance engineer 维修工程师

mechanic 机械工

technician 技师

Skills Requirements（技能需求）

1. Experience of working as a team leader 作为团队领导的经历

2. Skilled in using Word 2003 and Internet 擅长使用 Word 2003 办公软件以及网络操作

3. Served as class monitor for 3 years 当过 3 年班长

4. Get college diploma in… 在……获大专毕业证

5. Presentation and writing skills 演讲和写作技能

6. Knowledge of physical science and mathematics 物理和数学知识

7. Job/Professional certificates 工作/职业证书

8. Analytic and creative mind 分析和创造性思维

Section Five: Cultural Tips

埃德加·施恩的职业锚分类

职业锚理论产生于在职业生涯规划领域具有"教父"级地位的美国麻省理工大学斯隆商学院美国著名的职业指导专家埃德加·H·施恩（Edgar. H. Schein）教授领导的专门研究小组，是对该学院毕业生的职业生涯研究中演绎成的。职业锚，是指人们选择和发展自己的职业时所围绕的中心，是自我意识习得的一个部分；强调个人能力、动机和价值观三方面的相互作用与整合，是个人同工作环境互动作用的产物，在实际工作中是不断调整的。

1. 技术或功能型职业锚

这类人往往出于自身个性与爱好考虑，并不愿意从事管理工作，而是愿意在自己所处的专业技术领域发展。在我国过去不培养职业经理人的时候，经常将技术拔尖的科技人员提拔到领导岗位，但他们本人往往并不喜欢这样的工作，更希望能继续从事自己的专业。

2. 管理型职业锚

这类人有强烈的愿望去做管理人员，同时经验也告诉他们自己有能力达到高层领导职位，因此，他们将职业目标定为有相当大职责的管理岗位。成为高层管理人员需要的能力包括三方面：①分析能力：在信息不充分或情况不确定时，判断、分析、解决问题的能力；②人际交往能力：影响、监督、领导、应对与控制各级人员的能力；③情绪控制力：能够在面对危急事件时，不沮丧、不气馁，并且有能力承担重大的责任，而不被其压垮。

3. 创造型职业锚

这类人需要创建完全属于自己的东西，或是以自己名字命名的产品或工艺，或是自己的公司，或是能反映个人成就的私人财产。他们认为只有获得这些实实在在的事物才能体现自己的才干。

4. 自由独立型职业锚

有些人更喜欢独来独往，不愿像在大公司里那样彼此依赖，很多有这种职业定位的人同时也有相当高的技术型职业定位。但是他们不同于那些简单技术型定位的人，他们并不愿意在组织群体中发展，而是宁愿做一名咨询人员，或是自主创业，或是与他人合伙开业。其他自由独立型的人往往会成为自由撰稿人。

5. 安全型职业锚

有些人最关心的是职业的长期稳定性与安全性，他们为了安定的工作，可观的收入，优越的福利与养老制度等付出努力。目前我国绝大多数的人都选择这种职业定位，很多情况下，这是由于社会发展水平决定的，而并不完全是本人的意愿。相信随着社会的进步，人们将不再被迫选择这种类型。

译　文

第二部分：相关信息

职业规划

职业规划帮助你确定自己的技能和兴趣，确定什么职业最适合你的才能，和对于你所选择的职业需要什么技能和培训。职业规划是一个连续性的过程，这个过程中，你需要思考你的兴趣、价值观、技能和偏好；需要探索适合你自己的生活、工作和学习；确保你的工作符合你的个人情况；并能对你的工作和学习计划进行较好地调整，从而帮助你适应生活和工作的变化。职业规划具体包括以下四个步骤。

第一步：认识自己

首先想想你现在的位置，你想要的位置，以及如何达到你想要的那个位置。只有你考虑到现在的位置和你想要的位置，你才能开始了解你的技能，兴趣和价值观。

第二步：探索发现

这一步是探索你感兴趣的职业和学习领域。一旦你了解了自己的职业喜好，就可以研究那些职业所需的具体技能和资格。探索你感兴趣的职业，并问问自己如何将技能和兴趣与这些职业相匹配。

第三步：做出决定

这一步包括将你的选择进行比较并缩小选择范围，思考什么职业最适合你。在这一步之后，你就会缩小自己的选择范围，并且更多地考虑接下来需要做什么以帮助自己实现目标。

第四步：采取行动

此时，你要计划需要采取的步骤并把你的计划付诸行动。运用你所学到的所有技能，结合你的兴趣、价值观以及收集的关于工作的信息创建你的计划。完成这一步骤之后，你将拥有一个帮助你实现下一个学习或工作目标的计划。

第三部分：情境任务范例

情境：会计专业新生李欣，经过一周的新生入学教育，已经对自己的职业有了一个基本的想法。他为自己写了一份职业规划，以完善他的大学生活和未来的职业生涯。

我的职业规划		
姓　　名：李欣	计划时效：	
专　　业：会计	当前职位：大一新生	
长期目标：高级会计师		
当前技能与兴趣：		
1.	掌握基础会计技能	
2.	掌握一定的数学以及科学知识	
3.	做过团队领袖	
4.	擅长使用 Office 办公软件以及网络操作	
5.	做过 3 年班长	
职业需求：		
1.	大专毕业证书	
2.	演讲与写作技能	
3.	物理和数学知识	
4.	工作/职业证书	
5.	分析与创造性思维	
6.	计算机操作能力与外语能力	
教学活动：		
培训或课程：	开始日期	完成日期
基础会计	2017/9	2018/3
财务会计	2018/3	2018/9
会计实践	2018/9	2019/3

Unit Three   Application and Interview

3. 1   Write a Resume for Job Application

Section One: Tasks

Situation 1: Ma Weiwei majors in nursing, and she will graduate from the Nursing Division of Panjin Vocational & Technical College in July. She wants to be a nurse of Anxin Women Hospital. Suppose you were Ma Weiwei, please write a resume for the job application.

Situation 2: Peter is an assistant manager of HP Trade Company with 5-year working experience, and he wants to get the position as a sales manager of PMB International Trade Company. Suppose you were Peter, please write a resume for the job application.

Section Two: Related Information

Core Sections of a Resume for a Job Application

A resume is a document used by a person to present his/her backgrounds and skills. A typical resume contains a "summary" of relevant job and education experience. An effective resume speaks to the employer's needs and requirements and demonstrates a match between what you have to offer and requirements. [1] It stimulates interest in you by summarizing information: unique qualities, well developed skills, relevant work or academic experiences, or accomplishments.

There are three different kinds of resumes: chronological, skills-based, and combined resume.

Chronological resume: Highlights your work history and most recent job title first. It's the most commonly used format for resumes.

Skill-based resume: List your skills and accomplishment first, while shifting focus from your employment history.

Combination resume: A summary of qualifications or achievements highlights the most notable parts of your career, but your work history will still include details of your job description, skills, and other accomplishments.

Each type serves its own purpose, but the core sections for each kind of resumes are common, which will be explained as the followings.

Basic Information

This section should be at the top of your page, including your name, your phone number, your address, and your email.

Objective

The objective can be a sentence presented right after your Basic Information.[2] The objective includes job titles or descriptions.

Education

Starting with the latest college or university you graduated from, it is presented in a reverse chronological order and mainly includes your major, main courses and your expected degree year. Senior middle school should also be included if necessary.

Work Experience

Work experience includes the time spans you worked, the companies you worked, your job titles, and the description of your significant duties. Use keywords to describe work experience in bullet points with two to three bullets under each job in a reverse chronological order. If you are a new graduate, you can use "Activities" to introduce your college activities and social activities instead of work experience.

Honors and Awards

The section of honors and awards highlights the part which is relevant to your job. It mainly includes the year received, the name of the award and the organization of offering the award, which should be still presented in a reverse chronological order.

Skills

Language skills: *The section includes a list of the languages you have mastered and the level.*

Technical skills: *Technical skills include any specialized skills you have that is relevant to the job.*

Generally speaking, a perfect resume should ideally not be any longer than one page. If you have had a number of years of experience specific to the job you are applying for, two pages are also acceptable.[3]

Vocabulary

core [kɔː] *adj.* 核心的
section ['sekʃ(ə)n] *n.* 部分
resume ['rezjumeɪ] *n.* 简历
relevant ['reləvənt] *adj.* 相关的

applicant [ˈæplɪkənt] *n.* 申请人

chronological [ˌkrɒnəˈlɒdʒɪk(ə)l] *adj.* 依时间先后顺序而记载的

highlight [ˈhaɪlaɪt] *vt.* 突出

specialized [ˈspeʃəlaɪzd] *adj.* 专门的，专业的

optional [ˈɒpʃ(ə)n(ə)l] *adj.* 可选择的

objective [əbˈdʒektɪv] *n.* 目标；

span [spæn] *n.* 跨度

bullet [ˈbʊlɪt] *n.* 着重号

honor [ˈɒnə(r)] *n.* 荣誉

award [əˈwɔːd] *n.* 奖项

notable [ˈnəʊtəb(ə)l] *adj.* 显著的；

Notes

1. An effective resume speaks to the employer's needs and requirements and demonstrates a match between what you have to offer and requirements. 一份有效的简历需要满足雇主的需要和要求，呈现与需求相匹配的相关信息。"what you have to offer" 为 what 引导的宾语从句，与 requirements 一起作 match 的并列宾语。

2. The objective can be a sentence presented right after your Basic Information. 求职意向可以是一句话，置于基本信息之后。"presented right after your Basic Information" 为过去分词作后置定语修饰 "a sentence"。

3. If you have had a number of years of experience specific to the job you are applying for, two pages are also acceptable. 如果你有许多年的经验针对你所应聘的工作，两页也是可以接受的。此句为 If 引导的表示条件关系的主从复合句，其中 "you are applying for" 为省略关系代词的定语从句修饰从句中的 "the job"，"specific to the job you are applying for" 为形容词短语后置修饰 experience。

Section Three: Situational Task Samples

Sample 1: Li Xin is an accounting major who will graduate this July. He wants to be an accountant of Huawei Trade Company in Guangzhou. His basic information is included in the following Resume.

RESUME

Basic Information

Name: Li Xin

Address: 46 Yurun Lane, Pinghu Rd.

        Hunnan District

        Shenyang, Liaoning Province

Mobile Phone: 15998730628

E-mail: *Lixin1995@hotmail.com*

Birth Date[1]: Oct. 23, 1995

Gender[2]: Male

Marital Status: Single

Health: Excellent

Objective

To serve as an accountant in a foreign-capital enterprise

Education

September, 2014—June, 2017   Major in Accounting of Financial Division, Panjin Vocational & Technical College;

September, 2011—June, 2014   Shenyang 361 Senior Middle School

Work Experience

March, 2015—June, 2016   Part-time tourist guide for Jinqiu Traveling Agency;

December, 2014—December, 2015   Vice-chairman, Student Union of Financial Division, Panjin Vocational & Technical College

References

Professor Zhu Yu, Panjin Vocational & Technical College, Tel: 15842790522

Headmaster Li Yun, Shenyang 361 Senior Middle School, Tel: 15102439088

Sample 2: Li Xin is an accountant who has been working in a trade company for three years. He wants to be the Sales Manager of ABC Trade Company. His basic information is included in the following Resume.

RESUME

Basic Information

Name: Li Xin

Birth Date: Oct. 23, 1995

Gender: Male

Marital Status: Married

Health: Excellent

Phone Number: 15998730628

E-mail: *Lixin1995@hotmail. com*

Position Wanted[3]

To work as[4] a sales manager in an international trade company

Education

September, 2014—June, 2017   Major in Accounting of Financial Division, Panjin Vocational & Technical College

September, 2011—June, 2014   Shenyang 361 Senior Middle School

Work Experience

August, 2017—Present   An accountant in Huawei Trade Company

March，2015—June，2016　Part-time tourist guide for Jinqiu Traveling Agency

December，2014—December，2015

Vice-chairman，Student Union of Financial Department，Panjin Vocational & Technical College

Honors

May，2018　Excellent Staff，Huawei Trade Company

June，2017　Excellent Graduate，Panjin Vocational & Technical College

Reference

Will be furnished upon request.

Notes

1. "Birth Date" 翻译为出生日期，有时也可替换为 "Date of Birth"；但不可以用 Birthday，因为出生日期只有一个，而生日则年年都有。

2. "Gender" 表示性别，比 sex 更加得体；正式文体一般选用 gender 表示性别，而 sex 表示 "性"。

3. "Position Wanted" 翻译为求职意向，也可替换为 "Objective"。

4. "To work as" 或者 "To serve as" 为大纲型简历中阐述求职意向的常用短语。

Section Four: Functional Expression Bank

Basic Information（个人资料）

date of birth 出生日期

birth date 出生日期

birth place 出生地点

nationality 民族，国籍

native place 籍贯

province 省

city 市

district 区

autonomous region 自治区

prefecture 专区

county 县

street 街

lane 胡同，巷

road 路

postal code 邮政编码

home phone 住宅电话

business phone 办公电话

male 男

female 女

height 身高

weight 体重

marital status 婚姻状况

single 单身

married 已婚

separated 分居

divorced 离异

widowed 丧偶

health condition 健康状况

excellent 良好

Education（教育经历）

curriculum included 所学课程

courses taken 所学课程

refresher course 进修课程

student union 学生会

commissary in charge of entertainment 文娱委员

commissary in charge of sports 体育委员

commissary in charge of physical labor 劳动委员

commissary in charge of organization 组织委员

commissary in charge of publicity 宣传委员

party branch secretary 党支部书记

league branch secretary 团支部书记

graduate 毕业生

undergraduate 大学肄业生，（尚未取得学位的）大学生

freshman 大学一年级学生

sophomore 大学二年级学生

Junior 大学三年级学生

senior 大学四年级学生

B. A. Degree in（major）（专业名称）专业学士

Master's Degree in（major）（专业名称）专业硕士

Work Experience（工作经历）

1. Make logistics bills. 制作物流运单。

2. Produce import and export trade financial statements. 制作进出口贸易财务报表。

3. Analyze financial performance of…分析财务业绩……

4. Execute credit and financial analyses of 执行信贷和金融分析……

5. Remote diagnosis and maintenance of vehicle 远程汽车诊断与维护

6. Analyze logging data from a well 测井数据分析

7. Intern preschool classrooms observing kids 幼儿园课堂教学观摩……

8. Produce marketing plan to…制作……营销计划

Objective（目标描述）

To serve/work as…作为……

Awards & Honors（所获荣誉）

scholarship 奖学金

tri-excellent student 三好学生

excellent League member 优秀团员

excellent leader 优秀干部

prize fellow 奖学金生

advanced worker 先进工作者

working model 劳动模范

Reference（证明材料）

1. Will be furnished upon request. 以上将根据要求提供相关证明材料。

2. Available upon request. 以上将根据要求提供相关证明材料。

Section Five: Cultural Tips

HR 眼中的完美求职简历

什么样的简历能突出自我，展现自我，能在雪片般的求职简历中脱颖而出，吸引 HR 的眼球、留下深刻的印象呢？

1. 简洁、清新、明了、用数据体现业绩

简历的排版和设计清新、自然、大方、不失庄重。短短一份"成就纪录"，远胜于长长几页的"工作经验"。

2. 明确职业定位、职业目标，展现核心能力

对新岗位的工作职责、工作内容、任职资格要求进行仔细阅读，并将自己在学历、经验、技能及背景等方面能够吸引 HR 的核心优势突显出来。

3. 重点突出、经历引人注目

在职人士一定要突出职场经历、工作经验与比较优势及教育背景、荣誉、特殊技能和成就；而应届大学生的重点则放在对想获得职位的理解、感悟、态度、学历、社团经验、所获荣誉、特殊技能及训练等方面。

4. 形式突出，个性品格跃然纸上

简历的设计要突出个性。职业动机、兴趣爱好等方面，要展现出自信、诚实的个性，清晰的工作思路、稳健的工作作风等品格，这些都是企业 HR 最感兴趣和最想了解的。

5. 强化未来目标，流露求职意向

如果你对未来公司有信心、对所从事的职位很有兴趣，要在简历中体现出来，表达你很想加盟的愿望和理由，站在对方企业的角度去看待这个岗位，表明你的意向和决心，能促使 HR 向你发出应聘通知。

译　文

第二部分：相关信息

求职简历核心内容概述

简历是用于表现个人背景以及技能的文件。一份典型的简历包含一个相关工作和教育经历"简介"。一份有效的简历需要满足雇主的需要和要求，呈现与需求相匹配的相关信息。简历要概括诸如你独特的品质、良好的技能、相关工作或学术经历以及富有竞争力的成绩，从而让雇主对你产生兴趣。

主要有三种类型的简历，分别是时间顺序型简历、突出能力型简历和综合型简历。

时间顺序型简历：首先突出你的工作经历与最近的职位，是最常用的简历形式。

突出能力型简历：首先列出你的技能与成就，行文重点从工作经历转向能力介绍。

综合型简历：资质或成就总结要突显在职业生涯中最显著的部分，但是你的工作经历仍然要包含工作描述、技能和其他成就等详细信息。

每种简历都有其独特的写作目的，但是就内容而言，三种简历有其共同的核心内容。下文将对其进行解释说明。

基本信息

这部分应该放在页面的顶部，包括你的名字、电话号码、地址和电子邮件。

求职意向

求职意向可以是一句话，置于基本信息之后。包含职位名称或职位具体描述。

教育经历

这个部分一般从你最后毕业的大学或学院开始阐述，以倒序的时间顺序呈现，主要包括你的专业、主修课程和学制。如果有必要，高中的经历也应包含在内。

工作经历

工作经历包括你工作的时间段、公司的名称、工作职位、主要的工作职责描述。用关键词来描述工作经历要点，以倒序的时间顺序在每个工作下列举 2~3 条。如果你刚大学毕业，你可以用"活动"代替工作经历介绍你参与的校园活动和社会活动。

荣誉和奖励

荣誉和奖励部分要突出与你的工作有关的部分。该部分主要包括获奖时间、奖项名称、发证机关，该部分呈现依然遵从时间倒序的方式。

相关技能

语言能力：这部分包括一系列的你所掌握的语言和掌握程度。

技术技能：技术技能包括你拥有的与工作相关的任何专业的技能。

一般来说，一份完美的简历理想情况下应该不超过一页。如果你有许多年的经验针对你所应聘的工作，两页也是可以接受的。

第三部分：情境任务范例

范例 1： 李欣是会计专业学生，即将于今年 7 月毕业。他想成为华威贸易公司广州分公司的一名会计师。他的基本信息如下面简历所述。

简　历

基本信息

姓名：李欣

地址：辽宁省沈阳浑南区平湖路雨润巷 46 号

移动电话：15998730628

电子邮箱：*Lixin1995@hotmail.com*

出生日期：1995 年 10 月 23 日

性　　别：男

婚姻状况：单身

健康状况：良好

职位意向

在外资企业担任会计

教育经历

2014 年 9 月至 2017 年 6 月　　于盘锦职业技术学院财经分院主修会计专业

2011 年 9 月至 2014 年 6 月　　就读于沈阳 361 高中

工作经历

2015 年 3 月至 2016 年 6 月　在金秋旅行社任兼职导游

2014 年 12 月至 2015 年 12 月　担任盘锦职业技术学院财经分院学生会副主席

证明人

朱玉教授，盘锦职业技术学院，电话：15842790522

李云校长，沈阳 361 高中，电话：15102439088

范例 2：李欣是一位在贸易公司工作三年的会计。他想成为 *ABC* 贸易公司的销售经理。他的基本信息如下文简历中所述。

简　历

基本信息

姓　　名：李欣

出生日期：1995 年 10 月 23 日

性　　别：男

婚姻状况：已婚

健康状况：良好

电话号码：15998730628

电子邮箱：*Lixin1995@hotmail.com*

求职意向

在一个国际贸易公司做销售经理

教育经历

2014 年 9 月至 2017 年 6 月　于盘锦职业技术学院财经分院主修会计专业

2011 年 9 月至 2014 年 6 月　就读于沈阳 361 高中

工作经验

2017 年 8 月至今　在华威贸易公司任会计

2015 年 3 月至 2016 年 6 月　金秋旅行社做兼职导游

2014 年 12 月至 2015 年 12 月　担任盘锦职业技术学院财经分院学生会副主席

获得荣誉

2018 年 5 月　优秀员工　华威贸易公司

2017 年 6 月　优秀毕业生　盘锦职业技术学院

证明材料

以上将根据要求提供相关证明材料。

3. 2   Write a Cover Letter for Job Application

Section One: Situational Tasks

Situation 1: *Ma Weiwei*, *who majors in nursing*, *will graduate from the Nursing Division of Panjin Vocational & Technical College in July. She wants to be a nurse of Anxin Women Hospital. Suppose you were Ma Weiwei*, *please write a cover letter for job application.*

Situation 2: *Peter is an assistant manager of HP Trade Company with 5-year working experience. He wants to get the position as a sales manager of PMB International Trade company. Suppose you were Peter*, *please write a cover letter for job application.*

Section Two: Related Information

How to Organize a Cover Letter for a Job Application

A cover letter provides a great opportunity to cover qualifications that can't be fully explained in the resume. [1] In the cover letter, the applicant needs to introduce himself, mention the job he's applying for, match his skills and experiences with the skills and experiences required by the job. To take full advantage of a cover letter, please follow these steps below.

Add a letterhead at the top of the letter

Letterhead, also called "Heading", refers to the applicant's address and the date of writing the letter. [2] It is positioned on the top of the page, including your address, telephone number, e-mail and date. The date is usually placed two lines below the applicant's information, which is usually shown in the order day/month/year (English Practice) or month/day/year (American Practice). [3]

Address the recipient

The address of the recipient is typed on the left corner of the letter one or two lines below the applicant's address and the date. Be sure to refer to the recipient by his or her proper title (Mrs. , Mr. , Dr. , etc.).

State your purpose

Tell the employer why you are writing to him/her in two or three sentences. State the position for which you are applying. If you are writing an inquiry letter, in which you are asking about positions that might be available, specify why you are interested in working for the employer.

Outline your qualifications

Make a research on the company in which you are applying for a job and make your qualifications jump out at the reader. This will also be useful if you get an interview. Some questions to keep in mind as you write are:

What is the history of the company?

How has the business evolved?

What are the main highlights of the company's performance over the past few years?

Who is their target audience?

Write an appropriate closing

Make this closing paragraph between two to four sentences. Direct the employer to your enclosed resume and make sure you specify that you're available for an interview. Finish off by thanking the recruiter for their time and consideration, and welcome them to get in touch with you. After that, write "Sincerely," "Respectfully," or "Regards," leave several spaces, and print your name.

Add your signature

If you are submitting your cover letter digitally, it's a good idea to scan and add your signature, write it in with a digital writing pad, or make a digital signature stamp with appropriate software.

Make a notation of the enclosures

If you enclose something, such as a resume, with the letter, you should indicate that it contains enclosures by making the notation "Enclosure" or "Enclosures" at the bottom of the letter.

Vocabulary

letterhead ['letəhed] *n.* 信头

recipient [rɪ'sɪpɪənt] *n.* 收信人

recruit [rɪ'kruːt] *vt.* 征募招聘

specify ['spesɪfaɪ] *vt.* 详细说明

outline ['aʊtlaɪn] *vt.* 概述

submit [səb'mɪt] *vt.* 呈递

enclosure [ɪn'kləʊʒə] *n.* 附件

notation [nəʊ'teɪʃ(ə)n] *n.* 注释

signature ['sɪgnətʃə] *n.* 署名

digital ['dɪdʒɪt(ə)l] *adj.* 电子的

stamp [stæmp] *n.* 印记

appropriate [ə'prəʊprɪət] *adj.* 合适的

indicate ['ɪndɪkeɪt] *v.* 表明

finish off 结束，完成；

refer to 参考

Notes

1. A cover letter provides a great opportunity to cover qualifications that can't be fully explained in the resume. 求职信为申请人提供了一次完整介绍相关资历的好机会，从而弥补了简历内容的不充分性。"that can't be fully explained in the resume" 为修饰性成分，修饰 qualifications。

2. Letterhead，also called "Heading"，refers to the applicant's address and the date of writing the letter. 信头，也称为"标题"，一般包含申请人的地址与写信日期。"also called 'Heading'" 为 "letterhead" 的同位语，起到解释说明的作用。

3. The date is usually placed two lines below the applicant's information，which is usually shown in the order day/month/year (English Practice) or month/day/year (American Practice). 日期通常置于申请人信息之下两行，通常以日/月/年（英式体例）或者月/日/年（美式体例）顺序书写。后半句为 which 引导的非限定性定语从句，对前面的主句进行补充说明。

Section Three: Situational Task Samples

Sample 1：*Li Xin is an accounting major who will graduate this July. He wants to be an accountant of Huawei Trade Company in Guangzhou. The following is his cover letter for the job application.*（*Identified Style*[1]）

Li Xin

46 Yurun Lane，Pinghu Rd.

Hunnan District

Shenyang，Liaoning Province

June 6，2017

Miss Smith

Personnel Manager

Huawei Trade Company

Dongguan Trade District

Dear Miss Smith，

My name is Li Xin. I am thrilled to apply for the accountant role in your company. [2] After reviewing your job description，I learn that you're looking for an enthusiastic applicant who can be relied upon. [3] Given these requirements，I believe I am the perfect candidate for the job.

I am an enthusiastic college student who majors in accounting and will graduate from Panjin Vocational & Technical College. I have been consistently praised as an excellent student by my professors and peers. I have developed my Microsoft Word-processing and Financial Software-applying skills，which I hope to leverage into the accountant role in your company. [4]

After reviewing my resume，I believe you will agree that I am the type of positive and driven candidate you are looking for. I am excited to elaborate on my specific skills and abilities. If you are interested in my qualifications，please contact me at（024）85822658/15124285578 or via email at *87012343@qq. com* to arrange for a convenient meeting time.

Thank you for your consideration, and I look forward to hearing from you soon.

Sincerely yours,
Li Xin

Enclosure：Resume

Sample 2：*Li Xin is an accounting major with 3-year working experience in a trade company. He wants to be a sales manager of ABC Trade Company. The following is his cover letter for the job application.（Semi-blocked Style）*

> Li Xin
> Rm. 313，Building B
> 5 Xuefu Lane，Shiyou Ave.
> Guangzhou，Guangdong
> June 6，2020

Mr. Green
Personnel Manager
ABC Trade Company
Dongguan Trade District

Dear Mr. Green，

My name is Li Xin. Please accept my application for the sales manager in your company. After reviewing your job description，I believe that I have the necessary skills and abilities to fill the role.

I am an excellent accountant with 3-year experience who has been consistently praised as the best staff by my co-workers and management. Over the course of my 3-year career，I've developed a skill set directly relevant to the sales manager role you are looking for，including financial management and business statistics. Overall，I have demonstrated managerial abilities in every aspect of my accountant role，and I invite you to review my detailed achievements in the attached resume.

After reviewing my resume，I believe you will agree that I am the type of competent and reliable candidate that you are looking for. I can assist your business to achieve its goals. Please contact me at（020）37384537/15124285578 or via email at *87012343@qq.com* to arrange for a convenient meeting time.

Thank you for your consideration，and I look forward to hearing from you soon.

Sincerely yours,
Li Xin

Enclosure：Resume

Notes

1. 信函格式主要有两种：齐头式（Identified Style）、缩进式（Blocked Style）。一般采用缩进式，格式美观、逻辑清晰。在齐头式中，文件或书信中的每个部分都从左边界开头，段落之间以空行的方式隔开。缩进式是比较老式的商务书信格式。在缩进式中，每个段落的首行要缩进，每个段落缩进的距离要一样，段与段之间不用空行分开。采用缩进式时，最重要的是要前后一致。

2. I am thrilled to apply for…我很高兴申请贵公司的……句中过去分词 thrilled 相当于形容词的用法，表达陈述者自身的心理感受。

3. I learn that you're looking for an enthusiastic applicant that can be relied upon. 我得知贵公司正在寻找一位富有热情并值得信赖的申请人。此句主干部分为 "I learn that you're looking for an enthusiastic applicant"。其中 "that can be relied upon" 为 that 引导的定语从句，修饰先行词 applicant。

4. I have developed my Microsoft Word-processing and Financial Software-applying skills，which I hope to leverage into the accountant role in your company. 我已经掌握了 Microsoft Word 处理软件以及财务软件应用技术，我希望加入到您的公司担任会计。其中 "which I hope to leverage into the accountant role at your company" 为 which 引导的非限定性定语从句，修饰前面的部分，起到补充说明前文的作用。

Section Four: Functional Expression Bank

Beginning Description（开头部分描述）

1. On looking over today's *News Daily* my attention was attracted by your advertisement for a sales manager. Now as I am desirous of obtaining such a position，I would like to apply for it.

拜读贵公司在今日的《每日新闻》报上所刊登的广告，得悉贵公司欲招聘一位销售经理，本人现在正寻找这一类职位，特此修函应征。

2. I have heard that you might need an executive secretary with considerable experience who have worked in the companies like yours.

据悉贵公司有意招聘一名在类似公司工作过的有足够工作经验的行政秘书。

3. I must say that I have long been hopeful of working for your hospital after graduation，I am sure that I have the privilege of serving in your hospital, and I will greatly increase my experience and abilities.

我早已渴望能毕业后进入贵院工作，如有这份荣幸，我确信，对我增加经验和提高行医能力必有极大裨益。

4. Your organization is more than just a business house. It is a famous institution in the minds of the local public. It has a reputation for fair play and honesty with both employees and customers.

贵公司不仅仅是一个商业机构，还是当地的一个知名组织。贵公司的公正和诚实无论在雇员心中还是在顾客心中都享有崇高美誉。

5. For the past four years, while specializing in international trade at college, I have had a secret ambition to work for your organization. I will graduate in July this year.

在大学主修国际贸易的四年中，我一直有一个心愿，盼望能到贵公司工作。我即将在今年七月毕业。

Closing Description（结尾部分描述）

1. If you offer me an interview, I shall be happy to join in it, on any day and at any time you may appoint. 如贵公司有意面试，本人一定遵照所指定的时日，前往拜访。

2. Should you accept my application favorably, I would come over all the difficulties to make myself best to your satisfaction.

假如本人的应聘能得青睐，并能进入而为贵公司服务，本人必以排除万难的决心，为贵公司工作，以符厚望。

3. If there is further information that you wish in the meantime, please let me know. I can always be reached at the address given at the beginning of this letter.

如果需要有关本人的更详细资料，请按本函上方所载地址发函告知。

4. I would be very happy to work under your supervision if it is possible. Thank you very much for your kind attention. Please send me an answer at your earliest convenience.

如能为贵公司效力，本人将不胜荣幸。您能耐心读完这篇申请，本人不胜感激，并请尽快发函告知。

5. If there are additional application procedures, please advise me. I will be in this area from April 5 to April 14 and would like to arrange an interview with you during that time. I will call your office to set an interview date. Thank you for your consideration.

如果应聘还有其他程序，请告知。我将在 4 月 5～14 日在本地，希望届时能与您会面。我会致电您的办公室，确定面试日期。谢谢。

Purpose Description（求职意向描述）

1. I fit the candidate specifications as detailed in your ad.

我符合贵公司招聘广告中所提出的要求。

2. As a vocational college student at accounting I want to apply for an accounting assistance. 作为职业院校会计专业的学生，我想申请一份会计助理的职位。

3. In response to your September 15 ad in *News Daily* for an accountant, I have enclosed my resume.

获悉贵公司在 9 月 15 日《每日新闻》报上刊登的招聘会计的广告，我随信附上我的个人简历。

4. I believe that my enclosed resume will demonstrate that I have the characteristics and experience you seek.

我相信我随函附上的个人简历将会表明我具有贵公司所寻求的个性特征和经验。

Qualification Description（能力资质描述）

1. With my strong knowledge on computer, I am capable and competent.

我电脑知识扎实、能力强可以胜任工作。

2. I think I am skilled in computer operation and maintenance.

我认为我非常精通电脑操作和维修。

3. I believe I can make some positive contributions to your company in the future.
   我相信我能为公司的将来做出积极的贡献。

4. I am young and have more energy，so I think I can handle it well.
   我年轻、精力充沛，所以我想我能很好应对。

5. I have the ability to deal with multitasks/solve problems/communicate well.
   我有多任务处理能力/解决问题能力/良好沟通能力。

6. I'm good at/skilled at multitasking/working under pressure/working to a deadline.
   我擅长同时处理多个任务/在压力下工作/按时完成任务。

7. My strength is that I have high ability to solve problems/I am enthusiastic/I can speak fluent English. 我的优点是能高效解决问题/充满热情/能说一口流利的英语。

8. I can speak English and write in English well. I believe that such foreign language proficiency will be taken into favorable consideration.
   我的英语口语水平以及写作能力都不错，我相信我的外语水平值得贵公司给予认真考虑。

9. I passed the national College English Test（Band 4）in 2015（Photocopies of Certificate enclosed）. 我于 2015 年通过了全国大学英语考试（四级）（复印件证书附上）。

Education Background Description（教育背景描述）

1. I am now a（senior student/third-year student/sophomore/freshman）in Financial Division of Northeast University. 我现在是东北大学财经系的（大四、大三、大二、大一）学生。

2. I went to Liaoning University in 2015 and studied there for half a year.
   我于 2015 年去了辽宁大学，在那里学习了半年。

3. I was trained at Northeast University in management（subject）from April to July in 2015. 我于 2015 年 4～7 月在东北大学接受了管理学培训。

4. I major/specialize in accounting. 我的专业是会计。

5. I graduated from Panjin Vocational & Technical College in 2015 with excellent grade in accounting. 我以优异成绩于 2015 年从盘锦职业技术学院会计专业毕业。

Working Experience Description（工作经历描述）

1. I worked in retailing for seven years and was promoted to manager in my second year.
   我在零售行业做过七年，第二年就被提升为经理。

2. I worked for Anderson Assoc. as a lawyer. 我曾任职于艾德森协会，是一名律师。

3. After completing my studies，I joined TBM Company and worked as a sales assistance.
   完成我的学业后，我加入了 TBM 公司做销售助理工作。

4. On finishing my training，I took up the position of sales manager in Sales Department，
   and I have been at that post ever since. 在完成了培训后，我担任销售部销售经理至今。

5. For the last 5 years，I have been working as a sales assistant.
   过去 5 年，我一直做销售助理。

Awards Description（获奖情况描述）

1. I was awarded the prize of the Best Salesman in TMB Company for my outstanding performance in vehicle sales.

因为我在汽车销售方面的出色表现，我被授予 TMB 公司最佳销售员工奖。

2. I won/received the prize/award of the Best Designer in HP Company. 我在 HP 公司获得过最佳设计师奖。

Section Five: Cultural Tips

求职信的注意事项

1. 逻辑清晰

求职信最忌讳散乱无章，用逻辑性的顺序将必备的内容组合起来：为什么选择这份工作，为什么你是合适人选，如何能联系到你。

2. 短小精悍

求职信不宜过长，应该概括的介绍，而不是事无巨细，否则会增加 HR 的工作量，易使其产生厌烦感。

3. 个性突出

简历用语比较公式化，求职信用语可以个性化一些。但是注意不要太随便，或者过于亲昵，既有特色又不失专业水准为佳。

4. 联络信息

在求职信的开头部分务必要写清楚求职人的联系方式，因为有些应聘者把重要的联络信息都放在求职信封面上。然而，等到简历被传到人事部门管理人员手中，可能已经没有了封面，也就相应丢失了求职者的联络信息，以致人事人员无法联络到求职者。

译　文

第二部分：相关信息

如何拟写求职信

求职信为申请人提供了一次完整介绍相关资历的好机会，从而弥补了简历内容的不充分性。在求职信中，申请人需要介绍自己、介绍自己申请的工作、介绍与工作要求相匹配的技能和经历。为了充分发挥求职信的优势，请遵循以下步骤。

在信件顶部添加信头

信头，也称为"标题"，一般包含申请人的地址和写信的日期。信头位于页面顶部，包括你的地址、电话号码、电子邮箱和日期。日期通常置于申请人信息之下两行，通常以日/月/年（英式体例）或月/日/年（美式体例）的顺序书写。

提及收件人地址

收件人地址书写于信件的左上角，在申请人地址、日期下方一到两行。一定要使用收件人的适当头衔（夫人、先生、博士等）。

说明你的目的

用两到三句话告诉雇主你为什么要写信给他/她，阐释你正在申请的职位。如果你写的是一份询问信，在信中询问自己能申请的职位，请具体阐述你为什么对为这个雇主工作感兴趣。

概述你的资格

研究你正在申请工作的公司并让你的资格立刻吸引读者。如果你有机会参加面试，这也是有用的。在书写时要记住以下几个问题：

公司的历史是什么？

业务是如何发展的？

过去几年公司业绩的主要亮点是什么？

他们的目标受众是谁？

写一个合适的结尾

结束段落在两到四句之间，引导雇主查阅你的简历，并一定详细说明你可以接受面试。最后要感谢招聘者花时间认真阅读，并表达出希望他们与你进一步联系的意愿。之后，写上"真诚地""尊敬地"或"致意"，留下几个空格，并打上你的姓名。

添加签名

如果你要以电子方式提交你的求职信，最好扫描并添加你的签名，用写字板写入，或使用适当的软件制作数字签名。

标注随信附带简历

如果你随信附上一些东西，例如一封简历，你应该通过在信件底部标记"Enclosure"或"Enclosures"来表示该信包含附件。

第三部分：情境任务范例

范例1：*李欣是今年7月毕业的会计专业学生，他想成为华威贸易公司广州分公司的一名会计师。以下是他的求职信。（齐头式）*

李欣

辽宁沈阳浑南区平湖路雨润巷46号

2017年6月6日

史密斯小姐

人事经理

东莞贸易区华威贸易公司

尊敬的史密斯小姐：

我叫李欣，很高兴申请贵公司的会计师一职。在查看贵公司的工作描述后，我得知贵公司正在寻找一位富有热情并值得信赖的申请人。鉴于这些需求，我相信我是这个工作的完美候选人。

我是一名热情的大学生，即将从盘锦职业技术学院毕业，主修会计专业。在我的学生生涯中，我一直被我的教授和同学认为是一名优秀的学生。我已经掌握了 Microsoft Word 处理软件以及财务软件应用技术，我希望加入到您的公司担任会计。

在查看我的简历后，我相信您会认可，我就是贵公司正在寻找的积极和富有进取心的候选人类型。我很高兴能详细说明我的具体技能和能力。如果您对我的资历感兴趣的话，请通过电话（024）85822658/15124285578 或电子邮箱 *87012343@qq.com* 与我联系，从而安排方便的会面时间。

感谢您的考虑，期待着尽快收到您的回复。

您真诚的朋友
李欣

附件：简历

范例2：李欣是一名在一家贸易公司有3年工作经验的会计师。他想成为ABC贸易公司的一名销售经理。以下是他的求职信。（缩进式）

李欣
广东省广州市西楼大街5号学府巷；
石油大道B座313室
2020年6月6日

格林先生
人事经理
东莞贸易区ABC贸易公司

尊敬的格林先生：

我叫李欣，请接受我做贵公司销售经理的申请。在查看贵公司的工作描述后，我相信我有能力胜任这个职位。

我是一名优秀的会计师，有3年工作经验，一直被我的同事和领导称赞为最好的员工。在我3年的职业生涯中，我掌握了与贵公司正在招聘的销售经理一职直接相关一系列的技能，包括财务管理和商务统计。总的来说，在我做会计师期间，我在各个方面都展示了一定的管理能力。我期待您能阅读我随信附带的简历，进一步了解我的详细工作业绩。

看完我的简历后，我相信您会赞同我是贵公司正在寻找的、有能力胜任的、值得信赖的候选人。我有能力帮助您的企业实现公司的发展目标。请通过电话（020）37384537/15124285578或通过电子邮箱87012343@qq.com与我联系，从而安排方便的面谈时间。

感谢您的考虑，我期待着尽快收到您的回复。

您真诚的朋友
李欣

附件：简历

3.3 Have a Job Interview

Section One: Tasks

Situation 1: Wu Zixuan majors in preschool education and will graduate from Panjin Vocational & Technical College in July this year. Two weeks ago, she sent her resume to ABC Kindergarten to apply for a job by email. Wu Zixuan received the interview offer from ABC Kindergarten yesterday. Make a conversation on the job interview, and then act it with your partner.

Situation 2: Li Lei is a bank clerk with 5-year working experience, and he wants to apply for a higher position to challenge himself. Last week, he read the job-wanted advertisement of ICBC Bank in the newspaper and emailed his resume and application letter. He received the interview offer call this morning. Make a conversation on the job interview, and then act it with your partner.

Section Two: Related Information

How to Succeed in the Job Interview

In the ever tighter job market, great importance has been attached to the job interview. The interview has become indispensable for obtaining a satisfactory job. The interviewer can take the advantage to learn about the candidates, such as their working experience, education background and personalities. The interviewee can make use of the opportunity to get to know the job which he is going to take up, the credibility of the firm which he has applied for, and the working conditions as well. [1] If the interviewee has made full preparations for the interview and performed fairly confidently and honestly, success can be ensured. The following tips from experts will help the interviewee to maximize potential employment opportunities.

Dress smart

To dress smart is the best way to ensure a good first impression. If you are being interviewed for a job in an office, it is usually best to wear a dark-colored, conservative suit for both men and women; if you are interviewing for a job where the dress code is more casual such as at a factory or a construction site, nice slacks and a collared button-down shirt with a tie for men and a nice dress or blouse and slacks or skirt for women are usually appropriate. You should avoid wearing excessive jewelry, perfume, and flamboyant clothes. Most experts agree it is better to be overdressed than dressed too casually. What you are wearing tells employers a lot about how serious you are about getting the job. [2]

Be positive

Employers do not want to hear a litany of excuses or bad feelings about a negative experience. If you are asked about a low grade, a sudden job change, or a weakness in your background, don't be defensive. Focus instead on the facts briefly and emphasize what you learned from the experience. Be prepared to market your skills and experiences as they relate to the job described. Work at positioning yourself in the mind of the employer as a person with a particular set of skills and attributes, and work to describe your qualifications appropriately.

Research information

Some important information to look for includes what activities are carried out by the employer, how financially stable the employer is, and what types of jobs exist with the employer.[3] Researching an employer during the job search can help determine more about that organization and your potential place in it. Know how you can help the company and prepare questions to ask the interviewer about the company well.

Arrive early

Plan to arrive for your interview 10~15 minutes before the appointed time. Arriving too early confuses the employer and creates an awkward situation. By the same token, arriving late creates a bad first impression and may doom your chances. Ask for directions when making arrangements for the interview and carry useful portfolio for the interview.

Vocabulary

tight [taɪt] *adj.* 紧的

indispensable [ˌɪndɪˈspensəb(ə)l] *adj.* 不可缺少的；绝对必要的

satisfactory [ˌsætɪsˈfækt(ə)rɪ] *adj.* 满意的；符合要求的

candidate [ˈkændɪdeɪt; -dət] *n.* 候选人，应试者

credibility [ˌkredɪˈbɪlɪtɪ] *n.* 可信性；确实性

maximize [ˈmæksɪmaɪz] *vt.* 取……最大值；对……极为重视

conservative [kənˈsɜːvətɪv] *adj.* 保守的

casual [ˈkæʒjʊəl] *adj.* 随便的；非正式的

appropriate [əˈprəʊprɪət] *adj.* 适当的；恰当的

excessive [ɪkˈsesɪv; ek-] *adj.* 过多的，过分的

flamboyant [flæmˈbɔɪənt] *adj.* 艳丽的

overdressed [ˌəʊvəˈdrest] *adj.* 过分打扮的；讲究的

litany [ˈlɪt(ə)nɪ] *n.* 冗长而枯燥的陈述

defensive [dɪˈfensɪv] *adj.* 防御的

portfolio [pɔːtˈfəʊlɪəʊ] *n.* 文件

take advantage of 利用

Notes

1. The interviewee can make use of the opportunity to get to know the job which he is going to take up, the credibility of the firm which he has applied for, and the working conditions as well. 求职者可以利用这个机会了解他将要担任的工作，他所申请的公司的信誉，以及工作条件。此句主干为 "The interviewee can make use of the opportunity to get to know the job…, the credibility of the firm…and the working conditions as well"。"which he is going to take up" 和 "which he has applied for" 为定语从句，分别修饰先行词 job 和 firm。

2. What you are wearing tells employers a lot about how serious you are about getting the job. 你的穿着可以告诉雇主你对得到这份工作的重视程度。此句中 "What you are wearing" 为 what 引导的名词性从句，位于句首作全句的主语，"how serious you are about getting the job" 为 how 引导的名词性从句，在句中作介词 about 的宾语。

3. Some important information to look for includes what activities are carried out by the employer, how financially stable the employer is, and what types of jobs exist with the employer. 要搜集的重要信息包括雇主所从事的重要活动、雇主的财务稳定性，以及与雇主存在什么样的工作关系。此句中 "to look for" 为动词不定式短语，作 information 的后置定语，"what activities are carried out by the employer, how financially stable the employer is, and what types of jobs exist with the employer." 三个从句作为并列结构作谓语动词 includes 的宾语。

Section Three: Situational Task Samples

Sample 1: *An international hotel is looking for an accountant of Financial Division who is familiar with the hotel business and proficient in English.* [1] *Li Xin just graduated from Financial Division in Panjin Vocational & Technical College, and he wanted to apply for this position. The personnel manager of the hotel hosted the interview.* (*M*: *Personnel Manager*; *L*: *Li Xin*)

M: Nice to meet you.

L: Nice to meet you, too. My name is Li Xin.

M: Take it easy! Please have a seat.

L: Thank you.

M: We've received your resume in answer to our advertisement, and your qualifications for the accountant of Financial Division of our hotel are fit for our requirements, but we thought it necessary to ask you to come here for an interview. [2]

L: Thank you for your appreciation. It is my honor to have an opportunity for this interview.

M: Do you have experience in this field since you are just a graduate from Panjin Vocational & Technical College?

L: Well, our college pays much attention to practical experience. When I was in college, we were required to spend two months on practical work each year.

M: As an accountant of our hotel, you also need to be familiar with the hotel management. Have you mastered relevant knowledge?

L: Yes. At college I selected hotel management courses. And I am the monitor of our class. I can speak English fluently and operate the computer well.

M: Can you drink wine?

L: Yes, a little, but I never drink too excessively.

M: OK. Thank you for your coming. We'll inform you of the result next Monday. Your telephone number is 15124285578, right?

L: Yes. I'll be waiting for your reply.

Sample 2: PKM Trading Company is providing a post of sales manager. Li Xin is an accountant with 3-year practical experience who graduated from Financial Division in Panjin Vocational & Technical College, and he sent his application by email. The company's boss is personally interviewing him this Thursday. (B: Boss; L: Li Xin)

B: Please have a seat.

L: Thank you.

B: Are you Li Xin?

L: Yes, I am.

B: Do you bring any paper or certificate with you?

L: This is a copy of my diploma, and this is the recommendation letter[3] from my previous company.

B: Why do you want to leave your previous company?

L: Because the company wanted to establish the factory in a southern city, and it is far away from my family.

B: Your major is accounting, isn't it?

L: Yes, I graduated from Financial Division in Panjin Vocational & Technical College. My major is accounting.

B: Ours is a foreign trade company. Do you have any experience?

L: Yes. My previous company is a Sino-American joint venture enterprise, and it deals with many fields including trade.

B: What was your responsibility in previous company?

L: I was in charge of checking cost price and the rate of profit.

B: Well, if you don't mind, can you tell me how much you got in your previous company?

L: They gave me 2,000 yuan a month without bonus.

B: How about 2,500 yuan per month? If you are required to work in holidays, we'd pay you extra. Besides we will buy you medical insurance.

L: It is fine. I am sure I would do my best to work well for our company. Then, when am I supposed to start working?

B: Start from July 1. Please remember to bring with you the original diploma and your ID

70

card when you come, and report to the Human Resources Department first.

L: Thank you. Goodbye.

B: Goodbye.

Notes

1. An international hotel is looking for an accountant of Financial Division who is familiar with the hotel business and proficient in English. 一家国际酒店正在寻找一位熟悉酒店业务并且精通英语的财务部会计师。此句中 "who is familiar with the hotel business and proficient in English" 为 who 引导的定语从句，修饰先行词 accountant。

2. …we thought it necessary to ask you to come here for an interview. 我们认为有必要让你来这里参加面试。此句中 it 为形式宾语，"to ask you to come here for an interview" 为整句的真正宾语。

3. recommendation letter 意为推荐信。一般而言，求职者为增加求职成功的机会，往往会邀请较有资质的前辈，一般为大学教师或者原公司领导给写一封推荐信。

Section Four: Functional Expression Bank

Q&A Samples for Interview（面试应答范例）

Question 1: Can you tell me something about yourself?

问题1：能介绍一下你自己吗？

1. As a college student, I worked in KFC part-time and found that I could sell things easily. I'm very competitive and it means a lot to me to be the best.

作为一名大学生，我在肯德基做过兼职工作，发现自己可以轻松地销售商品。我具有很强的竞争意识，对我来说，这段经历让我受益良多，我要努力做到最好。

2. I have been working as a computer programmer for five years. To be specific, I do system analysis, trouble shooting and provide software support, but I am looking for a new challenge right now.

我做了五年的程序员。具体来说，我做系统分析，故障排除和提供软件支持，但是我现在正在寻求新的挑战。

Question 2: Why did you apply for this job?

问题2：你为什么应聘这个工作？

1. As the saying goes, "well begun is half done". Your company is a famous one in the industry and enjoys a high reputation. I hope to choose your company at the beginning of my career. Then I can not only learn new things, but set a solid foundation for my future career as well.

俗话说 "良好的开端是成功的一半"。贵公司是业内知名的企业，享有很高的声誉。我希望选择贵公司作为我职业生涯的开始。那么我不仅可以学习新事物，而且可以为未来的事业打下坚实的基础。

2. I am interested in the job description and the working duties on this position. I believe to be a perfect match for the job and a potential asset for your team. I have similar working

experience, too. That's why I submitted my application. 我对这个职位关于工作和工作职责的描述真的很感兴趣。我相信我可以完美胜任公司的工作并成为公司团队一名有价值的成员。因为我也有类似的工作经验，这就是我提交申请的原因。

Question 3：Why did you leave your last job? /Why are you planning to leave your present job?

问题 3：你为什么离开上一家公司？ /你为什么想离开现在的公司？

1. My last job was not challenging enough. I was not motivated to wake up to work anymore. I liked my colleagues and boss, but I simply can't keep myself motivated anymore. Based on the job description I really believe that I can find new motivation and challenges in your company. 我的上一份工作没有足够的挑战性，我几乎连起床工作的动力都没有了。我喜欢我的同事和老板，但我无法保持自己的积极性。根据工作描述，我相信我可以在贵公司找到新的动力和挑战。

2. There was a downsizing in our company. Similarly to most people from Financial Department, my contract was terminated. However, it is the past. I am ready to utilize all the knowledge and experience I gained there to start my new career, possibly in your corporation. 我们公司正在裁员。与大多数财务部门人员一样，我的合同也被终止了。然而一切都已经过去了。若有可能，我准备利用我在那里获得的所有知识和经验在贵公司开始我的新事业。

Question 4：Can you tell me something about your education?

问题 4：能和我说一说你的教育背景吗？

1. I graduated from Panjin Vocational & Technical College. My major is business administration. I am especially interested in Marketing. My major subject is Management and my minor subject is Practical Mathematics. I have studied in an English training, a computer training and finance training programme at a training school since I graduated from college. 我毕业于盘锦职业技术学院。我的专业是工商管理，我特别感兴趣的是营销科目。我的主修科目是管理，我的辅修科目是实用数学。自从大学毕业以后，我在培训学校分别进行了英语、计算机和金融课程的培训。

2. I have studied at Panjin Vocational & Technical College. I acquired knowledge of statistics and process management. I was active during my studies and took part in practical projects and courses. My studies were pretty practical and I believe to be ready for the job of a project manager. 我曾就读于盘锦职业技术学院，学习了统计和过程管理的相关知识。在读书期间，我积极参与实践项目以及相关课程。我的研究非常实用，我认为我已经为项目经理这份工作做好了准备。

Question 5：Can you tell us something more about your working experience?

问题 5：你能不能多跟我们说说你的工作经历？

1. I am working in a pharmaceutical factory. My present job is to inspect the quality of products. Comparatively speaking, quality control is rather simple. Although I do my job well, I am looking for a new job which is more challenging.
我在一家制药厂工作，目前负责检查产品的质量。相对而言，质量控制是相当简单的。尽管我的工作做得很好，但我希望寻找一个更具挑战性的新工作。

2. From 2010 to 2014 I worked as a project manager for Siemens. We were working mostly on small energy projects.

从2010～2014年，我担任西门子公司一名项目经理，主要负责小型的能源项目。

Question 6：Why should we hire you?

问题6：我们为什么要聘用你？

1. I have relevant experience and I am strongly motivated to work for your company, as it has always been my dream to work here.

我有相关的经验，我拥有强大的动力为贵公司工作，因为在贵公司工作一直是我的梦想。

2. I fulfill all the job requirements. However, I am sure some other applicants do fulfill it, too. But I am a nice guy and always try to create a good atmosphere in the workplace.

我符合这份工作所有的要求。不过，我相信其他一些申请人也确实符合。但我是一个优秀的人，一直努力在工作场所营造一个良好的氛围。

Question 7：What are your strengths?

问题7：你的优点是什么？

1. I'm very responsible and always accomplish all my duties on time. I'm pretty organized and I have good communication skills. I believe that communication skills are crucial in every job, especially in this one.

我非常有责任心，并且总是按时完成任务，而且我有较强的组织能力和良好的沟通技巧。我相信沟通技巧在每一项工作中都是至关重要的，尤其是在这个职位上。

2. I know a lot about how the Chinese economy works, and how business is done here. Secondly, I speak English fluently. And I am a hard-working worker when I have something challenging to do. 我对中国经济如何运作以及如何做生意非常了解。其次，我能说流利的英语。而且，当我面对一些具有挑战性的事情时，我是一个努力工作的人。

Question 8：What are your weaknesses?

问题8：你的缺点是什么？

1. I am not very patient. That's obviously bad. But I am working on it every day, trying to control myself and be more tolerant to others. It's not easy, but I have definitely made good progress in recent years. 我不是很有耐心，这显然是不好的。但是我每天都在努力控制自己，对别人更加宽容。这并不容易，但近年来我确实取得了很好的进展。

2. Sometimes I struggle to concentrate on work. However, I practice every day and my concentration has improved over the years. I try to eliminate other thoughts and focus purely on my job. 有时我难以专注于工作，但是我每天都在练习，几年来我的专注力有所提高。我会尽力消除杂念，完全专注我的工作。

Question 9：What are your goals in five-year horizon?

问题9：五年内，你想达到什么目标？

1. My goal is to become a better manager and to help my employer to achieve exceptional results for the company.

我的目标是成为一名更好的经理，并帮助我的雇主为公司取得卓越的业绩。

2. I would like to have a really good job in five-year time. However, I understand that

firstly I need to learn a lot and I believe that this position is a perfect start for me.

我想在五年的时间里真正把工作做好。但是我明白，首先我需要学习很多，并且我相信这个职位对我来说是一个完美的开始。

Question 10: What are your salary expectations?

问题 10：你期望的薪资是多少？

1. Since I am a recent graduate, there will be a transition period after I enter the company. Therefore, at the beginning, the profits I make for the company will be limited and I don't have specific requirements. But man has to survive. I hope the salary will be enough to help me to be economically independent from my parents.

因为我刚刚毕业，所以进入公司后会有一段过渡期。因此，一开始我为公司创造的利润将是有限的，在薪酬方面我没有具体的要求。但是人必须生存下去，所以我希望薪水足以帮助我在经济上独立。

2. Money is important, but the responsibility that goes along with this job is what interests me most. I would expect an appropriate pay for a person with my experience and educational background. Why don't we discuss salary after you decide whether I'm right for the job?

金钱是重要的，但是与这份工作相关的责任是我最感兴趣的。我希望有一个与我的经验和教育背景相适应的报酬。为何我们不在您决定我是否适合这份工作之后再讨论薪水呢？

Section Five: Culture Tips

面试技巧：面试之中的言语表达方法

言语表达最常见的有三种类型，分别是演讲、情景模拟、串词。演讲题型往往是给定主题的，这里就需要明确"以什么为题"和"以什么为主题"，这两者是有区别的，前者说明题目是既定的，后者说明题目是可以更换的；情景模拟题型则不同，往往是要确定论点，是以安抚劝服为主，还是以工作汇报为主，还是新闻报道的形式，不同的基调决定了后面答题的方向；而串词题型在这一方面类似于演讲，题目往往会说明以什么为题，或者题目自拟，面试人员需要根据给定内容，结合自己的知识储备，合理的命题。

演讲题型侧重的是逻辑，尤其是演讲的内容要有内在逻辑性，其逻辑重点体现在内容是有层次性的，要么由大及小，要么由表及里，要么由浅入深，要么由古至今等；情景模拟题型突出的是逻辑和条理，逻辑方面与演讲题型相似，条理方面需要注意解决问题的步骤，比如安抚劝服需要注重"以情感人、以理服人、解决问题"三个环节，再比如工作汇报重点在于说明"工作进展情况、优点在哪里、缺点有哪些、请领导指示"四个环节；串词题型重点在于逻辑，面试人员要能够将几个词用有逻辑的内容联系在一起，而不是简单地堆砌词句。

译　文

第二部分：相关信息

如何在面试中取得成功

在形势日益紧张的就业市场中，工作面试非常重要。面试已经成为获得一份令人满意的工作不可或缺的部分。面试官可以利用这个机会了解候选人，如他们的工作经验、教育背景和个性。求职者可以利用这个机会了解他将要担任的工作，他所申请的公司的信誉，以及工作条件。如果求职者已经为面试做了充分的准备并且表现相当自信，那么就能确保面试成功。专家的以下提示将帮助求职者最大限度地获得潜在的就业机会。

穿着得体

穿着得体是确保获得良好第一印象最好的方式。如果你正在面试的工作是在办公室的工作，无论男女通常最好穿一套深色、保守的西装；如果你正在面试的工作着装要求比较随意，如在工厂或建筑工地，对于男士来说漂亮的休闲裤、带领子和纽扣的衬衫搭配一条领带或对于女士来说一条漂亮的连衣裙或女衬衫配休闲裤或短裙通常都是适当的。你应该避免佩戴过多的珠宝，喷过量香水以及穿着艳丽的衣服。大多数专家认为，穿得讲究比穿得太随意更好。你的穿着可以告诉雇主你对得到这份工作的重视程度。

态度积极

雇主不想听到一些关于负面体验的冗长枯燥借口或不良感受。如果你被问到诸如职位低、突然的工作变动薄弱的背景等问题时，不要回避，要专注于事实，并强调你从这段经历中学到的东西。准备好介绍你的技能和工作经历，因为它们涉及你要应聘的工作。将自己定位在雇主的思考角度上，把自己看作是一个具有特定技能和特质的人，适当地描述你的任职资格。

搜集信息

要搜集的重要信息包括雇主所从事的活动、雇主的财务稳定性，以及雇主想雇佣的职位类型。在搜集工作信息期间，研究雇主可以帮助确定更多关于该公司和你潜在职位的信息，知道如何帮助公司，并且能更好地准备好问题向面试官询问公司的状况。

提前到达

要在指定时间前10~15分钟到达面试地点，但是过早到达会使雇主困惑造成尴尬的局面。同样的道理，迟到会造成很坏的第一印象，可能会让你失去机会。在安排面试时询问好方位并带好面试所需的文件材料。

第三部分：情境任务范例

范例1：一家国际酒店正在寻找一位熟悉酒店业务并且精通英语的财务部会计人员。李欣刚毕业于盘锦职业技术学院财经分院会计专业，他想申请这个职位。酒店的人事经理主持了面试。（M：人事经理；L：李欣）

M：很高兴见到你。

L：我也很高兴见到您。我是李欣。

M：放轻松！请坐。

L：谢谢。

M：我们收到了你回复我们招聘广告的简历。你的资质符合我们酒店财务部会计职位的要求，但是我们认为有必要让你来这里接受面试。

L：谢谢您的认可。我很荣幸有机会接受这次面试。

M：你刚刚毕业于盘锦职业技术学院，因此你在这个领域有相关的实践经验吗？

L：我们学院非常注重实践经验。在校就读期间，每年我们都要花两个月的时间来做专业实训。

M：作为我们酒店的会计师，你还需要熟悉酒店的管理。你有学过相关知识吗？

L：是的。在大学里，我选修过酒店管理课程。而且，我是我们班的班长。我能流利地说英语，并且熟悉电脑操作。

M：你能喝酒吗？

L：是的，能喝一点儿。但我从来不喝太多。

M：好的，感谢你的到来。我们将在下周一通知你结果。你的电话号码是 15124285578，对吗？

L：是的。我会等您的回复。

范例 2： PKM 贸易公司正在招聘一名销售经理。李欣是一位具有 3 年实践经验的会计师，毕业于盘锦职业技术学院财经分院。他通过电子邮箱发送了求职申请。这周四该公司的老板正在亲自面试他。（B：老板；L：李欣）

B：请坐。

L：谢谢。

B：你是李欣吗？

L：是的，我是。

B：你带相关证件了吗？

L：这是我的文凭副本，这是我以前公司的推荐信。

B：你为什么想离开你以前的公司？

L：因为公司想在南方建立工厂，新工厂离我家很远。

B：你的专业是会计吗？

L：是的，我毕业于盘锦职业技术学院财经分院会计专业。

B：我们是一家外贸公司。你有什么经验吗？

L：是的。我以前的公司是中美合资企业，它涉及贸易在内的许多领域。

B：在之前的公司，你的工作职责有哪些？

L：我负责核算成本价格和利润率。

B：嗯。如果你不介意，你能告诉我你在以前的公司工资吗？

L：不算奖金，他们给我每月 2,000 元。

B：每月 2,500 元如何？如果你想在非工作日工作，我们会有额外的补助。此外，我们将为你购买医疗保险。

L：好的。我一定尽最大努力为我们的公司工作。我什么时候可以开始工作？

B：从 7 月 1 日开始。请带上文凭原件和身份证原件，先到人力资源部报到。

L：谢谢。再见。

B：再见。

Unit Four　Vocational Training

4.1　Company Presentation

Section One: Tasks

Wang Lin is employed as the Sales Manager of ADM Trade Company, which intends to establish business cooperation with Coca-Cola China.

Situation 1: *Wang Lin has to collect the historical materials and pictures of Coca-Cola. Please search the data or information that he needs through the internet.*

Situation 2: *According to the collected materials and pictures of Coca-Cola, please help Wang Lin create a new slide in PowerPoint, and then insert the information about Coca-Cola that you selected into the new slide.*

Situation 3: *Wang Lin has to prepare a brief presentation of Coca-Cola China to the staff of the company, please help him give a slide presentation of Coca-Cola China.*

Section Two: Related Information

How to Make an Effective Business Presentation

Most business presentations range from incredibly boring to just plain boring. [1] It doesn't have to be this way, [2] though. This paper draws on published advice from expert presenters around the world, which will help to take your presentations from merely "good" to "great". [3] Whether you are an experienced presenter, or just starting out, there should be ideas here to help you improve. [4]

1. Focus on your audience's needs

As you prepare the presentation, you always need to bear in mind what the audience needs and wants to know, not what you can tell them. [5] While you're giving the presentation, you also need to remain focused on your audience's response, and react to that.

2. Keep it simple: concentrate on your core message

When planning your presentation, you should always keep in mind the question: What is the key message for my audience to take away? Some experts recommend "a 30-second elevator pitch"[6], others recommend that you can write it on the back of a business card, or say it in no more than 15 words. Whichever rule you choose, the important thing is to keep your core message focused and brief.

3. Smile and make eye contact with your audience

This sounds very easy, but a surprisingly large number of presenters fail to do it. If you smile and make eye contact, you are building rapport, which helps the audience to connect with you and your subject. To help you with this, make sure that you don't turn down all the lights so that only the slide screen is visible.

4. Remember the 10-20-30 rule for slide shows[7]

This is a tip from Guy Kawasaki of Apple. He suggests that slideshows should:

- Contain no more than 10 slides;
- Last no more than 20 minutes;
- Use a font size of no less than 30 point.

This last is particularly important as it stops you trying to put too much information on any one slide. A good set of slides should be no use without the presenter, and they should definitely contain less, rather than more information. If you need to provide more information, create a bespoke handout[8] and give it out after your presentation.

5. Relax, breathe and enjoy

If you find presenting difficult, it can be hard to be calm and relaxed about doing it. One option is to start by concentrating on your breathing. Slow it down, and make sure that you're breathing fully.

If you can bring yourself to relax, you will almost certainly present better. If you can actually start to enjoy yourself, your audience will respond to that, and engage better. Your presentations will improve significantly, and so will your confidence.[9] It's well worth a try.

Vocabulary

effective [ɪˈfektɪv] *adj.* 有效的，起作用的；实际的

presentation [ˌpreznˈteɪʃn] *n.* 演讲；陈述，报告

merely [ˈmɪəli] *adv.* 只是；仅仅，只不过

remain [rɪˈmeɪn] *vi.* 保持；依然；留下

response [rɪˈspɒns] *n.* 反应；回答，答复

core [kɔː(r)] *n.* 核心，精髓；果核

recommend [ˌrekəˈmend] *vt.* 推荐；劝告 *vi.* 推荐；建议

contact [ˈkɒntækt] *vt.* 使接触；与……联系 *vi.* 联系，接触

rapport ［ræ'pɔ:(r)］ *n.* 友好关系；融洽，和谐

slide ［slaɪd］ *vi.* 滑落；下跌   *n.* 幻灯片

visible ［'vɪzəbl］ *adj.* 看得见的；可察觉到的

particularly ［pə'tɪkjələli］ *adv.* 特别；尤其；异乎寻常地

breathe ［bri:ð］ *vi.* 呼吸   *vt.* 呼吸

option ［'ɒpʃn］ *n.* 选项；选择权

engage ［ɪn'geɪdʒ］ *vi.* 从事；保证   *vt.* 聘用；使参加

significantly ［sɪg'nɪfɪk(ə)ntlɪ］ *adv.* 显著地；相当数量地

focus on   专心于，将……集中于……   同 concentrate on 同意

keep in mind   牢记，记住，同 "bear in mind" 同意

draw on   借鉴

respond to   响应；对……做出反应

Notes

1. …incredibly boring 乏味到难以置信；…plain boring 平淡乏味

2. It doesn't have to be this way. 并不一定要这样。

3. This paper draws on published advice from expert presenters around the world, which will help to take your presentations from merely "good" to "great". 本文借鉴世界各地的专业演讲人发表的建议，帮助你使商业演讲从只是 "不错" 到 "棒极了"。这里 which 引导非限制性定语从句，补充说明前面的主句部分。

4. Whether you are an experienced presenter，or just starting out，there should be ideas here to help you improve. 无论你是一个经验丰富的演讲人，或是个新手，本文应该会有一些观点，有助于你改进自己的介绍演讲。whether…or… 引导让步状语从句，译为 "不论，不论如何"。

5. You always need to bear in mind what the audience needs and wants to know，not what you can tell them. 当你准备演讲的时候，你需要永远牢记听众的需要和想知道什么，而不是你能告诉他们什么。what 引导宾语从句，其本身在从句中充当宾语成分。e. g. I wonder what he does. 我想知道他是做什么工作的。

6. a 30-second elevator pitch "电梯游说" 是比喻可以 30 秒内在电梯里准确清晰地向客户解释说明一个产品或创意。这是麦肯锡公司检验员工陈述咨询报告的方法之一。

7. the 10-20-30 rule for slide shows 这是由苹果公司的盖伊·川崎所提出幻灯片演示法则。他认为幻灯片的播放应该不超过 10 张幻灯片，持续不超过 20 分钟，所用字体不小于 30 磅。

8. bespoke handout 定制的讲义

9. Your presentations will improve significantly，and so will your confidence. 你的演讲效果会显著提高，你的自信也会如此。这很值得一试。"so + 助动词/情态动词/be 动词 + 主语" 为部分倒装结构，表示 "主语也怎么样"，这里 So will your confidence 意思是 "你的自信也会如此"。

Section Three: Situational Task Samples

Situation 1: *Li Xin is employed as the Sales Manager of ABC Trade Company. He has to prepare a presentation of his company to the sales representatives[1] from branch offices.* [2]*Now he is asking his friend, Anne, for help. (A: Li Xin; B: Anne)*

Introducing yourself and your presentation

A: Hi, Anne! I have to prepare a presentation of my company. Could you help me with it?

B: Certainly, I'd be glad to.

A: How can I make a good start of a presentation?

B: You can first introduce yourself.

A: OK, here goes… On behalf of ABC Trade Company, I'd like to welcome all of you here today. My name is Li Xin, what I'd like to do today is to present our company profile[3].

B: Well, I think you may add your position or your responsibilities.

A: Ok, let me put it in this way. My name is Li Xin, and I am responsible for the management of the regional sales teams. Is that OK?

B: Yeah, that's better. You should also introduce your presentation from a couple of aspects.

A: From what aspects can I introduce?

B: You can introduce the topic, the purpose, the time and the main parts of the presentation.

A: Um-hum, I see.

Talking about the company profile

A: Anne, I'm preparing a presentation of my company. Can you give me some advice on the company profile?

B: Of course, I'd love to.

A: My presentation will be divided into 2 parts.

B: Excuse me, who will be invited to this conference?

A: Our sales representatives from our branch offices will be invited to come.

B: That's good. I'm sure your presentation can help them gain a better understanding of your company.

A: And that's why we need everyone to be informed.

B: OK, continue…

A: Firstly, we'll run through the history and the overall scale of the company[4]. Secondly, I'll talk about the line of business[5] and our marketing strategy[6].

B: That sounds good.

A: At the end of this presentation, a short advertisement will be shown to give them an idea of where we are going.

B: Good job.

Situation 2: *Li Xin's presentation of the company*

Introducing yourself and your presentation

Good afternoon, ladies and gentlemen. On behalf of ABC Trade Company, I'd like to welcome all of you here today. My name is Li Xin, and I am responsible for the management of the regional sales teams. What I'd like to do today is to present our company profile. My presentation will be divided into 2 parts: firstly, we'll run through the history and the overall scale of the company. Secondly, I'll talk about the line of business and our marketing strategy.

Hopefully, this introduction can help you gain a better understanding of our company. The presentation will last about five minutes. If you have any questions, please don't hesitate to ask.

Talking about the company profile

First, I'm going to introduce our company.

ABC Trade Company is an international trade company from America. It was founded in Redwood City, California in 1997 and specializes in the development of international markets. We have developed strong business networks in numerous major cities in the world, and we entered China's market in 2001. At present, we have established some branch offices in Shanghai, Beijing, Shenzhen and Guangzhou in China.

We have approximately 16,000 employees. Our annual revenue is about 6 billion dollars, and our services include e-business platform, e-business suite, consulting, education and support services. Our mission is to promote business opportunities involving the target country's manufacturers and American partners. We let you do business faster and reduce the cost of exploring international business opportunities.

This is the information about our company. Thank you!

Notes

1. sales representatives 销售代表
2. branch offices 分公司
3. company profile 公司概况
4. overall scale of the company 公司的整体规模
5. the line of business 业务范围
6. marketing strategy 营销策略

Section Four：Functional Expression Bank

Greeting and self-introduction（问候和自我介绍）

1. Welcome to…I'm…I'm in charge of…欢迎来到……我是……我负责……
2. I'd like to welcome all of you here today. 欢迎大家今天来到这里。
3. Ladies and gentlemen, good morning! It's an honor to address such a distinguished audience.

   女士们，先生们，早上好！很荣幸为诸位演讲。

4. My name is…And I am in charge of…我的名字是……我负责……

5. Ladies and gentlemen, good morning! I'm honored to have this opportunity to…女士们，先生们，早上好！我很荣幸有这个机会……

Introducing your presentation（介绍演讲）

Topic/Subject（主题）

1. The subject/topic of my presentation/speech is…我演讲/讲话/的主题是……

2. I'd like to tell you something about…我想告诉你一些关于……的事。

3. I'd like to introduce…to you. 我想向你介绍……。

Purpose/Objective（目的）

1. We are gathered here today to discuss/decide/review…

   我们今天应邀聚集在这里讨论/决定/回顾……

2. The purpose/aim of my presentation is to…我演讲的目的是……

3. This talk is designed with a view to…这个演讲的目的是为了……

4. Hopefully, my talk can serve as a catalyst/springboard for our discussion.

   希望我的讲话可以作为我们讨论的催化剂/跳板。

Time（演讲时间）

1. I shall take only 10 minutes of your time. 我只占用您 10 分钟的时间。

2. It will last about 15 minutes and I will be using the PPT/flip chart.

   本演讲将持续大约 15 分钟，我将利用 PPT/图表进行演示。

Main parts（主要部分）

1. There are 3 parts in my presentation. They are the company's history, main markets, and staff. 我的演讲有 3 个部分，分别为介绍公司的历史、主要市场以及公司员工情况。

2. My presentation is in 3 parts. First, we'll run briefly through the history of the company. Next, I'll tell you something about our main markets. Last, I'll come to the people. 我的演讲分为 3 个部分。首先，我们将简要地回顾下公司的历史。接下来，我会讲一些我公司的主要市场情况。最后，我会介绍一下公司的员工情况。

3. My presentation will be divided into 2 parts：ADM and ADM overseas.

   我的演讲将分为 2 个部分：ADM 公司简介和 ADM 海外公司简介。

Questions（相关问题）

1. Since there's quite a lot to cover, I'd be grateful if you hold your questions until the end of my talk. 因为要论述很多问题，如您在我的演讲后发问，我将不胜感激。

2. I will leave ten minutes for Q&A at the end of my talk.

   我将在演讲结束后留下十分钟的问答环节。

3. If you have any questions, please feel free to ask me at the end of my presentation.

   如果您有任何问题，请在我演讲结束后随意提问。

Talking about the company profile（谈论公司概况）

Company history（公司历史）

1. Our company was established/founded/set up in…我们公司成立于……

2. The company is an export-oriented company with a 15-year history.

本公司是一家具有 15 年历史的出口公司。

3. The company started out as a workshop with four workers.

这家公司起初是一个有四个工人的车间。

4. Last year, it merged with a multinational company. 去年，它与一家跨国公司合并。

Line of business（业务范围）

1. Our company engages in the production/trading of electronic products.

我们公司从事电子产品的生产/贸易。

2. We are in insurance line. 我们的产品都有承保。

3. We carry out business operations in the following areas… 我们在以下领域开展业务……

4. We deal exclusively in cosmetics. 我们专门经营化妆品。

Others（其他情况）

1. Our company covers/occupies /has an area of 66,000 square meters.

我们公司占地面积 66,000 平方米。

2. This is a Japanese company with its headquarters in Tokyo.

这是一家日本公司，总部在东京。

3. It has a staff of more than 3,000. 本公司有员工 3,000 多人。

4. The company has a production capacity of 80,000 cars every year.

本公司拥有每年 80,000 辆汽车的生产能力。

5. Our company has an annual turnover of ＄8 billion. 我们公司的年营业额为 80 亿美元。

6. Our main products are laptop computers. 我们的主要产品是笔记本电脑。

7. Our market share in Canada has increased by 4.5% this year, accounting for 20% of the total sales. 我们在加拿大的市场份额今年增长了 4.5%，占总销售额的 20%。

8. Our sales last quarter were 5 million dollars. 我们上个季度的销售额是 5 百万美元。

9. Our company has been certified by the ISO 9002 system.

我们公司已通过 ISO 9002 体系认证。

Ending（结尾）

1. This is all I want to say about ADM and ADM overseas, and I hope this brief introduction can help you shed some light on our company.

这就是我想说的关于 ADM 公司和 ADM 海外公司的情况，我希望这个简短的介绍会使大家对我们的公司有所了解。

2. So, are there any questions you'd like to ask me before we move on?

所以，在我们继续讨论之前，还有什么问题想问我吗？

Section Five：Culture Tips

企业文化

企业文化，或称组织文化（Corporate Culture 或 Organizational Culture），是一个组织由其价值观、信念、仪式、符号、处事方式等组成的其特有的文化形象。企业文化是企业的灵魂，其核心是企业的精神和价值观。美国的企业文化以个人主义为核心，强调个人的独立性、能动性、个性和个人成就。因此，美国企业对员工的评价也是基于能力主义原则，加薪和升职也只看能力和工作业绩，不考虑年龄、资历和学历等因素。

谷歌公司是一家美国的跨国科技企业，致力于互联网搜索、云计算、广告技术等领域，开发并提供大量基于互联网的产品与服务。谷歌是第一个被公认为全球最大的搜索引擎，在全球范围内拥有无数的用户。公司注重鼓励员工大胆创新，允许工程师们将20%的工作时间用于自己喜欢的项目，让他们去做自己认为更重要的事情。谷歌办公楼随处散落着健身设施、按摩椅、台球桌、帐篷等有趣的东西。整个办公空间采用了不同的色调搭配，明亮鲜活，让人感到轻松自在。

人性化的工作环境、小团队的工作方式、20/80法则的运用，以及每年1,000万美元的创新大奖，在这些政策的激励下，谷歌团队不断创新，产品已经从单纯的搜索引擎扩展到地图、图书、新闻等多个领域，并且开始全球化运营，诞生了一系列如Gmail邮箱、Orkut社区网络站点等对谷歌的发展有重大意义的项目和产品。

译　文

第二部分：相关信息

如何进行有效的商业演讲

大多数的商业演讲都平淡无奇甚至乏味到难以置信。然而，商业演讲并不一定要这样。本文借鉴世界各地的专业演讲人发表的建议，帮助你使商业演讲从只是"不错"到"棒极了"。无论你是一个经验丰富的演讲人，或是个新手，本文应该会有一些观点，有助于你改进自己的演讲。

1. 关注听众的需求

当你准备演讲的时候，你需要永远牢记听众的需要和想知道什么，而不是你能告诉他们什么。而当你发表演讲时，你也需要一直关注听众的反应，并给予相应的回应。

2. 保持简单：专注于你的核心信息

当你计划你的演讲时，你应该永远记住这个问题：我的听众获取的关键信息是什么？一些专家推荐一种名为"30秒钟电梯游说"法，另外一些专家建议你可以将关键信息写在一张名片背面，或用不超过15个字做总结。不管你选择哪一种方法，重要的是使你的核心信息集中和简短。

3. 保持微笑并与听众进行眼神交流

这听起来很容易，但仍有数量惊人的演讲人没有做到这一点。如果你保持微笑并与听众进行眼神交流，你就与听众建立了融洽的关系，这有助于听众关注你和你的演讲主题。为了帮你做到这点，请确保不要关闭所有灯光，因为那样听众就只能看到幻灯片的屏幕了。

4. 谨记幻灯片播放的10-20-30法则

这是由苹果公司的盖伊·川崎所提出的幻灯片演示法则。他认为幻灯片的播放应该：

- 不超过10张幻灯片；
- 持续不超过20分钟；
- 使用字体不小于30磅。

最后一点尤为重要，因为它会阻止你试图把太多的信息放在任何一张幻灯片上。一组好的幻灯片应当是在没有主讲人的情况下没有任何用处的，它应当肯定包含更少的信息，而不是更多的信息。如果你需要提供更多的信息，那就在你的演讲后创建一份定制的讲义，分发出去。

5. 放松、呼吸和享受

如果你发现演讲困难，那么你很难平静并且放松地去演讲。你可以选择开始专注于你的呼吸节奏。放慢速度，并确保充分呼吸。

如果你能让自己放松，几乎肯定你会表现得更好。如果你真的可以开始享受演讲的乐趣，那么你的听众会有所回应，并更好地参与你的演讲。你的演讲效果会显著提高，你的自信也会如此。这很值得一试。

第三部分：情景任务范例

范例 1：李欣是 ABC 贸易公司的销售经理。他需要准备给分公司的销售代表做一个公司简介。现在，他正向他的朋友安妮寻求帮助。（A：李欣；B：安妮）

自我介绍和演示文稿

A：嗨，安妮！我得准备做一个公司简介。你能帮我吗？

B：当然，我很乐意。

A：公司简介怎样才能有个好的开头呢？

B：你可以先自我介绍一下。

A：好的，我要开始了！……我代表 ABC 贸易公司欢迎今天到场的各位。我叫李欣，今天我要介绍一下我们公司概况。

B：嗯，我想你可以加上你的职位或者职责。

A：好的，让我这样说。我叫李欣，负责区域销售团队的管理。这样行吗？

B：是的，这样好些了。你也应该从几个方面介绍你的演讲。

A：我可以从哪些方面介绍呢？

B：你可以介绍演讲的主题、目的、时间和主要内容。

A：嗯，我明白了。

谈论公司简介

A：安妮，我正在准备我的公司简介。就公司概况你能给我一些建议吗？

B：当然，我很愿意。

A：我的演讲将分为两个部分。

B：打扰一下，谁被邀请参加这次会议？

A：我们分公司的销售代表应邀前来。

B：那很好。我相信你的介绍可以帮助他们更好地了解你们公司。

A：这就是我们通知每个人到场的原因。

B：好的，继续……

A：首先，我将介绍公司的历史和整体规模。其次，我将谈论公司业务范围及我们的营销策略。

B：听起来不错。

A：在这个演讲结束时，我将播放一个简短的广告以展示公司未来的发展方向。

B：干得好。

范例 2：李欣的公司简介

介绍自己和演讲情况

下午好，女士们，先生们。今天，我代表 ABC 贸易公司欢迎各位的到来。我叫李欣，负责区域销售团队的管理。今天我想介绍一下公司的概况。我的演讲将分为两个部分：首先，我将介绍公司的历史和整体规模。其次，我将谈谈公司业务范围以及我们的营销策略。

希望，这个简介可以帮助你们更好地了解我们公司。这个演讲将持续约 5 分钟。如果你们有任何问题，请不要犹豫，随时发问。

谈论公司概况

首先，我来介绍一下我们公司。

ABC 贸易公司是一家来自美国的国际贸易公司。它 1997 年成立于加利福尼亚州的雷德伍德城，专营国际市场发展。我们在世界上的许多大城市都建立了强大的业务网络，并在 2001 年进入了中国市场。目前，我们已经在上海、北京、深圳和广州建立了一些分公司。

我们公司有大约 16,000 名员工，公司年收入约 60 亿美元。我们的服务包括电子商务平台、电子商务套件、咨询、教育和支持服务。我们的使命是促进目标国家的制造商和美国合作伙伴的商业机会。我们力求更快地发展业务，并减少开拓国际商业机会的成本。

这是我们公司的情况。非常感谢。

4.2　Position Responsibility

Section One: Tasks

Wang Lin is employed as the Sales Manager of ADM Trade Company.

Situation 1: When Wang Lin walked in the street, he happened to meet his good friend, Tracy, who hadn't seen him for a long time. Make a conversation on their talking about their jobs, responsibilities and each other's likes and dislikes about their jobs.

Situation 2: As the Sales Manager of ADM Trade Company, Wang Lin has to know about the common departments and main responsibilities of the common positions in a company. Draw a clear and comprehensive chart of a basic company, and introduce main responsibilities of some common positions.

Section Two: Related Information

How to Develop a Good Work Ethic

Whether you are working at a job or studying at school, developing a good work ethic can be critical to success. A strong work ethic endears you to your co-workers and management. It offers you the opportunity to promote and earn raises. A strong work ethic requires you to focus on your daily tasks and complete them to the best of your ability. Your work ethic starts from the time you wake up to the time you leave the workplace.

1. Go to work on time each day.

Arriving at the workplace late always starts your workday[1] badly. Take into consideration the daily traffic, the weather and so on, so you can leave and make it to work on time.

2. Write down your daily tasks for each day of the week.

Hang the list near your workplace and check off each task as you complete it. Writing down your daily tasks lets you visually witness your progress and reminds you of what you still need to do.[2]

3. Improve daily.

Rather than becoming satisfied with your results, take steps to improve your work and go beyond your typical performance each day.

4. Complete projects and tasks immediately; don't procrastinate.

One of the trademark behaviors of a worker with a poor work ethic is to delay his work until another day. Procrastination[3] usually leads to late or incomplete projects.

5. Evaluate your work.

To build a strong work ethic, you must identify your weaknesses and create a plan to improve on those weak areas.[4] One of the best ways to evaluate your work is to create a list that summarizes the requirements and skills of your job. For example, suppose you're a manager, create a list that consists of "Communication Skills", "Employee Relations",

"Time Management" and "Listening". Score yourself for each. You must remain honest with yourself when conducting a self-evaluation⁵.

6. Develop a positive attitude.

Make it a point to remain friendly at work, smile at co-workers and remain optimistic regardless of what happens.

Vocabulary

ethic ['eθɪk] *n*. 道德；伦理观

endear [ɪn'dɪə(r)] *vt*. 使受喜爱；使亲密

co-workers *n*. 共同工作者，同事

visually ['vɪʒuəlɪ] *adv*. 视觉上；外表上

witness ['wɪtnəs] *n*. 目击者，见证人 *vi*. 见证；做证人

procrastinate [prəʊ'kræstɪneɪt] *vi*. 拖延，耽搁

trademark ['treɪdmɑːk] *n*.（注册）商标；（人的行为或衣着的）特征，标记

behavior [bɪ'heɪvjə] *n*. 行为；态度

evaluate [ɪ'væljueɪt] *vt*. 评价；对……评价 *vi*. 评价，估价

identify [aɪ'dentɪfaɪ] *vt*. 识别，认出；确定

conduct [kən'dʌkt] *vt*. 实施；安排

positive ['pozɪtɪv] *adj*. 积极的；肯定的

optimistic [ˌɒptɪ'mɪstɪk] *adj*. 乐观的，乐观主义的

to the best of one's ability 尽其所能

take into consideration 考虑到，顾及；着想

check off 核对

make it a point to do 对……特别注意；努力做到……

regardless of 不管不顾，不拘

Notes

1. workday 日常工作

2. Writing down your daily tasks lets you visually witness your progress and reminds you of what you still need to do. 写下你的日常工作任务，可以使你直观地看到自己的进步，并提醒你还需要完成哪些任务。"Writing down your daily tasks" 是现在分词短语，在句中作主语成分。

3. procrastination 拖延症，指将今天的事情拖延到明天。拖延症总是表现在各种小事上，但日积月累，特别影响个人发展。拖延现象现已成为管理学家和心理学家研究的一个重要课题。

4. To build a strong work ethic, you must identify your weaknesses and create a plan to improve on those weak areas. 要建立良好的职业操守，你必须找出自己的弱点，并制订一个计划，以改善那些薄弱领域。"To build a strong work ethic" 是动词不定式，在句中

作目的状语。

5. self-evaluation 自我评价，是自我意识的一种形式。是指主体对自己的思想、愿望、行为和个性特点的判断和评价。

Section Three：Situational Task Samples

Situation 1：Job Description

Li Xin and Linda are friends, who haven't seen each other for years. One day, they came across on the road and talked about their jobs.（A：Linda；B：Li Xin）

Dialogue 1：Talking about Li Xin's job

A：Hi，Li Xin! It's you! I haven't seen you for a long time. How are you?

B：Very well，thank you. And you，Linda?

A：Not too bad. Dylan told me that you've got a new job. So，what do you do now?

B：I'm the Sales Manager of ABC Trade Company.

A：That's great. What do your responsibilities include?

B：I'm mainly responsible for developing sales strategies[1] and plans，building and maintaining relations with clients，and developing new client base[2].

A：So what are your working hours like?

B：Well，it's flexible on working hours，and working overtime[3] is very common in my company. I have to exceed sales quotas[4] each month，and push my team to achieve.

A：It sounds like the work is highly under pressure. Do you like your job?

B：Sure，I enjoy it because it involves a lot of challenges. I can work well under the circumstances.

Dialogue 2：Talking about Linda's job

B：Linda，can you tell me a little bit about your current work?

A：Certainly，what would you like to know?

B：First of all，what do you work as?

A：I work as a computer technician[5] in an IT company.

B：What do your responsibilities include?

A：I'm responsible for system administration[6] and in-house programming[7].

B：What sort of problems do you deal with on a day-to-do basis?

A：Oh，there are always lots of small system glitches[8]. I also provide information on a need-to-know basis[9] for employees.

B：Do you like your job?

A：The salary and benefits are not bad，but it is so fine that sometimes it feels kind of boring. You know，doing the same thing every day.

B：Have you been thinking about changing your job?

A：Probably not，because I've got no experience in other fields.

B：Oh，come on，just give it a try. A new environment could give you total great refreshment.[10]

A：Ok，I'll think about it. Thank you for your advice.

Notes

1. sales strategies 销售策略
2. develop new client base 开发新的客户群
3. work overtime 加班
4. sales quotas 销售配额
5. computer technician 电脑技术员
6. system administration 系统管理
7. in-house programming 内部编程
8. system glitch 系统故障
9. need-to-know 须知；on a basis 在一定基础上
10. refreshment 恢复活力；焕发精神

Situation 2：*It is a chart below showing some common departments and positions in the business world.*

Common Departments and Positions in a Company

Departments 部门	Job Titles 职位
Financial Department 财务部	Chief Accountant 总会计师
Personnel Department 人事部	Assistant Manager 助理经理
Sales Department 销售部	Salesperson 销售员
Purchasing Department 采购部	Buyer 采购员
Public Relations Department 公关部	Office Clerk 办公室文员
Human Resources Department 人力资源部	Trainee Manager 培训部经理
Research and Development（R & D）研发部	Programmer 程序员
Legal Department 法务部	Lawyer 律师
Administrative Department 行政部	Administrative Clerk 行政文员
Production Department 生产部	Quality Control Engineer 质量工程师
Export Department 出口部	Deputy Manager 副经理

The following is a rough indication of the typical responsibilities，but these can vary a lot in different companies.

Main Responsibilities of Some Common Positions

1. Sales Manager

Developing sales strategies and plans；
Building and maintaining relations with clients；
Developing new client base；
Preparing proposals and reports.

2. Human Resources Manager

Support the Business Head in setting strategies, directions and objectives with regard to personnel;

Responsible for hiring appropriate personnel and ensuring career progression;

Identify, interpret and apply key performance indicators and monitor business managers' use of such indicators.

3. Purchaser/Buyer

Responsible for supplier identification and pre-screening of materials;

Benchmark and negotiate pricing, terms, and other related issues with potential suppliers to ensure fair market pricing.

4. R&D Manager

Regular review on business development and proposal on improvement;

Business contest and convention deployment;

Sectional planning and development;

Staff training and career path planning;

Developing new products or services.

5. Administrative Manager

Managing the rear service of the company;

Coordinating the staff to exercise the centralized management;

Ensuring that the human and material resources are correctly utilized;

Providing specialized support to other department and managers.

Section Four: Functional Sentence Bank

Describing jobs and responsibilities（描述工作和职责）

Describing jobs（描述工作）

1. What do you do? 你是做什么的?

   I'm a manager in the Sales Department. 我是销售部的一名经理。

2. What do you work as? 你做什么工作?

   I work as a computer technician at ABC Trade Company. 我在 ABC 贸易公司当电脑技术员。

3. What's your job/profession/occupation? 你做什么工作?

   I'm a computer programmer. My company allows me to work on my computer at home.
   我是一名电脑程序员。我的公司允许我在家里操作电脑。

4. What company are you with? 你在哪家公司工作?

   I'm with a branch of a German company called… 我在一家叫……的德国公司分公司
   上班。

5. What company do you work for? 你在哪家公司工作?

   I work as a software engineer for a software company. 我在一家软件公司做软件工程师。

Describing responsibilities（描述职责）

1. What are you in charge of? 你负责什么工作?

I'm in charge of training employees. 我负责培训员工。

2. What do your responsibilities include? 你的工作职责包括哪些？

I am responsible for system administration and in-house programming.

我负责系统管理和内部编程。

3. What exactly are your duties? 你的工作职责确切是什么？

I run the Production Department. This includes ensuring that the production meets deadlines and dealing with customer queries.

我负责经营生产部，包括确保产品如期交付（或按期交货）及处理客户咨询等。

Describing positions and departments （描述职位和部门）

1. Which department are you in? 你在哪个部门？

I'm in the Human Resources Department. 我在人力资源部。

2. What position do you hold? /What position are you in? 你的职位是什么？

I work for/under the Sales Manager. 我为销售经理工作。

3. What are you responsible/accountable to? 你的工作职责是什么？

I'm responsible to the Marketing Manager. 我为市场经理工作。

Likes and dislikes of jobs （对工作的喜好）

Working hours and routines （工作时间和日常工作）

1. I'm on the day/night shift. 我上白班/上夜班。

2. I have to start work at nine. 我需要九点开始工作。

3. It's a regular nine-to-five job. 这是一个常规的朝九晚五的工作。

4. I do a lot of overtime every week. 我每周加班很多次。

5. We are on flexible time. 我们的工作时间很灵活。

Interpersonal relationships （人际关系）

1. My boss is quite nice. He gets on very well with us. 我的老板很好。他和我们相处得很好。

2. My boss is a very difficult person to work with. 我的老板是个很难相处的人。

3. Most of my colleagues are friendly and cooperative. 我的大多数同事都是友好和合作的。

Compensation （工资福利）

1. I get about $800 a month in commissions. 我每个月得到大约800美元的佣金。

2. The meals in the work cafeteria are subsidized. 在公司食堂有用餐补贴。

3. After tax and national insurance, I make 4,000 RMB a month.

在扣除税款和保险后，我一个月挣 4,000 元。

Promotion （职位晋升）

1. I've just been promoted to the head of Human Resources. 我刚被提升为人力资源部主管。

2. He is being groomed for a higher position. 他正接受专门的培训准备从事更高的职位。

3. I'm in line for the position of the Sales Manager. 我将获得销售经理的职位。

Job satisfaction （工作满意度）

1. I enjoy my job because it involves a lot of challenges.

我喜欢我的工作，因为它涉及很多挑战。

2. I hate my job because I can't stand/bear my boss.

我讨厌我的工作，因为我受不了我的老板。

3. I don't like what I'm doing right now because it's boring.

我不喜欢我现在所做的工作，因为它很无聊。

Section Five：Culture Tips

职业操守

职业操守是指人们在从事职业活动中必须遵从的最低道德底线和行业规范。它具有"基础性""制约性"的特点，凡从业者必须做到。职业操守是人们在职业活动中所遵守的行为规范的总和。它既是对从业人员在职业活动中的行为要求，又是对社会所承担的道德、责任和义务。一个人不管从事何种职业，都必须具备良好的职业操守，否则将一事无成。良好的职业操守包括：

1．诚信的价值观

在业务活动中一贯秉持守法诚信，这种价值观是通过每个员工的言行来体现的。良好的职业操守构成我们事业的基石，不断提高我们的声誉。

2．遵守公司法规

遵守一切与公司业务有关的法律法规，并始终以诚信的方式对人处事，是我们的立身之本，也是每个员工的切身利益所在。

3．确保公司的资产安全

确保公司的资产安全，并保证公司资产仅用于公司的业务。这些资产包括办公用品、专有的知识产权、秘密信息和其他资源等。

4．诚实地制作工作报告

正确并诚实地制作工作报告是每个员工的基本责任。任何不诚实的报告，例如虚假的费用报销单、代打卡等都是绝对禁止的。禁止向公司内部或外部组织提供不实的报告，或者误导接收资料的人员。

5．不要泄密给竞争对手

与竞争对手接触时，应将谈话内容限制在适当的范围。不要讨论定价政策、合同条款、成本、存货、营销与产品计划、市场调查与研究、生产计划与生产能力等内容，也要避免讨论其他任何联想的信息或机密。

译　文

第二部分：相关信息

如何养成良好的职业操守

无论你是在工作还是在学校学习，培养良好的职业道德都是成功的关键。良好的职业操守可以使你倍受同事和领导的喜爱。它会为你提供晋升和加薪的机会。良好的职业操守会要求你专注于日常工作，尽你所能完成任务。从起床到离开工作岗位，时时体现着你的职业操守。

1. 每天按时上班

上班迟到总会一开始就使你的工作变得很糟糕。考虑到日常的交通情况、天气状况等因素，那么你就能够准时出门按时到岗。

2. 写下你一周中每一天的日常工作任务

将任务表挂在工作场所，每完成一项任务后逐一勾除。写下你的日常工作任务，可以使你直观地看到自己的进步，并提醒你还需要完成哪些任务。

3. 每一天都有所进步

采取措施提升工作表现，并且每一天都超越自我，而不是变得只满足于目前的工作业绩。

4. 立即完成工作项目和任务；不要拖延

一个不敬业的工人的标志性行为之一就是将工作拖到另一天。拖延症通常会导致项目延期或不完工。

5. 评估你的工作表现

要建立良好的职业操守，你必须找出自己的弱点，并制订一个计划，以改善那些薄弱领域。评估工作表现的最好方法之一是创建一个总结工作需求和所需技能的清单。例如，假设你是一名经理，创建一个由"沟通技巧"、"员工关系"、"时间管理"和"倾听"所组成的清单，并给自己每一项进行打分。进行自我评估时，你必须始终对自己诚实。

6. 培养积极的工作态度

努力做到在工作中保持友好的态度，对同事保持微笑，并且无论发生什么事，都要保持乐观的心态。

第三部分：情境任务范例

情境1：工作描述

李欣和琳达是多年未见的朋友，一天，他们在路上偶遇并谈论起了各自的工作。（A：琳达；B：李欣）

对话1：谈论李欣的工作

A：嗨，李欣！是你呀！好久不见。你好吗？

B：我很好，谢谢！你呢，琳达？

A：还凑合。迪伦告诉我你有了一份新工作。那么，你现在做什么？

B：我是 ABC 贸易公司的销售经理。

A：太好了。你的工作职责包括哪些？

B：我主要负责制订销售策略和销售计划，建立和维护与客户的关系，以及开发新的客户群。

A：那么你的工作时间是怎么样的？

B：嗯，我的工作时间很灵活，而且加班在我们公司非常普遍。每个月我必须超额完成销售配额，并推动我的团队完成销售计划。

A：听起来工作压力很大。你喜欢你的工作吗？

B：当然，我非常享受它所带来的诸多挑战。在这样的情况下我能做得更好。

对话2：谈论琳达的工作

B：琳达，你能跟我讲一点儿你目前的工作吗？

A：当然，你想知道什么？

B：首先，你是做什么工作的？

A：我在一家 IT 公司做电脑技术员。

B：你的工作职责包括哪些？

A：我负责系统管理和内部编程。

B：你日常主要处理什么样的问题呢？

A：哦，总有很多小系统会出问题。我还要为员工们提供信息须知。

B：你喜欢你的工作吗？

A：薪水和福利是可以的，但有时会感觉有点无聊，你知道，每天都做同样的事情。

B：你考虑过换个工作吗？

A：还没有，因为我在其他领域没有工作经验。

B：哦，来吧，试一试。新的环境会使你精力充沛。

A：好吧，我会考虑的。谢谢你的建议。

情境 2： 下面是一张图表，展示了商界中一些常见的部门和职位。

公司的常见部门和职位（表略）

这些职位的职责在不同的公司中可能会有很大的不同，以下只是粗略地说明了一些典型的职责。

常见职位的主要职责

1. 销售部经理

制订销售策略和计划；

建立和维护与客户的关系；

开发新客户群；

准备建议书和报告。

2. 人力资源部经理

在关于人事制度的策略、方向和目标设置方面支持业务主管；

负责招聘合适的员工，确保职业发展；

识别、解释和应用关键绩效指标，并监督业务经理这些指标的实施。

3. 采购员

负责供应商的选择和材料的前期筛选；

与潜在供应商进行价格、条款，以及其他相关问题的协商，以确保公平的市场定价。

4. 研发部经理

定期回顾业务发展和改进建议；

商业竞赛和会议部署；

部门规划和发展；

员工培训和职业生涯规划；

开发新产品或服务。

5. 行政部经理

管理公司后勤工作；

协调员工实行集中管理；

确保人力物力得到正确利用；

为其他部门和管理人员提供专业支持。

4.3　Product Presentation

Section One：Tasks

Situation 1：*Mr. Wilde，a client who comes into the office of Furniture Retail Store，asks Wang Lin，a shop assistant，about photocopiers in the store. Make a conversation according to the following information.*

　　1. The features：an attractive design，relatively small in size，light in weight，easier to operate，save energy.

　　2. The measurements and weight：42cm wide，62cm long，40cm high，weights 15 kilograms，six colors available.

　　3. The functions：120 copies a minute，little noise.

Situation 2：Ask each group of students to choose one cellphone to talk about. Have different groups choose different brands and models，and make a list of advantages and disadvantages of the cellphone. Call on the group representatives to demonstrate some key functions of their cellphones and give presentations in class.

Section Two：Related Information

Tips on Product Presentation

When you are giving a presentation to introduce a new product or an existing product to a new buyer，there are some tips to keep in mind that will make your presentation more effective.[1] Remember that you are communicating information to the potential customer. For a successful presentation，think of how you can deliver your message clearly with an eye toward closing the sale.

Know What You Are Talking About

Make sure you know everything about your product，such as the history of the product，and the similar products. If there have been problems in the past，such as difficulties with shipping，you should know about it. In case an objection is raised during your presentation，you can be prepared to handle it.[2] By being well prepared，you can alleviate some of the anxiety that sometimes goes along with public speaking.[3]

Know Who You Are Talking to

Know about your audience，and whether they have experience with or knowledge of your product. It also helps to know if they are in the mindset to accept what you are about to tell them，or if you are likely to face objections that might hinder a sale.[4]

Structure the Presentation

A product presentation should have a beginning，the body and the end. Start off with an opening that introduces the product to customers in the presentation and briefly states the purpose of the meeting. The main part of the presentation，the body，should be divided into easily understood modules，each with a single focus. Use a short summary to reinforce main points.

Question and Answer

Allow time for the audience to respond to your presentation with questions about the product. This may give you the opportunity to elaborate on the features and benefits of the product. On the other hand, you may be asked something you don't have a ready answer for. Tell the audience you will look into it, and use this situation as an opportunity to follow up with the potential customer.

Presentation Techniques

Visual aids are very effective in getting your point across. Simple charts and graphs can be effective, or you may choose a PowerPoint presentation or state-of-the-art[5] audio visual effects. Make sure the images you use can be seen clearly by the entire audience. Handouts should be given at the end of the presentation, with your contact information clearly stated.

Vocabulary

objection ［əb'dʒekʃn］ n. 反对；反对的话

alleviate ［ə'liːvieɪt］ vt. 减轻，缓和

mindset ['maɪndset] n. 观念模式，思维方式

hinder ['hɪndə(r)] vt. & vi. 阻碍，妨碍

module ['mɔdjuːl] n. 组件，单元

reinforce ［ˌriːɪn'fɔːs］ vt. 加固；强化

elaborate ［ɪ'læbərət］ vi. 详尽说明；变得复杂

script ［skrɪpt］ n. 脚本，手迹

gesture ['dʒestʃə(r)] n. 手势，姿势

emphasize ['emfəsaɪz] vt. 强调，着重

enthusiasm ［ɪn'θjuːziæzəm］ n. 热情，热忱

highlight ['haɪlaɪt] vt. 强调，突出

controversy ['kɔntrəvɜːsi] n. 论战；公开辩论

controversial ［ˌkɔntrə'vɜːʃl］ adj. 有争议的，引起争议的

transition ［træn'zɪʃn］ n. 过渡，转变

polished ['pɔlɪʃt] adj. 磨光的，擦亮的

with an eye toward　着眼于

go along with　连同；以及；和……

in the mindset　在观念模式，思维倾向或心态上

look into　调查；观察

start off with　从……开始，用……开始

follow up with　跟进，继续

get across　（使）被理解；把……讲清楚

Notes

1. When you are giving a presentation to introduce a new product or an existing product to a new buyer, there are some tips to keep in mind that will make your presentation more effective. 当你向新买家推出新产品或介绍现有产品时，要记住以下几点建议，这将使你的演示更加有效。When 引导时间状语从句，that will make your presentation more effective 为 that 引导的定语从句，修饰先行词 tips。

2. In case an objection is raised during your presentation, you can be prepared to handle it. 假使在你陈述时有人提出异议，你可以有所准备，应付自如。In case 意为"假使；以免"，引导条件状语从句。

3. By being well prepared, you can alleviate some of the anxiety that sometimes goes along with public speaking. 通过充分的准备，你可以缓解公开演讲时所出现的一些焦虑情绪。By 是介词，用来表示方法、手段、方式，意思是"凭借；靠；用；通过"，后接动词-ing 形式。that 引导定语从句，修饰先行词 anxiety。

4. It also helps to know if they are in the mindset to accept what you are about to tell them, or if you are likely to face objections that might hinder a sale. 这也有助于知道他们是否在思维方式上接受你将传达给他们的内容，或者你是否可能面临有可能阻碍销售的反对意见。句中两个 if 分别引导并列的宾语从句，作动词 know 的宾语。

5. state-of-the-art 使用最先进技术的；体现最高水平的

Section Three：Situational Task Samples

Situation 1：*Product Promotion*

Li Xin is introducing the photocopiers to Mr. Brown，a purchasing manager of a company.

（A：Li Xin；B：Mr. Brown）

Dialogue 1：Introducing Products

A：Good morning.

B：Good morning. Have you got the ZOL IR-2420 photocopier?

A：Yes，sir. It's right here.

B：Great! How much is it?

A：Let me see⋯IR-2420，hmm，$1,450.

B：Woo，it's not cheap!

A：Yes，the price is a bit high，but it has been the best-seller[1] for 6 months.

B：I know it's good. But I'm afraid my boss won't like the price. Can you give discounts for bulk[2]? We want to buy 5 of them.

A：In that case，we can cut the price to $1,377.

B：$1,377⋯That's about a 5% discount. Is that right?

A：Yes，that's the lowest price we can offer.

B：OK. How long is the warranty? One Year?

A：Three years from the date of purchase.

B: Good. How about its after-sales service³? You know, photocopiers have jamming problems all the time. It's a real nuisance!⁴

A: I can assure you that you won't have any problems with this model. Besides, we offer free on-site service for the length of the warranty⁵, and then $120 a year after that. If there's something wrong with the machine, just contact us. We'll send a technician over as soon as possible.

B: Good. What about the guarantees?

A: Well, there's a 7-day money-back guarantee⁶ if you're not satisfied with the machine. Or if you have any problems, just bring it in and you can have a refund.

B: OK.

Dialogue 2: Comparing Products

B: One more thing, how soon can you deliver them to our office?

A: Well, I'm afraid there's a slight delay on orders at the moment. We could send them to you at the end of the month.

B: You mean we have to wait for 2 weeks!

A: I'm afraid so.

B: That will be too late! We need them next week.

A: Er, how about this one, IR-2220? We have plenty of these in stock. If you place the order now, you can have them by tomorrow afternoon.

B: I don't know. How does it compare with IR-2420?

A: They are similar in size and functions. The only difference is IR-2420 can print 120 copies a minute, while IR-2220 prints 20 copies less.

B: That doesn't matter. How much is this one?

A: 1,200 dollars each, if you buy 5.

B: 1,200 dollars, that's…

A: That's $177 less than the IR-2420.

B: Sounds not bad. I think we could have these.

Notes

1. best-seller 畅销的产品

2. discount for bulk 批量购买所提供的折扣

3. after-sales service 售后服务

4. It's a real nuisance! 真讨厌!

5. the length of the warranty 保修期限

6. money-back guarantee（如对货物不满可退回货款的）退款保证

Situation 2: Product Presentation
Li Xin, the sales manager of ABC Trade Company, is presenting the latest model of a smart phone to his sales staff.

Good morning, everyone. I've invited you here today to present to you the latest model of our smart phone. I would like to briefly run through the 3 Ps for the new model— the Product, the Place and the Price. Please stop me whenever you've got a question.

To start with, I'll focus on the features of this new model. Please look at the screen. This is the picture of Note 130 and its functions. You see, it's small enough to fit right in the palm of your hand. It measures $11.2cm \times 6.0cm \times 2.2cm$[1].

Isn't it too tiny to use? Well, you can try it when we finish. You'll find it surprisingly easy to use. The screen is $4.5 cm \times 4.5cm$. This phone makes both a great PDA[2] and a cellphone. You can make phone calls and browse on the web. It also allows you to perform certain tasks that you would normally need a computer for. For example, when you are in a meeting and someone needs a figure in a slide that you know you have received in an email, you can download the email and view the spreadsheet[3] and give the figure. Then you may find yourself rather grateful that your smart phone is more than a cellphone and a PDA.

Of course, it has all the normal features of a cellphone such as a clock, alarm, reminders, stopwatch, calculator, games, etc. plus a built-in camera[4] and speakerphone[5]. In a word, it has just about everything you can think of and it does more than you expect!

OK. Now, let me move on to the next point — the Place. I mean, how and where we are going to distribute the product. The launch date for the Note 130 will be January 1 st next year so that it will definitely be in the shops in time for the buying season[6] during the Spring Festival. It will be in stock in all retail outlets[7] throughout the country by then. We will also be making the phone available by mail order and online, with a guaranteed 7 days delivery[8].

Pricing comes along with the product going on the market. At present, the new model retails at $699. That should be quite a reasonable price considering the quality and the advanced features.

Right, I'll stop here. I hope you've got a clearer picture of the Note 130. And I hope you will be 100% behind this model.

Notes

1. $11.2cm \times 6.0cm \times 2.2cm$ 乘以用 multiplied by，口语可用 by，即 11.2 centimeter by 6.0 centimeter by 2.2 centimeter.
2. PDA 即 personal digital assistant 掌上电脑
3. spreadsheet 电子表格程序；电子表格
4. built-in camera 内置摄像头
5. speakerphone 扬声器
6. the buying season 购物旺季
7. retail outlet 零售网点
8. a guaranteed 7 days delivery 保证 7 天交货

Section Four: Functional Expression Bank

Giving General Information (介绍主要信息)

1. It's our best-selling… 这是我们最畅销的……

2. This is priced at… 定价为……

3. It can be used for… 它可用于……

4. This is equipped with… 这个配备了……

5. These are the latest styles. 这些是最新款式。

6. We have a large range of sizes. 我们有各种尺寸。

7. It's 20 inches long/wide/high/thick/deep. 它是 20 英寸长/宽/高/厚/深。

8. This size is in stock/out of stock. 这种尺寸库存充足/库存不足。

Comparing Products (产品比较)

1. Compared with other competing products, ours looks better and is lower in price.
   与其他竞争产品相比，我们的产品更好看，价格更低。

2. Our latest cellphone is much lighter and slimmer than its competitors.
   我们最新款的手机比竞争对手更加轻薄。

3. Our product is the best-selling model of its kind. 我们的产品是同类产品中最畅销的。

Asking for Product Information (咨询产品信息)

1. What does the guarantee cover? 担保的内容是什么？

2. Do you offer after-sales service? 你们提供售后服务吗？

3. How does it work? 如何使用呢？

4. How many colors does it come in? 它有多少种颜色？

5. How do you install it? 你如何安装它？

6. What's its length/width/height/thickness/depth? 它的长度/宽度/高度/厚度/深度是多少？

7. What's it made of? 它是由什么制成的？

8. What is it used for? 它是用来干什么的？

9. How much do/does…cost? 需要花费多少钱？

10. What sort of warranty do you offer on…? 关于……你们提供什么样的保证？

Product Presentation (产品介绍)

Opening Remarks (开场白)

1. Ladies and gentlemen. It's an honor to have the opportunity to address such a distinguished audience. 女士们先生们。我很荣幸有机会向尊敬的观众讲话。

2. Good morning, everyone. I appreciate the opportunity to be with you today. I am here to talk to you about… 早上好，各位。今天我很感激能有机会和你们聚在一起。我来这里是想和你们谈谈关于……

3. Good morning, everyone. I am very happy to have this chance to give my presentation. Before I start my speech, let me ask you a question. By a show of hands, how many of you own a car? 早上好，各位。我很高兴有这个机会演讲。在我开始演讲之

前，我问大家一个问题。你们当中有多少人有私家车？请举手。

Responding to Questions（应对问题）

1. If you have any questions，I will be pleased to answer them at the end of the presentation. 如果你有任何问题，我很乐意在演示结束时回答。

2. Don't hesitate to interrupt if you have a question. 如果你有问题，不要犹豫请打断我提问。

3. I think I said that I would answer questions at the end of the presentation—perhaps you wouldn't mind waiting until then. 我想我说过我会在演讲结束时回答问题——也许你不介意等到那时。

Telling the Topic（告知演讲主题）

1. The subject of my presentation is⋯我演讲的主题是⋯⋯

2. I shall be speaking today about⋯今天我要讲的是⋯⋯

3. Today we are here to talk about⋯Before we start，I'd like you meet my team members⋯ 今天我们在这里谈谈⋯⋯在我们开始之前，我希望你们见见我的团队成员⋯⋯

Telling Speech Length（告知演讲时长）

1. During the next ten minutes，I shall⋯在接下来的十分钟里，我将⋯⋯

2. I shall be speaking for about ten minutes⋯我要讲十分钟⋯⋯

3. My presentation will last for about ten minutes⋯我的演讲将持续约十分钟⋯⋯

Arousing the Audience's Interest（引起观众兴趣）

1. I'm going to talk about something that is vitally important to all of us.
我要讲的是对我们所有人来说至关重要的事情。

2. My presentation will help solve a problem that has puzzled people for years⋯
我的演讲将有助于解决多年来困扰人们的一个问题⋯⋯

3. At the end of this presentation you will understand why this company has been so successful for so long⋯在演示结束时，你们会明白为什么这家公司这么久一直如此成功⋯⋯

Telling Speech Content（告知演讲内容）

1. There are five main aspects to this topic（Firstly，⋯，⋯Secondly，⋯，⋯The third⋯，Another，⋯The final⋯）这个主题有五个主要方面：第一，⋯⋯第二，⋯⋯再一个，⋯⋯另一个，⋯⋯最后，⋯⋯）

2. I've divided my talk into five parts⋯我把我的讲话分成五个部分⋯⋯

3. I want to start with this particular topic，and then draw some more general conclusions from it. 我想从这个特别的话题开始，然后从中得出一些更普遍的结论。

Closing Remarks（结束语）

1. In conclusion，I'd like to⋯总之，我想⋯⋯

2. I'd like to finish by⋯我想以⋯⋯结束⋯⋯

3. I hope this has given you some ideas/clear ideas/an outline of⋯我希望这给了你们一些思路/清晰的思路/大纲⋯⋯

4. I hope I've managed to give you a clearer picture of …我希望我能让你们更清楚地了解……

5. Thank you for your attention …谢谢你们的关注……

Section Five：Culture Tips

芭比娃娃

芭比娃娃（Barbie），全名为芭比·密里森·罗伯兹（Barbie Millicent Roberts），是 20 世纪最广为人知及最畅销的玩偶，于 1959 年 3 月 9 日举办的美国国际玩具展览会（American International Toy Fair）上首次展出，后发展成为世界玩具市场上畅销最久的玩具。它的创立者露丝·汉德勒（Ruth Handler）创建了美泰玩具公司，是美国最成功的女性企业家之一。她发现她的女儿芭芭拉（Barbara，Barbie 是简称）喜欢玩像成人而不是婴儿或小孩的玩偶。在瑞士琉森一个店铺的橱窗中，露丝发现一种名为 Bild Lilli doll 的成人形象的德国玩偶，于是在工程师杰克·瑞恩（Jack Ryan）的协助下，着手设计玩偶，并以女儿芭芭拉的名字为玩偶起名为"芭比"。

在美国，有近 70 个芭比收藏俱乐部，会员来自各行各业，他们经常聚会，欣赏对方的藏品，交流收藏心得。早期的古董芭比在拍卖中是价格最高的。1959 年原版芭比当时售 3 美元，2004 年原版芭比在 eBay 的价格高达 3,552.5 美元。在 2006 年 9 月 26 日，一个芭比在伦敦佳士得拍卖会上以 9,000 英镑售出，创下世界纪录。

芭比的性感造型和完美体型一直遭欧美国家人们的诟病，被质疑会影响儿童成长。针对芭比最广泛的批评是她的腰围，媒体称她宣扬了不切实际的女性身体形象，容易让模仿芭比的女性患上厌食症。批评指出女性如果要有芭比的身材，她需要有 7 尺 2 寸高，重 115～130 磅，臀围 30～36 寸，腰围 18～23 寸，胸围 38～48 寸。在 1997 年芭比被重新设计后，腰围增加，美泰公司指出此改变会令芭比穿现代时装设计时更合适。

译　文

第二部分：相关信息

产品介绍技巧

当你向新买家推出新产品或介绍现有产品时，要记住以下几点建议，这将使你的演示更加有效。记住你是在向潜在客户传达信息。对于一个成功的产品介绍，着眼于达成交易，想一想你如何能清晰地传达你的信息。

了解推介的产品

确保你了解所有关于你的产品的情况，例如产品的历史，以及同类产品的情况。你应该了解产品曾存在的问题，如航运困难。假使在你陈述时有人提出异议，你可以有所准备，应付自如。通过充分的准备，你可以缓解公开演讲时所出现的一些焦虑情绪。

知道你在跟谁说话

了解你的观众，以及他们是否使用过或了解你的产品。这也有助于知道他们是否在思维方式上接受你将传达给他们的内容，或者你是否可能面临有可能阻碍销售的反对意见。

产品介绍结构化

产品介绍应该包含开头、主体和结尾。从开头起，要向与会的客户介绍产品，并简要陈述会议的目的。产品介绍的主体部分，即正文，应该分为易于理解的几个模块，每一模块都有一个重点。结尾用简短的总结加强要点。

问答环节

让观众有时间就产品问题发问。这样可能会给你机会阐述产品的特点和好处。另一方面，你可能会被问到你并没有准备回答的问题。告诉听众你会进行调查，并利用这种情况作为跟进潜在客户的机会。

演讲技巧

视觉教具对于表达观点非常有效。简单的图表展示就很有效，或者你可以选择利用演示文稿或使用最先进的视听效果来展现。确保所有观众可以清晰地看到你使用的图像。演示结束时应发放讲义，并明确说明你的联系方式。

第三部分：情境任务范例

情境 1：产品促销

李欣在向某公司的采购经理布朗先生介绍影印机。（A：李欣；B：布朗先生）

对话 1：产品介绍

A：早上好。

B：早上好。你这里有 ZOL IR-2420 影印机吗？

A：是的，先生。就在这里。

B：太棒了！多少钱？

A：让我看看……IR-2420，嗯，1,450 美元。

B：哦，不便宜啊！

A：是的，这款价格有点儿高，但 6 个月以来，它一直是畅销产品。

B：我知道这款很好。但是我的老板恐怕不会喜欢这个价格。批量购买你能提供折扣吗？我们想买 5 台。

A：那样的话，我们可以把价格降低到 1,377 美元。

B：1,377 美元……大约是 5％的折扣。对吗？

A：是的，这是我们能提供的最低价格。

B：好的。保修期是多长时间？1 年吗？

A：从购买之日起 3 年保修期。

B：好的。它的售后服务怎么样？你知道，影印机总是存在卡纸问题。真讨厌！

A：我可以向你保证，使用这款机器不会出现任何问题。此外，我们提供保修期内免费上门服务，保修期外上门服务每年需 120 美元。如果机器出现问题，请联系我们。我们会尽快派技术员过来。

B：好的。担保的内容是什么？

A：如果你对机器不满意的话，可享受 7 天免费退换。或者如果你有任何问题，只要把产品带过来，你就可以得到退款。

B：好的。

对话 2：产品比较

B：还有一件事，你多久能把产品送到我们办公室来？

A：嗯，恐怕目前订单有点儿延误。我们可以在月底把产品派送给你们。

B：你的意思是我们需要等两个星期！

A：恐怕是这样。

B：那就太晚了！我们下周就需要它们。

A：呃，这款怎么样，IR-2220？我们有大量现货。如果你现在下订单，在明天下午就可以收到产品。

B：我不知道。与 IR-2420 相比，这款有哪些不同？

A：它们在大小和功能上相似。唯一的不同是 IR-2420 一分钟可以打印 120 份，而 IR-2220 比前者每分钟少打印 20 份。

B：那没关系。这款多少钱？

A：如果你买 5 台，每台 1,200 美元。

B：1,200 美元，那是……

A：这款比 IR-2420 少 177 美元。

B：听起来不错。我想我们可以购买这款机器。

情境 2：*产品介绍*

ABC 贸易公司的销售部经理李欣在向本公司销售人员介绍最新型号的一款智能手机。

早上好，各位。今天我邀请你们来到这里是要向你们介绍我们公司最新型号的智能手机。我想通过 3 个 P，也就是产品、地点和价格这三方面，简单地演示这款新产品。有问题时请随时打断我的发言提出问题。

首先，我将重点介绍这款新产品的特点。请看屏幕。这是 Note 130 的图片和功能。请看，它的尺寸足够小，正好适合手掌的大小。尺寸为 12.2cm×6cm×2.0cm。

这款产品是不是太小而不好操作？我演讲后你们可以试用一下。你们会发现它的操作出奇地简单。屏幕是 4.5cm×4.5cm。这款手机兼具掌上电脑和手机的双重功能。你可以拨打电话，也可以上网浏览网页。它也可以执行某些需要使用电脑才能完成的任务。例如，当你在一个会议上，有人需要一个幻灯片里的数据，之前你知道是用电子邮箱接收的，你就可以下载电子邮件，查看电子表格，给出数据。那么你会发现你很感激你的智能手机兼具手机和掌上电脑的功能。

当然，它具有所有手机的正常功能，如时钟、闹钟、提醒、秒表、计算器、游戏等，再加上内置摄像头和扬声器。总之，它几乎拥有所有你能想到的功能，甚至比你期望的更多！

好，现在，让我转到下一个话题——地点。我的意思是，我们将如何以及在哪里发售这款产品。Note 130 的发售日期将在明年 1 月 1 日，所以在春节期间的购物旺季肯定会准时发售到各大商场。届时，本产品将在全国所有零售网点都有库存。我们也将使手机可通过邮购和网购方式进行销售，并保证 7 天交货。

价格根据产品的市场销售情况而定。目前，这款新产品零售价定为 699 美元。考虑到产品质量和先进的功能，这应该是一个相当合理的价格。

好，我就讲到这里。希望你们对这款 Note 130 有更清楚的了解。并希望你们能 100% 地支持这款新产品。

Unit Five   Office Automation

5.1   Use a Computer

Section One: Tasks

Situation 1: *Alice is a new employee of BMY Company. She is asking Bill about how to run a computer. Make a dialogue according to the situation.*

Situation 2: *Alice is talking with Bill about the Internet. Make a dialogue according to the situation.*

Situation 3: *Alice is asking customer service for help about the problem of his computer. Make a dialogue according to the situation.*

Section Two: Related Information

Carbon-based Error

"My computer may be out of order. When I enter the password, it is clear that I input the numbers, but it shows only stars on the screen. How could it be?[1]" When the IT Department staff receive such technical help information, they must be crazy, right? Well, this example may be extreme. However, it is said that most of the IT employees deal with the failures caused by human factors. [2]

A carbon-based error refers to a problem with a computer or a program that is caused by the user rather than the machine. [3] All life on the earth depends on carbon, which forms the molecular bonds that make life possible. Therefore, to say that an error is carbon-based is another way of saying it was caused by a computer's human user. Carbon-based errors are a common problem for IT professionals, particularly when it comes to inexperienced users.

This slang term[4] is most frequently used by IT professionals who are always being

106

called upon to fix errors that have nothing to do with the technology. But there are also some everyday technical failures that can be easily solved by some simple operations. Like anything electronic, your computer will occasionally encounter problems. Knowing some basic troubleshooting tips can help save you a lot of time and potentially money. [5] You don't have to be an expert, but knowing what to try first can be very beneficial.

The first thing you should try whenever you are encountering a problem is resetting your computer. Believe it or not, this will resolve a large number of issues you are having with a program or function. If you are having connectivity problems when browsing the internet, resetting your connection may fix your problem.

Another way to keep your computer in good condition is to uninstall troublesome programs. As you add more and more programs to your computer, you'll find that there are some you use more than others. If you have old programs installed that you no longer use, they're taking space on your computer that could be used for other things. Certain programs may be running in the background as well, even if you're not using them, which can significantly impact your computer's performance. Regularly uninstalling programs you no longer use is a good way to maintain your computer's health. [6]

Vocabulary

carbon ['kɑːbən] *n.* 碳；*adj.* 碳的

input ['ɪnput] *n.* 输入，投入；输入的数据；*vt.* 把……输入电脑

extreme [ɪk'striːm] *adj.* 极端的，过激的；极限的，非常的

molecular [mə'lekjulə] *adj.* 分子的，由分子组成的

bond [bɒnd] *n.* 纽带；联系

inexperienced [ˌɪnɪk'spɪərɪənst] *adj.* 无经验的；不熟练的

frequently ['friːkwəntlɪ] *adv.* 往往；频繁地；屡次地

fix [fɪks] *v.* 固定；修理

technical ['teknɪkl] *adj.* 技术（性）的；工艺的

electronic [ɪˌlek'trɒnɪk] *adj.* 电子的

troubleshoot ['trʌblʃuːt] *vt.* 故障排除

occasionally [ə'keɪʒnəlɪ] *adv.* 偶尔；偶然；有时候

encounter [ɪn'kaʊntə(r)] *vt.* 遭遇；不期而遇；对抗

potentially [pə'tenʃəlɪ] *adv.* 潜在地；可能地

beneficial [ˌbenɪ'fɪʃl] *adj.* 有利的；有益的

reset ［,ri:'set］vt. 重置；重新安装

resolve ［rɪ'vlɔv］vt. 使消释；使分解；使解体；解决

issue ［'ɪʃu:］n. 问题；（报刊的）期，号；发行物

connectivity ［,kɔnek'tɪvɪtɪ］n. 连通性

browse ［brauz］vt. 浏览

uninstall ［,ʌnɪn'stɔ:l］vt. 卸载

troublesome ［'trʌblsəm］adj. 令人讨厌的；令人烦恼的；引起麻烦的

install ［ɪn'stɔ:l］vt. 安装；安顿，安置

significantly ［sɪg'nɪfɪkəntlɪ］adv. 意味深长地；值得注目地

impact ［'ɪmpækt］n. 影响；碰撞，冲击，撞击；冲击力；vt. 撞击；挤入，压紧；对……
产生影响

performance ［pə'fɔ:məns］n. 表现；表演

regularly ［'regjələlɪ］adv. 定期地；有规律地；按部就班地；经常；不断地

maintain ［meɪn'teɪn］vt. 保持；保养

out of order 故障，违反规程

deal with 处理；应对

refer to 提到；针对；关系到

depend on 依赖；依靠；取决于……；随……而定

when it comes to 当提到……；当涉及……

call upon 召唤，拜访

Notes

1. How could it be? 怎么会这样呢？

2. However，it is said that most of the IT employees deal with the failures caused by human factors. 然而，据说大多数 IT 员工处理由人为因素造成的故障。"it is said that…" 据说……

3. A carbon-based error refers to a problem with a computer or a program that is caused by the user rather than the machine. 人为故障指因为用户而非机器的原因而导致的计算机或者程序问题。"refer to…" 指的是……，"…that is caused by…" 是由 that 引导的定语从句，意为"由……所引起的"。

4. slang term 俚语

5. Knowing some basic troubleshooting tips can help save you a lot of time and potentially money. 了解一些基本的故障排除技巧可以帮助你节省大量的时间和潜在的金钱。Knowing some basic troubleshooting tips 是现在分词作主语。

6. Regularly uninstalling programs you no longer use is a good way to maintain your computer's health. 定期卸载你不再使用的程序是让你的计算机健康的好方法。本句主句中省略 that 的定语从句，完整形式应该是 …programs that you no longer use，先行词在从句中作宾语时，that 可省略。

Section Three: Situational Task Samples

Situation 1 : The following dialogue is about how to use a computer. Li Xin is helping Carol , an old lady in his office who has never worked on a computer before. (A : Carol ; B : Li Xin)

A: I have never worked on a computer before. Could you tell me how to use it?

B: OK. Let me show you. First, you plug the computer in. Next press the power button and wait for the computer to go into the Windows 7 System[1].

A: What is the Windows 7 System?

B: Well, it's a very popular operating system developed by Microsoft Company[2]. Most PCs[3] in the world use this system except Macs[4].

A: Then what shall I do?

B: You will see some icons[5] on the screen of the monitor[6].

A: Oh, yes. What do they stand for?

B: They stand for different software. For example, this stands for Microsoft Word. Just double click the icon, and you can start to use it.

A: It seems quite simple.

B: Yes, that's it. But you need more practice to make it perfect[7].

A: I got it. Thank you.

Situation 2 : The following dialogue is about the Internet. Li Xin is talking with his colleague Carol about the Internet. (A : Carol ; B : Li Xin)

A: Nowadays the expression "Have you been online?" seems to be so popular. I wonder why so many people are crazy about[8] the Internet.

B: You mean you have never surfed the net[9] before?

A: That's right.

B: What a pity! Though the Internet has a short history, it has been developing very fast.

A: It seems we all have to learn how to use the Internet. Tell me, what can we do on the Internet?

B: Well, we can do a lot of things such as sending emails, chatting, watching movies and even doing online shopping[10].

A: It sounds interesting and helpful. But how can I have my computer connected to the Internet?

B: You need to find yourself an Internet supplier first.

A: Ok, I'll try. Can you help me when you're free?

B: Sure thing.

Situation 3 : The following dialogue is about customer service. Li Xin is talking with a customer service representative about the problem he faced. (B : Li Xin ; C : The representative)

C: Service Center[11] of HP[12]. May I help you?

B: The computer I bought from you does not work properly.

C: I'm sorry to hear that. What's the problem?

B：I don't know for sure. When I turn on the computer，nothing comes up on the screen.

C：How long have you had this trouble?

B：Since yesterday. Can you tell me what's wrong with my computer?

C：Well，I can't tell at the moment. We'll send a technician[13] to check on the problem.

B：I'd like to know if you'll charge me for the service.

C：When did you buy the machine，Sir?

B：Last December.

C：The guarantee[14] is valid[15] for one year. Your computer is still under warranty[16]. So you don't have to pay at all.

B：When can your technician come?

C：This afternoon.

B：I'll be waiting for him at home. Thank you.

Notes

1. Windows 7 System　Windows 7 系统，微软公司设计的一种计算机操作系统，类似的还有 Windows XP，Windows 10 等。

2. Microsoft Company 微软公司

3. PC personal computer 的缩写，个人电脑

4. Mac 特指苹果电脑

5. icon 电脑桌面上的图标

6. monitor 显示器

7. practice makes perfect 熟能生巧

8. be crazy about 痴迷于

9. surf the net 网上冲浪，上网

10. online shopping 网上购物

11. Service Center 客户服务中心

12. HP 惠普公司（Hewlett-Packard Development Company，L. P.，HP）

13. technician 技师，技术人员

14. guarantee 保证书，担保

15. valid 有效的；有法律效力的

16. under warranty 在保修期内

Section Four：Functional Sentence Bank

About hardware（关于硬件）

1. I'd like to buy a computer with up-to-date components. 我想买一台有最新配件的电脑。

2. I'm afraid this software is not compatible with the main board.
   恐怕这个软件和主板不兼容。

3. Your memory is too small to run this application software.
   你的内存太小，无法运行这个应用软件。

4. If you want your computer to run faster，do not install too many programs on the hard disk. 如果你想让你的电脑运行得快一点儿，就不要在硬盘上安装太多程序。

5. Do you want to buy a compatible computer or a name brand? 你想买一台兼容机还是品牌机？

6. What configuration of computer do you want to buy? 你要买什么配置的电脑？

About virus（关于病毒）

1. Virus is a self-duplicating computer program that interferes with a computer's hardware or operating system.
   病毒是一种自我复制的计算机程序，它干扰计算机的硬件或操作系统。

2. In order to protect your data，you need to install a powerful anti-virus program on the hard disk. 为了保护你的数据，你需要在硬盘上安装一个强大的杀毒程序。

3. These two documents have been infected with a virus. You have to clean them with an anti-virus program. 这两份文件已经感染了病毒。你必须用杀毒程序清理它们。

4. CIH is a very destructive virus with a payload that destroys data.
   CIH 是一种有效载荷，对数据有极大破坏性的病毒。

5. CIH virus triggers/strikes/breaks out on the 26th of April or any month.
   CIH 病毒触发/攻击/爆发在 4 月 26 日或任何一个月的 26 日。

6. Viruses operate，replicate，and deliver their payloads only when they are running.
   病毒只有当被运行时才会操作、复制并传播它们的有效载荷。

About the Internet（关于互联网）

1. Do you often go online? /Do you often surf the Internet? 你经常上网吗？

2. What kind of website do you often browse? 你经常浏览什么网站？

3. Our home page was attacked by hackers. 我们的主页被黑客攻击了。

4. Have you got an email address? 你有电子邮箱吗？

5. Do you often send emails on the Internet? 你经常在网上发电子邮件吗？

6. Do you do online shopping? 你网上购物吗？

7. You can download the latest driver of the sound card from the Internet.
   你可以从网上下载最新的声卡驱动。

8. I often use the search engine Google to search for information.
   我经常使用谷歌搜索引擎搜索信息。

About operation（关于操作）

1. My computer is down again. 我的电脑又死机了。

2. Key in your password. 输入你的密码。

3. I bought this computer one year ago and it's now out of date.
   我一年前买的这台电脑，现在它过时了。

4. A：Is this a compatible computer or a name brand? 它是兼容机还是品牌机？

   B：This is a compatible computer. It often breaks down.
   这是一台兼容机。它经常出故障。

5. Press the right button on the mouse. 单击鼠标右键。

6. Move the cursor here and double click the left button on the mouse.

移动光标到这里并双击鼠标左键。

7. Please key in/type in your password. 请输入密码。

8. Please log in/log out. 请进入系统/退出系统。

9. Remember to save the document before you exit. 退出前记得保存文件。

10. Please backup your important documents on a mobile hard disc.

请把你的重要文件备份到移动硬盘上去。

Giving instructions（给予指导）

1. Press the button once to start the machine. To stop it, press the same button once again.

按一下这个按钮来启动这台机器，再按一次即可停止运行。

2. First, plug in the computer. 首先，插上电脑电源。

3. Then, press the power button. 然后，按开关按钮。

4. Next, select the Microsoft Word icon, and double click it.

接下来，选择微软 Word 图标，双击一下。

5. Don't push the switch when the machine is running. 机器在运行时不要触碰开关。

6. If you press these two keys（Ctrl and Space Bar）at the same time, you can switch the status from English to Chinese, or vice versa. 如果你同时按这两个键（Ctrl 和空格键），就可以从英文输入法切换到中文输入法，反之亦然。

7. If you click this icon, you will save the document.

如果你点击这个图标，就可以保存文档。

8. If you select the Esc key, you will exit this system. 如果你选择 Esc 键，就可以退出系统。

Section Five：Culture Tips

微软公司

微软，是一家美国跨国科技公司，也是世界 PC（Personal Computer，个人计算机）软件开发的先导，由比尔·盖茨与保罗·艾伦创办于 1975 年，公司总部设在华盛顿州的雷德蒙德（Redmond，邻近西雅图），以研发、制造、授权和提供广泛的电脑软件服务业务为主。

微软最为著名和畅销的产品是 Microsoft Windows 操作系统和 Microsoft Office 系列软件，目前是全球最大的电脑软件提供商。

微软在 2013 年在世界 500 强企业排行榜中排名第 110 位，2014 年排名第 104 位。2016 年 6 月 8 日，"2016 年 BrandZ 全球最具价值品牌百强榜"公布，微软排名第 3 位。6 月 13 日，微软以每股 196 美元，合计 262 亿美元的全现金收购 LinkedIn 公司的全部股权和净现金。10 月，微软排 2016 年全球 100 大最有价值品牌第 4 名。2017 年 2 月，Brand Finance 发布 2017 年度全球 500 强品牌榜单，微软排名第五。

"Microsoft"一词由"Microcomputer"和"software"两部分组成。其中，"Micro"的来源是 Microcomputer"微型计算机"，而"soft"则是 software"软件"的缩写，是由比尔·盖茨命名的。

微软在 1999 年 12 月 30 日创下了 6,616 亿美元的人类历史上上市公司最高市值记录，如果算上通货膨胀，相当于 2012 年的 9,130 亿美元。由于 1999 年受到美国国会反垄断控制调查，微软股价极度受挫，不然预估能突破 8,500 亿美元。

截止 2013 年，微软公司几乎占据了美国市场的每一寸空间，将市场占领到了极致，几乎达到了瓶颈。微软的贡献是不能用金钱价值来衡量的。

译　文

第二部分：相关信息

人为故障

"我的电脑可能出问题了。我输入密码的时候明明输的是数字，但是怎么显示的全是星星啊？"当 IT 部门的员工接到这样的技术求助信息时，他们一定很崩溃吧？好吧，这个例子可能有些极端。不过，据说大部分 IT 员工处理的都是这些人为因素导致的故障。

人为故障指因为用户而非机器的原因而导致的计算机或者程序问题。地球上所有的生命都是在碳元素的基础上发展而来的，它是构成生命分子链的基本元素。因此，当我们说某个错误或故障是 carbon-based，其实就是说这个故障是人为导致的。很多 IT 专业人士面对的都是人为故障，尤其是当电脑使用者为新手的时候。

最常使用这个俚语的自然就是 IT 专业人士，因为他们经常被叫去处理一些跟技术一点儿关系都没有的故障。但也有一些日常的技术故障，可以通过一些简单的操作很容易地解决。像所有电子产品一样，你的电脑偶尔也会遇到问题。了解一些基本的故障排除技巧可以帮助你节省大量的时间和潜在的金钱。你不一定要成为专家，但知道先尝试去做什么可能是非常有益的。

无论何时你遇到问题，你应该尝试的第一件事就是重启你的电脑。信不信由你，这将解决大量的程序或功能问题。如果你在浏览互联网的时候有连接问题时，重置你的连接可能会解决你的问题。

另一种让你的计算机处于良好状态的方法是卸载麻烦的程序。当你把越来越多的程序装入你的电脑时，你会发现有些程序其实你并不经常使用。如果你有已经安装却不再使用的旧程序，它们在占用计算机的空间，而这些空间可用于其他事情。某些程序也可能在后台运行，即使你不使用它们，它们也会显著地影响计算机的性能。定期卸载你不再使用的程序是让你的计算机健康的好方法。

第三部分：情境任务范例

情境 1： 下面的对话是有关如何使用电脑的。李欣正在帮助卡罗尔，一位他办公室里的年长女士，她以前从没有在电脑上工作过。（A：卡罗尔；B：李欣）

A：我从没在电脑上工作过，你能告诉我怎么使用吗？

B：好的，让我给你演示一下。首先，插上电脑电源。然后按开机按钮，等待电脑启动至 Windows 7 系统。

A：什么是 Windows 7 系统？

B：嗯，它是由微软公司开发的一个很受欢迎的电脑操作系统。除了苹果电脑，世界上大多数电脑都是用的微软系统。

A：那么接下来我要怎么做？

B：你会看到电脑显示器的屏幕上出现一些图标。

A：哦，是的。它们代表什么？

B：它们代表不同的软件。比如，这个代表文字处理软件。只要双击这个图标，你就可以启动使用这个程序了。

A：这似乎很简单。

B：是的，就这样。你只需要熟能生巧。

A：我明白了，谢谢你。

情境 2： 下面的对话是关于互联网的内容。李欣正在跟他的同事卡罗尔讨论互联网话题。

（A：卡罗尔；B：李欣）

A：如今"你上网了吗？"这句话似乎很流行。我想知道为什么那么多人痴迷于互联网。

B：你的意思是你以前从来没有上过网吗？

A：是啊。

B：太遗憾了！虽然互联网的历史很短，但发展得很快。

A：看来我们都得学会如何使用互联网。告诉我，我们在网上能做什么？

B：嗯，我们可以做很多事情，如发送电子邮件、聊天、看电影、甚至网上购物。

A：听起来很有趣很有帮助。但我怎样才能让我的电脑连接到互联网呢？

B：你首先需要找一个互联网供应商。

A：好的。我试试看。你有空时能帮帮我吗？

B：当然可以。

情境 3： 下面的对话是有关客户服务的。李欣正在向一名客服代表咨询自己遇到的问题。

（B：李欣；C：客服代表）

C：惠普客服中心，我可以帮助你吗？

B：我从你们那儿买的电脑不正常工作了。

C：很遗憾听到这件事。有什么问题吗？

B：我不知道。当我打开电脑时，屏幕上什么也没出现。

C：这种情况有多久了？

B：从昨天开始。你能告诉我，我的电脑出了什么问题吗？

C：我现在说不出来。我们会派一个技术员去检查这个问题。

B：我想知道你们是否会向我收取服务费。

C：先生，你什么时候买的这台机器？

B：去年 12 月。

C：担保有效期为一年。你的计算机仍在保修期内。所以你不用付钱。

B：你们的技术人员什么时候能过来？

C：今天下午。

B：我会在家等他。谢谢你。

5. 2   Use a Printer

Section One: Tasks

Situation 1: *As a new employee of BMY Company, Alice is asking Bill about how to solve a problem on the printer caused by lack of paper. Make a dialogue according to the situation.*

Situation 2: *Alice is asking Bill about how to solve a problem on the printer caused by paper jamming. Make a dialogue according to the situation.*

Situation 3: *Alice is asking Bill about how to solve a problem on the printer caused by lack of ink. Make a dialogue according to the situation.*

Section Two: Related Information

3D Printing

3D printing, also known as increasing manufacturing technology, is a technology based on digital model files, which uses powder metal or plastic and other adhesive materials to construct objects by printing through layers. [1]

Generally speaking, 3D printing has considerable imagination. It can be widely applied in [2] many fields, such as traditional manufacturing, automobile, consumer electronics, medical devices, building engineering and so on. These fields can be better developed by combining with [3] 3D printing.

With the continuous maturity of 3D printing technology, its industrial potential is expected to be released rapidly and the market expansion can be expected. [4] According to the statistical analysis of *China's 3D Printing Industry Market Demand and Investment Potential Analysis Report* [5], in 2016, the global 3D printing market scale reached 15. 9 billion US dollars, and it is estimated that by 2020, the global 3D printing market will reach 35. 4 billion US dollars.

Although the 3D printing industry in China started late, the enthusiasm for development continues to rise, and the market size is also rising. It is expected that in 2020, the market size of China's 3D printers will be around 10 billion yuan.

Vocabulary

adhesive ［əd'hiːsɪv］ *adj*. 可黏着的，黏性的

construct ［kən'strʌkt］ *vt*. 构成；修建，建造；创立

considerable ［kən'sɪdərəbl］ *adj*. 相当大（或多）的；该注意的，应考虑的

apply ［ə'plaɪ］ *vt*. 申请；应用，运用

combine ［kəm'baɪn］ *v*. 使结合；使化合；兼有

continuous ［kən'tɪnjuəs］ *adj*. 连续的；延伸的

maturity ［mə'tʃuərəti］ *n*. 成熟；完备

potential ［pə'tenʃl］ *n*. 潜力，潜能

expansion [ɪk'spænʃn] n. 扩张；扩大

statistical [stə'tɪstɪkl] adj. 统计的；统计学的

analysis [ə'næləsɪs] n. 分析，分解

enthusiasm [ɪn'θju:zɪæzəm] n. 热情，热忱

Notes

1. 3D printing, also known as increasing manufacturing technology, is a technology based on digital model files, which uses powder metal or plastic and other adhesive materials to construct objects by printing through layers. 3D 打印又被称为增材制造技术，是一种以数字模型文件为基础，运用粉末状金属或塑料等可黏合材料，通过逐层打印的方式来构造物体的技术。

2. be applied in… 应用于……

3. combine with 与……结合

4. can be expected 可以预期

5. *China's 3D printing Industry Market Demand and Investment Potential Analysis Report*《中国 3D 打印产业市场需求与投资潜力分析报告》

Section Three：Situational Task Samples

Situation 1：*The following dialogue is about how to use a printer. Li Xin's colleague Carol is asking him about how to use a printer.*（A：Carol；B：Li Xin）

A：I have never worked on a printer before. Could you tell me how to use it?

B：OK. Let me show you. First, you plug the printer in. Next press the power button and wait for the printer to get started.

A：OK. Then what shall I do?

B：You select the file you want to print and double-click it with your mouse.

A：Oh, yes. What's next?

B：Put the cursor[1] on the page you want to print or select the part you want to print. Then select the "file" button and click "print".

A：It seems quite simple.

B：Yes, that's it. You may preview[2] the file you want to print first to make sure it is all right.

A：I got it. Thank you.

Situation 2：*The following dialogue is about how to solve a problem on a printer caused by lacking of paper. Li Xin's colleague Carol is asking him about how to deal with the printer problem.*（A：Carol；B：Li Xin）

B：Hi, Carol. You look upset there. What's the matter?

A：Oh, hi, Li Xin. It seems my printer doesn't work well.

B：Oh, really? Let me see. You are running out of paper.

A：So it is! How stupid I am!

B: Never mind, it happens. Just put some paper in it.

A: Thank you.

B: You are welcome.

Situation 3*: The following dialogue is about how to solve a problem on a printer caused by paper jamming. Li Xin's colleague Carol is asking him about how to deal with the printer problem. (A: Carol; B: Li Xin)*

A: Excuse me, Li Xin. Can you do me a favor?

B: Sure. What's up?

A: There's something wrong with my printer again.

B: Are you running out of paper again?

A: No, I got plenty of paper in it. But it just won't come out.

B: Well, let's check it out. Um…I got it.

A: What's the problem?

B: It's paper jamming.

A: Then what should I do?

B: Open the cover so you can exactly see where the paper jammed.

A: Yes, it's there.

B: Take it out slowly and carefully. Then try to print again.

A: Great, it works!

Situation 4*: The following dialogue is about how to solve a problem on a printer caused by lacking of ink. Li Xin's colleague Carol is asking him about how to deal with the printer problem. (A: Carol; B: Li Xin)*

B: Hi, Carol. Could you please print this file for me?

A: Sure. How would you like it, one side or double sides?

B: One side.

A: And would you like it black-and-white printing or color printing?

B: Black-and-white printing[3] is OK.

A: How many copies do you need?

B: Ten, please.

A: Well, here they are. But what's wrong with the machine? The printing is not clear.

B: I guess it is short of ink. You have to change the ink cartridge[4].

A: OK. It's done. Let's try again.

B: Well done. You can run the printer now.

A: Thanks to you.

Notes

1. cursor ['kɜːsə] 光标

2. preview ['priːvjuː] 预览

3. black-and-white printing 黑白打印

4. ink cartridge ['ka:tridʒ] 墨盒

Section Four: Functional Sentence Bank

Technical terms（技术术语）

1. needle printer 针式打印机

2. ink jet printer 喷墨打印机

3. laser printer 激光打印机

4. ink cartridge 墨盒

5. toner cartridge 硒鼓

Problems solving（解决问题）

1. It seems my printer doesn't work well. 我的打印机似乎不好用了。

2. You are running out of paper. 没纸了。

   It's short of paper. 没纸了。

3. What's the problem/matter? 怎么了？

4. There's something wrong with my printer. 我的打印机出故障了。

5. It's paper jamming. 卡纸了。

6. Open the cover so you can exactly see where the paper jammed.

   打开盖子，这样你就可以看清卡纸的位置了。

7. It is short of ink. 墨不够了。

8. You have to change the ink cartridge. 你得换墨盒了。

About Copying（关于打印）

1. A：Can you have this file copied? 你能把这份文件复印一下吗？

   B：Sure. How many copies would you like? 好的。你要复印多少份？

2. Would you copy these papers? 你能复印一下这些材料吗？

3. A：You can do double-sided copying. 你可以双面复印。

   B：That's great. 好极了。

4. Can this copy machine make double-sided copies? 这台复印机能双面复印吗？

5. A：Do you want color copies or black-and-white copies? 你想要印彩色的还是黑白的？

   B：Color copies，please. 请印彩色的。

Section Five: Culture Tips

打印机的种类

1. 针式打印机

针式打印机曾经在打印机历史上的很长一段时间占据着重要的地位，从 9 针到 24 针，可以说针式打印机的历史贯穿着几十年。针式打印机之所以在很长的一段时间内能盛行不衰，这与它极低的打印成本和良好的易用性以及单据打印的特殊用途是分不开的。当然，它较低的打印质量、很大的工作噪声也是它无法适应高质量、高速度的商用打印需要的根结，所以现在只有在银行、超市等用于票单打印的很少地方还可以看见它的踪迹。

2. 彩色喷墨打印机

彩色喷墨打印机有着良好的打印效果与较低的价位，因而占领了广大中低端市场。此外喷墨打印机还具有更为灵活的纸张处理能力，在打印介质的选择上，喷墨打印机也具有一定的优势：既可以打印信封、信纸等普通介质，还可以打印各种胶片、照片纸、光盘封面、卷纸等特殊介质。

3. 激光打印机

激光打印机则是近年来高科技发展的一种新产物，也是有望代替喷墨打印机的一种机型，分为黑白和彩色两种，它为我们提供了更高质量、更快速、更低成本的打印方式。其中低端黑白激光打印机的价格目前已经降到了几百元，达到了普通用户可以接受的水平。它的打印原理是利用光栅图像处理器产生要打印页面的位图，然后将其转换为电信号等一系列的脉冲送往激光发射器，在这一系列脉冲的控制下，激光被有规律地放出。与此同时，反射光束被接收到的感光鼓感光。激光发射时就产生一个点，激光不发射时就是空白，这样就在接收器上印出一行点来。然后接收器转动一小段固定的距离继续重复上述操作。当纸张经过感

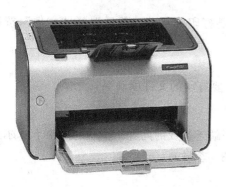

光鼓时，鼓上的着色剂就会转移到纸上，印成了页面的位图。最后当纸张经过一对加热辊后，着色剂被加热熔化，固定在了纸上，就完成了打印的全过程，整个过程准确而高效。虽然激光打印机的价格要比喷墨打印机昂贵得多，但从单页的打印成本上讲，激光打印机则要便宜很多。而彩色激光打印机的价位则很高，几乎都要在万元上下，应用范围较窄，很难被普通用户接受。

译　文

第二部分：相关信息

3D 打印

　　3D 打印又被称为增材制造技术，是一种以数字模型文件为基础，运用粉末状金属或塑料等可黏合材料，通过逐层打印的方式来构造物体的技术。

　　大体来说，3D 打印具有相当可观的想象空间，可应用领域十分广泛，像传统的制造业，以及汽车、消费电子、医疗器械、建筑工程等。这些领域都可以通过与 3D 打印结合，从而获得更好地发展。

　　随着 3D 打印技术的日益成熟，其产业潜力有望快速释放，市场规模扩张可期。根据《中国 3D 打印产业市场需求与投资潜力分析报告》的统计数据分析，2016 年，全球 3D 打印市场规模达到 159 亿美元，预计到 2020 年，全球 3D 打印市场规模将达到 354 亿美元。

　　我国 3D 打印产业虽然起步较晚，但发展热情持续高涨，市场规模也节节攀升。预计到 2020 年，我国的 3D 打印机市场规模将在 100 亿元左右。

第三部分：情境任务范例

情境 1：下面的对话是关于如何使用打印机。李欣的同事卡罗尔正在向李欣请教如何使用打印机。（A：卡罗尔；B：李欣）

A：我从未用过打印机，你能告诉我怎么使用吗？

B：好的，让我来给你演示一下。首先，插上打印机的电源。然后按下开机按钮，并等待打印机启动。

A：好，那么接下来我要怎么做呢？

B：选择你要打印的文件然后用鼠标双击它。

A：哦，是的。接下来呢？

B：把光标放在你要打印的那页上或者选择你要打印的部分。然后选择"文件"按钮里的"打印"选项，单击它。

A：这似乎很简单。

B：是的，就这样。你可以在打印之前预览一下要打印的文件以确保其无误。

A：我明白了，谢谢你。

情境 2：下面的对话是关于如何解决打印机纸张缺乏造成的问题。李欣的同事卡罗尔正在问他如何处理这个打印机的问题。（A：卡罗尔；B：李欣）

B：嗨，卡罗尔。你看起来很烦恼。怎么了？

A：噢，嗨，李欣。我的打印机好像不太好用。

B：哦，真的吗？我看一下。你的打印纸用完了。

A：原来是这样！我真笨啊！

B：没关系，这是常有的事。把纸放在打印机里即可。

A：谢谢。

B：不客气。

情境 3： 下面的对话是关于如何解决打印机卡纸造成的问题。李欣的同事卡罗尔正在问他如何处理这个打印机的问题。（A：卡罗尔；B：李欣）

A：打扰一下，李欣。你能帮我个忙吗？

B：当然可以。出什么事了？

A：我的打印机又出毛病了。

B：你的纸又用完了吗？

A：没有，里面有很多纸。但它就是打印不出来。

B：好吧，让我们检查一下。嗯……我知道了。

A：是什么问题？

B：是卡纸了。

A：那我该怎么办呢？

B：打开盖子，这样你就可以看清卡纸的位置了。

A：是的，在那儿。

B：慢慢地，小心地把纸拿出来。然后再打印试试。

A：太好了，它动了！

情境 4： 下面的对话是关于如何解决打印机墨水不足造成的问题。李欣的同事卡罗尔正在问他如何处理这个打印机的问题。（A：卡罗尔；B：李欣）

B：嗨，卡罗尔。你能帮我打印这个文件吗？

A：当然可以。你要单面打印的还是双面打印的？

B：单面的。

A：你想要黑白印刷还是彩色印刷的？

B：黑白打印就可以了。

A：你需要多少份？

B：10 份，请吧。

A：好，打出来了。但是这台机器怎么了？打印得不清楚啊。

B：我猜是墨水不够了。你得换墨盒了。

A：好的。换好了。让我们再试一次。

B：做得好。现在你可以运行这台打印机了。

A：谢谢你了。

Unit Six Meeting

6. 1   Organize a Meeting

Section One: Tasks

Situation 1: *As a monitor, Zhang Xue is organizing a class meeting on how to protect animals. Make a dialogue according to the situation.*

Situation 2: *As a director of ABC Company, Susan is organizing a meeting on how to increase sales. Make a dialogue according to the situation.*

Section Two: Related Information

How to Gain and Keep the Audience's Attention?

Experienced speakers always know how to capture the attention of the audience and how to maintain that attention during a presentation. [1] You can do this by trying these nine techniques.

* A promise. Begin with a promise that keeps the audience's expectant. For example, "by the end of the presentation I will show you how you can increase your sales by 50 percent!"

* Drama. [2] Open by telling a moving story or by describing a serious problem that involves the audience. Throughout your talk include other dramatic elements, such as a short pause after a key statement, or change your vocal tone or pitch. Professionals always use high-intensity emotions such as anger, joy, sadness, and excitement. [3]

* Eye contact. As you begin, command attention by surveying the entire audience to take in all listeners. Take two to five seconds to make eye contact with[4] as many people as possible.

* Movement. Leave the lectern area whenever possible. Walk around the conference table or between the aisles of your audience. Try to move toward your audience, especially at the beginning and end of your talk.

● Questions. Keep listeners active and involved with questions. Ask for a show of hands to get each listener thinking. The response will also give you a quick gauge of audience attention.

● Demonstrations. Include a member of the audience in a demonstration. For example，I'm going to show you exactly how to implement our four-step customer courtesy process，but I need a volunteer from the audience to help me. [5]

● Samples/gimmicks. If you're promoting a product，consider tossing them out to the audience or to award as prizes to volunteer participants. [6]

● Visuals. Give your audience something to look at besides yourself. Use a variety of visual aids in a single session. Also consider writing the concerns expressed by your audience on a flipchart or on the board as you go along.

● Self-interest. Review your entire presentation to ensure that it meets the critical what's-in-it-for-me audience test. [7] Remember that people are most interested in things that benefit them.

Vocabulary

audience ['ɔːdiəns] n. 观众；听众

capture ['kæptʃə(r)] vt. 引起（注意、想象、兴趣）；获得，捕获

attention [ə'tenʃn] n. 注意

presentation [ˌpreznˈteɪʃn] n. 陈述；展示；介绍

pitch [pɪtʃ] n. 音高

intensity [ɪnˈtensəti] n. 强烈；（感情的）强烈程度

lectern ['lektən] n. 小讲台

aisle [aɪl] n. 过道；通道

gauge [geɪdʒ] n. 评估

demonstration [ˌdemən'streɪʃn] n. 示范；证明

implement ['ɪmplɪment] vt. 实施；执行；实现

gimmick ['gɪmɪk] n. 噱头；花招；诡计；骗人的把戏

toss [tɔːs] vt.（轻轻或漫不经心地）扔；（使）摇荡；摇匀；投掷；（为……）掷硬币决定

flipchart [flɪpt'ʃɑːt] n. 挂图；翻转图

critical ['krɪtɪkl] adj. 批判性的；批评的；爱挑剔的

capture the attention of sb.   吸引住某人的注意力

make eye contact with sb.   与某人进行眼神交流

toss out   扔出

Notes

1. Experienced speakers always know how to capture the attention of the audience and how to maintain that attention during a presentation. 有经验的演讲者总是知道如何吸引听众

的注意力，以及如何在演讲中保持注意力。capture the attention of sb. 即 capture one's attention 抓住某人的注意力。

2. drama 原指戏剧，此处指戏剧效果。

3. Throughout your talk include other dramatic elements, such as a long pause aftter a key statement, or change your vocal tone or pitch. Professionals always use high-intensity emotions such as anger, joy, sadness, and excitement. 在你的讲话中还包括其他的戏剧性的元素，例如在关键陈述之后长时间停顿或改变你的语调或音高。专业人士常使用高强度的情绪，如愤怒、喜悦、悲伤和兴奋。vocal tone 语调；pitch 音高。

4. make eye contact with sb. 与某人进行眼神交流。

5. For example, I'm going to show you exactly how to implement our four-step customer courtesy process, but I need a volunteer from the audience to help me. 例如，我将确切地向你们展示如何实现对客户有礼貌的四个步骤，但我需要一名听众作为志愿者帮助我。

6. If you're promoting a product, consider using items to toss out to the audience or to award as prizes to volunteer participants. 如果你正在推销一个产品，那就考虑把这些物品扔给听众，或者把它们作为志愿参与者的奖品。

7. Review your entire presentation to ensure that it meets the critical what's-in-it-for-me audience test. 回顾你的整个演讲以确保满足听众批判性的测试"对我有什么用"。

Section Three: Situational Task Samples

Situation: The following dialogue is an example of a typical business meeting. As you can see from the dialogue, a typical business meeting can be divided into five parts.（C: Meeting Chairman Li Xin; J: Jack Peterson; T: Tom Robbins; S: Sam Stewart; A: Alice Jones; B: Bill Walker）

Introductions

C: If we are all here, let's get started. First of all, I'd like you to join me in welcoming Jack Peterson, our Southwest Area Sales Vice President. [1]

J: Thank you for having me, I'm looking forward to today's meeting.

C: I'm afraid our sales director, Anne Black, can't be with us today. She is in Kobe at the moment, developing our Far East sales force.

Review Past Business

C: Let's get started. We're here today to discuss ways of improving sales in rural market[2] areas. First, let's go over the report from the last meeting which was held on June 24th. All right, Tom, over to you.

T: Thank you, Mark. Let me just summarize[3] the main points of the last meeting. We began the meeting by approving the changes in our sales reporting system discussed on May 30th. After briefly revising the changes that will take place, we moved on to a brainstorming session[4] concerning after sales customer support improvements. You'll find a copy of the main ideas discussed in that session in the photocopies[5] in front of you.

Begin the Meeting

C: Thank you, Tom. So, if there is nothing else we need to discuss, let's move on to today's agenda[6]. Have you all received a copy of today's agenda? If you don't mind, I'd like to skip item 1 and move on to item 2: sales improvement in rural market areas. Jack has kindly agreed to give us a report on this matter. Jack?

Discuss Items

J: Before I begin the report, I'd like to get some ideas from you all. How do you feel about rural sales in your sales districts?

S: In my opinion, we have been focusing too much on urban customers and their needs. I think we need to return to our rural base by developing an advertising campaign to focus on their particular needs.

A: I'm afraid I can't agree with you. I think rural customers want to feel as important as our customers living in cities. I suggest we give our rural sales teams more help with advanced customer information reports.

S: I don't quite follow you. What exactly do you mean?

A: Well, we provide our city sales staff with database information[7] on all of our larger clients. We should provide the same sort of knowledge on our rural customers to our sales staff there.

J: Would you like to add something, Bill?

B: I must admit I never thought about rural sales that way before. I have to agree with Alice.

J: Well, let me begin with this Power Point[8] presentation (Jack presents his report).

S: I suggest we divide into groups and discuss the ideas we've presented.

Finish the Meeting

C: Unfortunately, we're running out of time. We'll have to leave that to another time.

J: Before we close, let me just summarize the main points:

Our sales teams need more accurate information on our customers.

A survey will be completed to collect data on spending habits in these areas.

The results of this survey will be delivered to our sales teams.

C: Thank you very much, Jack. All right, it looks as though we've covered the main items. Is there any other business?

A：Can we fix the next meeting, please?

C：Good idea, Alice. How does Friday in two weeks' time sound to everyone? Let's meet at the same time, 9 o'clock. Is that OK for everyone? …Excellent. I'd like to thank Jack for coming to our meeting today. The meeting is closed.

Notes

1. Sales Vice President 销售副总裁；vice 副手，副职
2. rural market 农村市场
3. summarize 总结
4. brainstorming session 头脑风暴会议；brainstorming 指的是无限制的自由联想和讨论，其目的在于产生新观念或激发创新设想
5. photocopy 复印件，可数名词
6. agenda 会议日程
7. database information 数据库信息
8. Power Point 幻灯片，课件

Section Four：Functional Expression Bank

The Chairman Declared the Meeting Open（主席宣布会议开始）

1. Good morning, ladies and gentlemen. 女士们，先生们，早上好。
2. Good morning, Mr. President and members of the society/association. 主席、各位协会成员，早上好！
3. May I have your attention, ladies and gentlemen? 女士们，先生们，请注意。
4. Ladies and gentlemen, please be seated. 女士们，先生们，请坐下。
5. The meeting is now declared open. 会议现在开始。
6. I'd like to call the meeting to order. 我宣布会议开始。
7. I declare the 10th General Assembly of…is now open.

   ［正式］我宣布第十届……全体会议现在开始。
8. Let's begin our meeting. 开会吧。

   Let's get started.［非正式］咱们开始吧。

   Let's make it start.［非正式］咱们开始吧。
9. Shall we get down to business?［非正式］让我们进入正题吧？

Declare the Purpose of the Meeting（宣布会议目的）

1. Today we are to discuss the proposal to start a football club.

   今天我们要讨论筹建一个足球俱乐部的建议。
2. The purpose of this meeting is to make a general review of our activities during last year, and to propose new plans for activities during the coming year.

   本次会议的目的是对我们去年的活动做一次总的回顾，并提出新的一年的活动计划。

Issues and Agenda（议题与议程）

1. We have three questions on the agenda. 按照议程，我们有三个问题要讨论。

2. The agenda is as follows：… ［正式］会议的议程如下：……

3. The issue we have to discuss this afternoon is…今天下午我们要讨论的问题是……

4. The first item on the agenda is… ［正式］议程上的第一项是……

5. Are there any additions or amendments to the proposed agenda?
   对所提的议程有没有增加或修改?

6. If I hear no objection，I shall consider the agenda adopted. 如果没有人反对，议程就通过了。

7. There being no objection，the agenda is adopted. ［正式］无人反对，议程通过。

8. I would like to limit the time of each speaker to 15 minutes.
   我想把每位发言者的时间限制在 15 分钟内。

9. After the presentation by the panelists，we are going to have a 20-minute discussion.
   在专门小组成员发言后，我们要讨论 20 分钟。

10. It is not open for discussion. 对此不展开讨论。

The Chairman Introduces the Spokesman（主席介绍发言人）

1. Ladies and gentlemen，I have great pleasure in introducing Mr. Brown，the famous…
   Mr. Brown will give us a lecture about…
   ［正式］女士们，先生们，我很高兴介绍布朗先生，他是著名的……，布朗先生将给我们
   做有关……的讲座。

2. And now，I'd like to present our next speaker to you，Professor Lin Yan.
   现在，我向大家介绍我们的下一位发言人，林艳教授。

3. Mr. Smith will now address you. ［正式］现在请史密斯先生给大家讲话。

The Chairman Asks Sb. to Speak（主席请某人发言）

1. Who will be the first speaker? 谁将第一个发言?

2. Mr. Black，give us your views first. 布莱克先生，您先发表意见。
   Mr. Black? ［用升调］布莱克先生?
   I'd like to call Mr. Black to present his views. ［委婉］我想请布莱克先生发表他的意见。
   Mr. Black，would you care to comment? ［正式］布莱克先生，您愿意发表意见吗?

3. Mr. York has the floor for the report on Item 2 of the agenda.
   ［正式］约克先生就议程第二项做报告。

4. Dr. White，you may have the floor. ［正式］怀特博士，您可以发言了。

5. I give the floor to the representative of… ［正式］我请……的代表发言。

The Opening Remarks of a Personal Statement（个人发言的开场白）

1. I appreciate your words of introduction. ［正式］我很感谢您的介绍。

2. Thank you for your kind introduction. The subject of my paper is…
   感谢您的介绍。我论文的题目是……

3. I would like to take this opportunity to express… ［委婉］我愿借此机会表达……

4. It's a great honor for me to be given this opportunity to address you on the occasion of
   this special meeting. ［正式］我很荣幸能有此机会在这个特别会议上发言。

5. Allow me to speak on behalf of the Chinese delegation.
   ［正式］请允许我代表中国代表团发言。

6. Thank you，Mr. Chairman. Good evening，ladies and gentlemen. I'm delighted to be here to speak about this very interesting subject.

［正式］谢谢您，主席先生。晚上好，女士们，先生们，我很高兴来这里谈谈这个非常有趣的话题。

The Closing Remarks of a Personal Statement（个人发言的结束语）

1. I would like to conclude with the hope that… ［委婉］我最后希望……

2. Because of shortage of time，I'll have to omit the next point.

   由于时间关系，我只得略去下面一点。

3. There're only a few minutes left，I'll give you right away my conclusions.

   只有几分钟的时间了，我马上就给大家讲一下我的结论。

The Chairman Controls the Discussion（主席掌控讨论）

1. We shall now proceed to the discussion.［正式］我们现在开始讨论。

2. After Professor Clinton speaks briefly about the actual situation，we shall enter into discussion.［正式］在克林顿教授简单地介绍实际情况之后，我们将进行讨论。

3. Could you tell us briefly?［委婉］您可以给我们简要讲一下吗？

4. Dr. Steward will be pleased to answer your questions now.

   斯图尔特博士现在将很高兴回答你们的问题。

5. Please don't interrupt，Mr. Jackson. You'll have a chance to speak later.

   杰克逊先生，请不要打断，您稍后会有机会发言的。

6. Order，order! One at a time. 秩序！秩序！一个一个发言。

7. Please continue，Dr. Port. 请继续，波特博士。

8. Let's go back to the theme. 让我们回到主题上来。

9. Now I'd like to bring up another point.［委婉］现在我想提出另一个问题。

End the Meeting（会议结束）

1. I would like to close this meeting now.［委婉］我想现在结束会议。

2. The meeting is now adjourned.［正式］会议现在休会。

3. As there are no further questions on the agenda，I declare the meeting closed.

   ［正式］由于议程上没有其他问题需要讨论了，我宣布会议结束。

4. Thank you very much for your earnest cooperation in carrying out this seminar.

   ［正式］非常感谢你们在举办此次研讨会中的真诚合作。

Section Five：Culture Tips

会议组织流程

1. 前期工作

（1）确定召开会议的时间、地点、人员、议程、接机、就餐、住宿等。

（2）根据会议的规模，确定会务组的成员，并对成员进行具体分工。

① 会务组成员名单及联系方式。

② 会务组成员需要开展的工作：如接机、住宿安排、会场布置、就餐安排、购买物资、收发材料、结账等。

（3）提前了解会场情况：

① 该时间段有几间会议室及能容纳多少人。

② 每间会议室提供哪些硬件设备以及易耗品（水、会议用纸、笔等）的数量等信息。

③ 会议上会标、背景、横幅等的使用。

④ 是否提供服务员以及保留对方负责人以及会场联系人的联系方式。

（4）提前了解住宿情况：

① 该时间段均能提供的各种房型的房间数量、价格等信息。

② 明确入住流程、早餐券的使用方式及酒店提供的免费项目。

③ 与会人员如需使用收费项目，酒店需要和会务组的何人确认。

④ 要求保留对方联系人以及酒店的联系方式。

（5）提前了解就餐情况：

① 就餐场地的桌席分布图（酒店提供）、主桌的安排。

② 就餐场地的背景布置。

③ 确认菜单的内容以及上菜的顺序、速度。

④ 会务人员的就餐安排。

（6）如果是在外地召开会议，需要当地提供支持，包括人员支持、车辆支持等。

（7）确认是否需要接机，接机车辆的安排与租赁，从机场到会场，出租车的行驶距离、时间以及大概费用。

（8）参会人员的机票预订方式（各自预订还是统一预订）。

2. 到达会场前的工作

（1）会场预订合同、酒店住宿以及就餐合同等的流转以及预付款的及时支付。

（2）参会人员的最终确认名单及联系方式。

（3）根据名单安排住宿房间表。

（4）会场座位示意图的确认与打印。

（5）大会主席人员座席卡的打印与座次安排确认。

（6）打印好签到表（2-3 份）。

（7）准备好常用物品（签到笔、信纸、小信封、透明胶、剪刀、订书机、笔记本电脑、U 盘等）。

3. 住宿安排

（1）提前确认所有房间是否已经准备就绪，发现问题及时纠正。

（2）提前办理好重要宾客的入住手续，安排专人在大堂等候，到酒店直接入住。

（3）将会务资料提前发放至各与会人员的房间。

（4）入住签到以及就餐券的发放。

4. 会议前安排

（1）确认座位的摆放、张贴与会人员座次标签以及按照要求设置演讲台。

（2）在会议室入口醒目处张贴好大会座位安排表，并由专人引导。

（3）调试话筒设备、笔记本、投影仪、电源等设备，确保处于正常工作状态。

（4）确认会场方应提供的鲜花、纸、笔等均已摆放完毕。

（5）如果酒店和会场之间需要接送车辆，应提前安排好。

（6）安装确认会场背景。

5. 会议中安排

(1) 定期提醒服务人员添加饮用水。

(2) 注意会场内的需求，有问题及时解决。

6. 会务用餐安排

(1) 在就餐前确认所有席位都已经准备完毕。

(2) 在餐厅入口处醒目位置张贴用餐示意图。

(3) 摆放主桌桌卡（红色）和其他桌次的桌卡。

(4) 如果是自助餐，在餐厅入口处发放就餐券（视情况决定）。

(5) 安排好领导随行人员就餐。

译　文

第二部分：相关信息

如何获得和保持听众的注意力？

有经验的演讲者总是知道如何吸引听众的注意力，以及如何在演讲中保持注意力。你可以通过尝试这九种技巧来做到这一点。

●承诺。从保证听众期待的承诺开始。例如，"在演讲结束时，我会告诉你们如何提高百分之五十的销售额！"

●戏剧效果。通过讲述一个感人的故事或描述一个与听众相关的严肃问题来展开。在你的讲话中还包括其他戏剧性的元素，例如在关键陈述之后的短时间停顿，或改变你的语调或音高。专业人士总是使用高强度的情绪，如愤怒、喜悦、悲伤和兴奋。

●眼神交流。当你开始时，通过观察所有听众来吸引他们的注意力。花两到五秒钟与尽可能多的人进行眼神交流。

●活动。尽可能离开讲台，在会议桌周围或过道来回走动。尤其是在你开始和结束讲话时，尽量走向你的听众。

●问题。让听众们积极参与问题。要求听众举手示意来让他们都思考。听众的回应也会给你一个对他们注意力的快速评估。

●示范。让听众参与示范。例如，我将确切地向你们展示如何实现我们对客户礼貌的四个步骤，但我需要一名听众作为志愿者帮助我。

●样品/噱头。如果你正在推销一个产品，那就考虑把这些物品扔给听众，或者把它们作为志愿参与者的奖品。

●视觉。除了你自己之外，再给听众一些可看的东西。在一场会议中使用多种视觉辅助工具。同时考虑在演讲过程中将听众关注的问题写在翻转图或写字板上。

●个人兴趣。回顾你的整个演讲以确保满足听众批判性的测试"对我有什么用"。记住人们最感兴趣的是对他们有益的事情。

第三部分：情境任务范例

情境：下面的对话是典型商务会议的一个例子。从对话中可以看出，一场典型的商务会议

可以分为五个部分。（C：会议主席李欣；J：杰克·皮特森；T：汤姆·鲁宾斯；S：山姆·斯图尔特；A：爱丽丝·琼斯；B：比尔·沃克）

介绍

C：既然大家都到了，咱们就开始吧。首先，我想请你们和我一起欢迎我们西南地区销售副总裁杰克·皮特森。

J：谢谢邀请我来，我很期待今天的会议。

C：恐怕我们的销售总监安妮·布莱克今天不能和我们一起开会了。她目前在科比发展我们的远东销售团队。

回顾过去的业务

C：我们开始吧。我们今天在这里讨论改善农村市场销售状况的方法。首先，让我们回顾一下上次在 6 月 24 日举行的会议报告。汤姆，接下来交给你了。

T：谢谢你，马克。让我总结一下上次会议的要点。首先，我们批准在 5 月 30 日会议上讨论的有关销售报告制度变更。在简要地回顾将要发生的变更后，我们进行了一次关于提升售后服务的头脑风暴会议。放在你们面前的是那次会议上讨论的主要内容的复印件。

会议开始

C：谢谢你，汤姆。如果没有其他内容需要讨论的话，咱们就来讨论今天的会议议程吧。你们都收到今天会议议程的复印件了吗？如果大家不介意的话，我想跳过第 1 项，转到第 2 项：改善农村市场的销售状况。杰克已经答应给我们做一个关于这个问题的报告。杰克？

讨论项目

J：在我开始做报告之前，我想了解你们所有人的一些想法。你们对各自所在销售地区的农村销售状况有何感想？

S：在我看来，我们一直都太注重城市顾客和他们的需求了。我认为我们需要通过开展一场广告活动，关注农村顾客的特殊需要来返回我们的农村基地。

A：恐怕我不能赞同你的观点。我认为农村顾客想要感觉到他们和城市顾客一样重要。我建议给农村销售团队在提供最新的客户信息报告方面给予更多的帮助。

S：我不太明白你的意思。

A：好的，我们为城市销售人员提供各大客户数据库信息。我们应该向我们的农村销售人员提供同样的有关农村顾客的信息。

J：比尔，你有什么要补充的吗？

B：我必须承认我以前从来没有那样考虑过农村销售。我不得不同意爱丽丝的观点。

J：好吧，让我来开始展示幻灯片（杰克做报告）。

S：我建议大家分成小组，讨论我们提出的意见。

会议结束

C：不幸的是，我们的时间不够了。我们将不得不下次再讨论这个问题。

J：在会议结束之前，让我来总结一下要点：
我们的销售团队需要更准确的客户信息。

将完成一项收集这些地区消费习惯数据的调查。

调查的结果将传达给我们的销售团队。

C：非常感谢，杰克。好的，看来我们已经涵盖了会议的主要议题。还有没有其他事情？

A：请问我们能定一下下次开会的时间吗？

C：好主意，爱丽丝。两周后的星期五大家觉得怎么样？同一时间，九点钟。大家都可以吗？……很好。我要感谢杰克今天来参加我们的会议。会议到此结束。

6.2　Meeting Agenda

Section One: Tasks

Situation 1: *Li Xin is a clerk of ABC Company, please help him write an agenda of the weekly meeting.*

Situation 2: *UTT Company planned to organize a two-day meeting to make a market outlook of mobile phone products, please write a meeting agenda for this company.*

Section Two: Related Information

How to Write a Meeting Agenda

A meeting agenda is a list of topics of meeting activities that has to be addressed during a meeting. We always follow these principles when we write a meeting agenda.

Start with a title. The title of a meeting agenda tells the reader two things: first, he is reading an agenda, and second, what topic the meeting is covering. The title doesn't have to be flowery or complicated——in a business context, simple and direct titles are usually the best.

Use a plain, dignified font like Times New Roman or Calibri, and make your title the same size as the rest of the lettering on the document (or only slightly larger). [1] Remember, the purpose of your title is to inform readers of what they are viewing, not necessarily to amuse or distract them.

Include "when", "where", "who" information in the header. There is always a header located about one line below the title. Generally speaking, in the header, you'll always want to include brief information about the meeting, such as date, time, location, attendees etc. Job titles of attendees are usually optional, and not necessarily required.

Briefly state the meeting objective(s). The objectives of a meeting agenda usually tell us what to talk about in a meeting. Then, describe the items of discussion for the meeting in a few concise and to-the-point sentences. For instance, if you want to write an objective for a budget meeting, you might write like this: "Objective: Outline key budget goals for the 2018—2019 fiscal year and discuss long-term, cost-cutting measures. Additionally, R&D[2] Director Marcus Feldman will present the results of a recent competitiveness study."

Outline the main topics of the meeting with a schedule. The topics in an agenda are listed in the order they are supposed to be taken up and should be associated with a time slot to ensure that each meeting activity is addressed. [3]

If any guests are coming to your meeting to discuss important topics, you'll want to devote a chunk of the meeting time to these people. It is best to contact the guests ahead of time to figure out how much time each one will need for their discussion topics.

Leave extra time at the end of the meeting for Q&A[4]. During this time, people can ask for clarification about confusing topics of discussion, offer their own opinions, suggest topics for future meetings, and make other comments.

Check the agenda for errors before distributing it. Because some attendees may rely heavily on the meeting agenda, it's wise to proofread it for errors and completeness before giving it out. Doing so isn't just a courtesy to the attendees——it also reflects positively on your attention to details and the respect you have for them. [5]

Vocabulary

agenda [ə'dʒendə] n. 议程；日程表

address [ə'dres] vt. 提出；处理

flowery ['flaʊəri] adj. 辞藻华丽的，花哨的

context ['kɔntekst] n. 语境；上下文

dignified ['dɪgnɪfaɪd] adj. 庄重的；有尊严的；高贵的

font [fɔnt] n. 字体

amuse [ə'mjuːz] vt. 娱乐；逗乐；使人发笑

distract [dɪ'strækt] vt. 使分心

attendee [ˌæten'diː] n. （会议等的）出席者；与会人员

optional ['ɔpʃənl] adj. 可选择的

objective [əb'dʒektɪv] n. 目标，任务；   adj. 目标的；客观的

concise [kən'saɪs] adj. 简明的；简洁的

budget ['bʌdʒɪt] n. 预算

fiscal ['fɪsk(ə)l] adj. 财政的；会计的

competitiveness [kəm'petətɪvnəs] n. 竞争力；竞争性

outline ['aʊtlaɪn] n. 梗概；大纲；   vt. 概述；略述

slot [slɔt] n. 位置；狭槽；时段

devote [dɪ'vəʊt] vt. 奉献；把……奉献（给）；把……专用（于）

chunk [tʃʌŋk] n. 一块；大量，大部分

clarification [ˌklærəfɪ'keɪʃn] n. （意义等的）澄清，说明

confusing [kən'fjuːzɪŋ] adj. 混淆的；令人困惑的

distribute [dɪ'strɪbjuːt] vt. 散发；分发

proofread ['pruːfriːd] vt. 校对；校正

courtesy ['kɜːtəsi] n. 礼貌

positively ['pɔzətɪvli] adv. 明确地；肯定地

generally speaking   一般来说

for instance   例如

be associated with   与……相关联

time slot   时间段

a good chunk of time   一大块时间

Notes

1. Use a plain，dignified font like Times New Roman or Calibri，and make your title the same size as the rest of the lettering on the document（or only slightly larger）. 使用像 Times New Roman 或 Calibri 这样简单而庄重的字体，并使你的标题与文档上其他内容字体大小相同（或字体仅略大于其他内容）的字号。Times New Roman 和 Calibri 都为办公软件中的字体名称；the same…as… 与……一样。

2. R&D：即 Research and Development Department 研发部

3. The topics in an agenda are listed in the order they are supposed to be taken up and should be associated with a time slot to ensure that each meeting activity is addressed. 议程中的议题按照它们应被处理的顺序列出，并应与时间段相关联，以确保每个会议活动都得到解决。in an agenda 为介词短语作后置定语；they are supposed to be taken up 为定语从句，先行词是 order；take up 开始处理，讨论；that each meeting activity is addressed 是 ensure 的宾语从句；be supposed to do…应该做某事；are listed 由于其主语是非人的抽象名词，所以这里采用被动语态 be done 结构。

4. Q&A：即 questions and answers 问答

5. Doing so isn't just a courtesy to the attendees——it also reflects positively on your attention to details and the respect you have for them. 这样做不仅仅是对与会者的礼貌，他也明确地反映了你对细节的关注和对与会者的尊重。you have for them 为省略了 that 的定语从句，先行词是 respect。

Section Three：Situational Task Samples

Situation 1：*Here is a meeting agenda of MC Company on March 6，2018.*

Agenda

Topic	Start Time	End Time	Presenter
Meeting Agenda	14:00	16:00	
1. Welcome/Opening remarks[1]	14:00	14:15	Peggy Olson
2. Review and discussion of outstanding issues[2] from last meeting	14:15	14:30	Joan Holloway
3. Topic 1	14:30	14:45	Ken Cosgrove
4. Topic 2	14:45	15:00	Bertram Cooper
5. Topic 3 etc.	15:00	15:10	Herman Phillips
6. Any other business（AOB[3]）	15:10	15:20	Roger Sterling
7. Schedule of next meeting	15:20	15:30	Pete Campbell
8. Closing remarks	15:30	15:40	Peggy Olson

Situation 2：*Here is a three-day conference agenda of PND Company.*

Conference Agenda

Monday, February 12, 2018	
7:00 p. m. to 9:00 p. m.	Registration and reception
Tuesday, February 13, 2018	
7:30 a. m. to 8:00 a. m.	Continental breakfast[4]
8:00 a. m. to 8:20 a. m.	**Opening ceremony**[5]
8:20 a. m. to 10:30 a. m.	Presentation: **Marketing**
10:30 a. m. to 10:45 a. m.	Break
10:45 a. m. to 11:30 a. m.	Group discussion
11:30 a. m. to 1:00 p. m.	Lunch
1:00 p. m. to 3:00 p. m.	Presentation: **Competition in the Industry**
3:00 p. m. to 3:15 p. m.	Break
3:15 p. m. to 5:00 p. m.	Group discussion
6:00 p. m. to 8:00 p. m.	Evening reception
Wednesday, February 14, 2018	
7:30 a. m. to 8:00 a. m.	Continental breakfast
8:00 a. m. to 9:30 a. m.	Presentation: **Employee Motivation**
9:30 a. m. to 9:45 a. m.	Break
9:45 a. m. to 10:10 a. m.	**Closing ceremony**[6]

Notes

1. remark 言辞；话语。welcome remarks 欢迎辞；opening remarks 开幕致辞，开场白；closing remarks 结束语，闭幕词

2. outstanding issues 悬而未决的问题，尚未解决的问题。outstanding 突出的，关键的，尚未解决的

3. AOB：为 any other business 三个单词的首字母缩写，其他事宜

4. continental breakfast 欧式早餐。主要食品有茶、咖啡、面包卷和果酱，主要为冷食。相对而言 English breakfast 指英式早餐，主要食品为熏肉、煎蛋、烤面包和果酱，主要为热食。在西方国家出版的书籍中，提到 continent 或 continental 这类词语时，多指欧洲大陆。

5. opening ceremony 开幕仪式

6. closing ceremony 闭幕仪式

Section Four: Functional Expression Bank

Apenda Words & Phrases（议程词汇）

1. agenda/schedule 日程安排

2. registration 会晤登记

3. check in 入会

4. roll call　点名

5. Welcome and opening address will be given by…由……致欢迎辞

Closing address will be given by…由……致闭幕词

6. chairman/chairwoman　主持人

7. lecturer　主讲人，主讲嘉宾

8. topic report　主题报告

9. under the auspices of…由……单位主办；在……赞助/支持/保护下

undertaken by…由……单位承办

10. tea break　茶歇

11. lunch and break　午餐及午休

12. banquet/dinner party　晚宴

13. refreshment　宴会或会议中提供的饮料或小点心

Agenda Template（议程模板）

【Group Name】	【会议组织名称】
【Location】	【地点】
【Date：start time～end time】	【日期：起止时间】
1. Welcome and introduction from the chairman；	1. 主席致欢迎辞；
2. Roll call of attendance and apologies for non-attendance；	2. 清点到会人员及未到人员；
3. Minutes from the last meeting；	3. 回顾上次会议内容；
4. Matters arising from the last meeting；	4. 上次会议项目跟进；
5. Officers' reports；	5. 领导做报告；
6. Specific agenda items；	6. 具体议题；
7. Any other business；	7. 其他事宜；
8. Date of next meeting	8. 下次会议时间

Section Five：Culture Tips

会议议程的最佳安排方法

1. 首先安排最重要的议题

在安排会议时，通常将最重要的议题预先安排在时间表里，这样能确保两件事情：首先，每个人都能够在会议开始时，也是头脑最清楚的时候讨论最重要话题；第二，它确保了在会议必须提前结束或某些与会者在散会前需要离开的情况下，已经讨论完了最重要的议题。

2. 灵活安排会议议程

在安排和举行会议时，很可能会发生会议时间过长的情况。一般来说，员工们厌恶过长的会议，并且有他们自己的理由：一是会议内容可能非常无聊；二是冗长无效的会议延误了他们处理紧迫的工作。可以通过关注时间确保会议按计划进行。

但是，会议通常不按计划进行，因此如果会议的某一部分持续时间比你预想的要长，则需要做灵活安排。例如，如果会议的某一部分持续了很长时间，可以通过缩短会议其他部分的讨论时间，或者取消相对不重要的部分，以确保及时得出结论。

3. 在会议之前撰写议程

议程至关重要：它可以让与会者知道你珍惜他们的时间以及你对公司所做的贡献。因此，确保你有足够的时间并尽早撰写会议议程。

你可以在会议前对议程进行意见征集并细化。与同事或主管分享你的议程草案并请求他们提出意见，这样可以帮助你弥补议程中存在的缺陷并补充被忽视的细节。如果你等到最后一刻才写下议程，那就没有时间征求和整合反馈意见了。虽然对于一些日常会议，你可以在会议召开的前一天写出议程，但重要的会议可能需要提前几周的时间进行准备。

4. 在会前与与会者分享议程

这样可以确保每个人都能够充分了解会议要讨论的主题。根据不同的公司文化，这可能意味着要打印大量的副本并亲自交付，或者简单地以电子方式共享，例如通过附件的形式发送议程。无论采用哪种方式，请确保在共享之前内容没有错误。

译　文

第二部分：相关信息

如何撰写会议议程

会议议程是会议期间必须处理的一系列议题或会议活动的清单。我们在写会议议程时总是遵循以下这些原则。

从标题开始。会议议程的标题告诉读者两件事：第一，他正在阅读一份议程；第二，会议的主题是什么。标题不必花哨复杂，在商务语境中简单直接的标题通常是最好的。

使用像 Times New Roman 或 Calibri 这样简单而庄重的字体，并使你的标题与文档上其他内容字体大小相同（或字体仅略大于其他内容）字号。记住，你的标题的目的是告知读者他们正在查看什么，而不是为了娱乐或分散他们的注意力。

页眉信息要包含时间、地点、和与会人员。议程标题下方一行左右处通常都有一个页眉。一般来说，页眉这部分通常需要包括与会议相关的简要信息，如日期、时间、地点、与会人员等。与会人员的职位通常是有选择性的，只做必要性添加。

简要说明会议目的。会议议程的目的通常告知我们会议即将探讨的问题。然后，用一些简明扼要的句子来描述讨论项目。例如，如果你想为一次预算会议写一个目的，那么你可以这样写，"目的：概述 2018～2019 财政年度的关键预算目标，并讨论长期的成本削减措施。另外，研发总监马库斯·费尔德曼将讲解近期竞争力研究的结果。"

用一个时间表概述会议的主要议题。议程中的议题按照它们应被安排的顺序列出，并应与时间段相关联，以确保每个会议活动都得到解决。

如果有客户来参加会议，讨论重要议题，那么你将需要分出大块的会议时间给这些人。最好提前联系客户，以了解他们需要多少时间来讨论他们的议题。

在会议结束时留出额外的时间进行问答。在此期间，人们可以要求澄清讨论中令人困惑的议题，提出他们自己的观点，为以后的会议提出建议，以及提出其他建议。

在下发前检查议程是否有误。因为一些与会者可能会非常依赖会议议程，所以明智的做法是在发放之前，校对错误和其完整性。这样做不仅仅是对与会者的礼貌，也明确地反映了你对细节的关注和对与会者的尊重。

第三部分：情境任务范例

情境 1： 这是 2018 年 3 月 6 日 MC 公司的一次会议议程。

议题	开始时间	结束时间	演讲人
会议议程	14:00	15:40	
1. 欢迎/开幕致辞	14:00	14:15	佩吉·奥尔森
2. 上次会议审议和讨论悬而未决的问题	14:15	14:30	琼·赫各维
3. 议题一	14:30	14:45	肯·科斯格罗夫
4. 议题二	14:45	15:00	伯特伦·库珀
5. 议题三等	15:00	15:10	赫尔曼·菲利善斯
6. 其他事宜	15:10	15:20	罗杰·斯特林
7. 下次会议的时间表	15:20	15:30	皮特·坎贝尔
8. 结束语	15:30	15:40	佩吉·奥尔森

情境 2： 这是 PND 公司一个三天的会议议程。

会议议程

2018 年 2 月 12 日周一	
晚上 7:00—9:00	会晤登记与接待
2018 年 2 月 13 日周二	
上午 7:30—8:00	欧式早餐
上午 8:00—8:20	**开幕式**
上午 8:20—10:30	报告:**市场营销**
上午 10:30—10:45	休息
上午 10:45—11:30	小组讨论
上午 11:30—下午 1:00	午餐
下午 1:00—3:00	报告:**行业竞争**
下午 3:00—3:15	休息
下午 3:15—5:00	小组讨论
下午 6:00—晚上 8:00	晚宴
2018 年 2 月 14 日周三	
上午 7:30—8:00	欧式早餐
上午 8:00—9:30	报告:**激励员工**
上午 9:30—9:45	休息
上午 9:45—10:10	**闭幕式**

6.3 Meeting Minutes

Section One: Tasks

Situation: *Anna works as a secretary for UTT Import & Export Co. Ltd. At a recent sales meeting, people in the sales department discussed how the customers pay their bills. Write the minutes according to the following information: Ordinary customers usually pay by cash, debit cards, credit cards or even by WeChat, while wholesale clients prefer to pay by check.*

Section Two: Related Information

Tips for Writing Meeting Minutes

Before the meeting

• Review the agenda. The agenda lists the names of attending participants and topics to be discussed at the meeting. In other words, it lists who will say what. Therefore, the more you know about the upcoming discussions and participants, the more efficiently you will write the minutes. [1]

• Make a template. With the help of the agenda, it is possible to make a template, or an outline of major topics to be discussed. Leave plenty of space in between the topics for notes to be filled in. It is also important to include all necessary information such as the date and time, agenda, participants, time adjourned, next meeting date, etc.

During the meeting

• Take notes in your own way. Accurate notes should be capable of describing the main points of the discussion and any decision that was reached. The way of note-taking may vary from person to person. You can take down only a few key words so long as you understand the words afterwards. Or you can use abbreviations or even symbols to help with note-taking.

• Use a recorder if necessary. The key to successful minutes is accurate note-taking. However, this is sometimes impossible if speakers talk too fast or unclearly in a heated discussion. It's much better to use a recorder than to ask for clarification either during or after the meeting. [2]

After the meeting

It is necessary to make a draft of the minutes immediately after the meeting while everything is still fresh in mind.

• Read the notes. It is helpful to read through the notes taken during the meeting to refresh the memory before actually writing the minutes. [3]

• Use headings, numbers and bullet points. Topics discussed at a meeting may be complicated. Headings, numbers and bullet points are common devices to help build up a logic structure. It will be very helpful when someone wants to read the minutes long after the meeting.

• Attach what is necessary. Any materials distributed at the meeting should be enclosed in the minutes.

- Revise the draft. As the final step of all writings, revising gives the minutes-taker the last chance to correct possible errors in spelling, grammar and punctuation. Then check the draft according to the general 5-C principle. [4] The use of past tense is necessary because minutes are records of what already happened in the meeting. [5]

Vocabulary

minutes　['mɪnɪts]　n. 会议记录

upcoming　[ˈʌpkʌmɪŋ]　adj. 即将来到的；即将出现的

template　['templeɪt]　n. 模板

adjourn　[əˈdʒɜːn]　vt.（使）休会

accurate　['ækjərət]　adj. 精确的；准确的

afterwards　[ˈɑːftəwədz]　adv. 之后；以后

abbreviation　[ə.briːviˈeɪʃn]　n. 省略；缩写

symbol　['sɪmbl]　n. 符号；记号

clarification　[.klærəfɪˈkeɪʃn]　n. 澄清；说明

refresh　[rɪˈfreʃ]　vt. 使恢复；使振作

bullet　['bulɪt]　n. 着重符号；子弹；弹药

device　[dɪˈvaɪs]　n. 方法；手段

attach　[əˈtætʃ]　vt. 附上

distribute　[dɪˈstrɪbjuːt]　vt. 分配；分发

enclose　[ɪnˈkləuz]　vt. 附入；附上

revise　[rɪˈvaɪz]　vt. 修改；修正

draft　[drɑːft]　n. 草稿

punctuation　[.pʌŋktʃuˈeɪʃn]　n. 标点符号

so long as　只要

bullet point　项目符号

Notes

1. Therefore, the more you know about the upcoming discussions and participants, the more efficiently you will write the minutes. 因此，对即将要进行的讨论和与会者的了解得越多，你就越能有效地撰写会议记录。the more…the more…越……越……，more 后面可以接名词、部分双音节形容词、副词或几乎所有的多音节形容词、副词，该句型可以提炼成：the + 比较级，the + 比较级。

2. It's much better to use a recorder than to ask for clarification either during or after the meeting. 使用录音设备进行记录要比会中或会后要求讲话人进行解释说明好得多。much better…than…………比……要好得多；It's better to do sth. than to do sth. 在用法上前后两部分要保持形式一致，都用不定式 to do，表示比较含义；either…or…或者……或

者……，不是……就是……表示两者选一，连接两个并列的成分。

3. It is helpful to read through the notes taken during the meeting to refresh the memory before actually writing the minutes. 在真正撰写会议记录之前，通读在会议期间所记录的笔记帮助回忆是很有益处的。It is + *adj.* + to do sth. 做……（事情）是怎么的。taken during the meeting 在句中为过去分词短语作后置定语，修饰 notes。

4. Then check the draft according to the general 5-C principle. 然后根据普遍的五个 C 原则检查草稿。5-C principle，五个 C 原则，指的是一般性商务文体的写作原则，即：clarity 明确性，correctness 准确性，conciseness 简洁性，completeness 完整性，courteousness 礼貌性。

5. The use of past tense is necessary because minutes are records of what already happened in the meeting. 使用过去时态是有必要的，因为会议记录是记录会议中已经发生的事情。past tense 过去时态，类似的还有 present tense 现在时态，future tense 将来时态；because 引导原因状语从句。

Section Three：Situational Task Samples

Situation 1：Here is a simple board meeting minute[1] taken by Li Xin.

Board Meeting Minutes

Date：July 15，2020，9：00 a.m.

Present：Jim Baker
   Sam Anderson
   Steve Nichols
   Jane Webster
   Mike Smith

Apologies for Absence：Babara White

Minutes from the Last Meeting

 The minutes of the last meeting of the quarterly meeting of Board of Directors on July 2, 2020 were read and confirmed by Mr. Anderson.

Mr. Anderson's Report

 1. After the meeting was declared open，Mr. Anderson，chairman of the Board，made a report on the work and total sales of the company in this quarter.

 2. After a heated discussion, all the directors agreed to hold a press conference[2] for the company next week.

New Business

 The meeting suggested inviting experts from Australia to give a training course to all the employees of the company.

Adjournment
 The meeting adjourned at 11：50 a.m.

Li Xin
Secretary

Situation 2 : Here is a formal meeting minute taken by Anna Brown.

Greenland Travel Agency

MINUTES OF FINANCIAL MEETING

Friday 12 December 2020

Royal Garden Hotel

Chairman : Alice Black

Present

David Bedford

Judith Brown

Zoe Wilde

Dr. Stephen Thomas

Also present

Tom Adams

Bill Pakey

Absent

Hugh Mckown

Agenda item 1 : Opening remarks

David Bedford reviewed the agenda and welcomed everyone to the meeting, especially welcomed Dr. Stephen Thomas as a legal counsel[3].

Agenda item 2 : Confirmation of minutes of last meeting

Minutes of Midterm Financial Conference held at Royal Garden Hotel, on 23 July, 2020.

(a) Correct record

The minutes were approved as a correct record.

(b) Matters arising

Paragraph 16 : Plan of pension fund[4].

Agenda item 3 : Update development of company finance

Judith Brown reviewed, trends and issues from the balance sheet, income statement and cash flow statement. [5] Particular concerns were the $2.2 million deficit in the company's pension fund and its impact.

Resolved :

(a) The content of the paper be approved;

(b) A further update report should be submitted to[6] the Board on 30 December 2020, once satisfactory financial investigations were completed.

Agenda item 4 : Recruitment of Head of Finance

It was recommended that a qualified accountant should be recruited with sufficient status to complete the implementation of financial controls and keep the Board and management of the company informed with timely and pertinent[7] financial information.

The meeting agreed that:

A full-time accountant be recruited in the position of Head of Finance.

Agenda item 5: Any other business

Zoe Wilde confirmed that both external and internal auditors would be reviewed before the next AGM[8] in 2020.

Agenda item 6: Date and place of the next meeting

The next meeting was scheduled for 5 January, 2021, at Greenland Hotel at 9:00 a. m.

Agenda item 7: Adjournment of meeting

Meeting adjourned at 5:00 p. m.

Respectfully submitted,

Anna Brown

Notes

1. board meeting minute 董事会会议记录
2. press conference 新闻发布会
3. legal counsel 法律顾问
4. pension fund 退休基金，养老基金
5. Judith Brown reviewed, trends and issues from the balance sheet, income statement and cash flow statement. 朱迪斯·布朗根据公司的资产负债表、损益表和现金流量表，回顾了公司所存在的突出问题和未来发展趋势。balance sheet 资产负债表；income statement 损益表；cash flow statement 现金流量表。
6. be submitted to 把……提交给……
7. pertinent 有关的，相干的
8. AGM，即 annual general meeting 年会

Section Four: Functional Expression Bank

Words & Phrases for meeting（会议词汇）

1. propose v. 提议；建议
   proposal n. 建议；提议
2. solution n. 解决办法；解决方案
3. participant n. 参与者；参加者
4. effective adj. 有效的；生效的
5. session n. 会议；一段时间
6. cut in 打断别人的话；插嘴
7. call it quits 结束争论或争吵
8. in charge 主管；负责

Minute Template（会议记录模板）

(Name of Company)	(公司名称)
Minutes of (Name of Meeting)	(会议名称)的记录
(Date of Meeting)	(会议日期)
(Place of Meeting)	(会议地点)
Chairman：(Name of Chairman)	主持人：(主持人姓名)
Present	出席
(names of people present)	(出席人员的姓名)
Also present	列席
(names of other people present)	(列席人员姓名)
Absent	缺席
(names of people absent)	(缺席人员姓名)
Agenda item 1：Opening Remarks	议程第 1 项：开会致辞
(content of remarks)	(讲话的内容)
Agenda item 2：Confirmation of Minutes of Last Meeting	议程第 2 项：确认上次会议的记录
Minutes of (name of last meeting) held at (place of last meeting) on (date of last meeting).	在(上次会议的地点)于(上次会议的日期)召开的(上次会议的名称)的记录。
(a) Correct record	(a)修改记录
The minutes were approved as a correct record.	上次会议的记录被修改通过。
(b) Matters arising	(b)产生的问题
Paragraph (number)：(name of matters arising)	上次会议记录的第(数字)段：(问题的名称
(update development of matters of last meeting)	上次会议所议事项的最新发展情况)
Agenda item 3：(Name of New Item)	议程第 3 项：(新议事项的名称)
(Contents of Discussion)	(讨论内容)
Resolved：	会议形成决议：
(a) (Content of Approval)	(a)(决议内容)
(b) (Content of Approval)	(b)(决议内容)
Agenda item 4：(Name of New Item)	议程第 4 项：(新议事项的名称)
(Speeches of the Committee)	(与会人员的发言)
The meeting agreed that：	会议同意：
(a) (Content of Approval)	(a)(决议内容)
(b) (Content of Approval)	(b)(决议内容)
Agenda item 5：Any Other Business	议程第 5 项：其他事项
(Content of other business)	(其他事项的内容)
Agenda item 6：Date of the Next Meeting	议程第 6 项：下次会议日期
The next meeting was scheduled for (date of next meeting)，at (place of next meeting) commencing at (time of next meeting).	下次会议定于(下次会议的日期)在(下次会议的地点)举行。
Agenda item 7：Closing Remarks	议程第 7 项：结束语
(content of remarks)	(讲话的主要内容)
Agenda item 8：Adjournment of meeting	议程第 8 项：散会
Meeting adjourned at (time of adjournment).	会议在(散会时间)结束。
Respectfully submitted，	由……提交：
(name of secretary)	(秘书的姓名)

Section Five：Culture Tips

做好会议记录的技巧

1. 提高自己的书写速度

要做好会议记录，首先要有一定的书写速度，书写运笔要快，字要写得小些、轻一点儿，多写连笔字。要顺着肘、手的自然走势，斜一点儿写。在平日里多写东西，有意识地提高自己的书写速度。

2. 提前了解会议的主要内容

在开会以前，可以通过会议通知了解一下会议的大体内容，然后在会前就将一些可以写上的东西写好，比如时间、地点、与会人员等，等会议正式开始后，就只需要记录与会人员的观点了。

3. 借助录音笔、手机 App 等工具

在做会议记录的时候，即使是书写速度再快的人，也会有疏忽漏写的情况发生。这个时候，我们在会议前准备的录音笔或手机里实用的会议记录 App 就派上用场了。会议结束后，我们就可以使用录音笔、手机 App 来完善自己的会议记录。

4. 择要而记

所谓的会议记录是要记录与会人员的不同观点，不是每一句话都要记录，而是择要而记。就记录一次会议来说，要围绕会议议题、会议主持人和主要领导发言的中心思想，与会者的不同意见或有争议的问题、结论性意见、决定或者决议等做记录。就记录一个人的发言来说，要记其发言要点、主要论据和结论，论证过程可以不记。就记一句话来说，要记录这句话的中心词，修饰语一般可以不记。要注意上下文的连贯性，一篇好的会议记录应当独立成篇。因为在做会议记录的时候，我们完全可以先聆听发言人的发言，归纳总结后再记录。

5. 认真聆听

做会议记录最忌讳的就是会议过程中开小差，一心二用。一旦自己有一个地方跟不上，那么其他地方就会随之跟不上，导致严重影响会议记录的完整性。因此，做会议记录时一定要保持精神高度集中。

6. 一点没记完，果断跳过

很多人在第一次做会议记录的时候，都会想着一点一点记好，不想漏掉任何一点。可是，在开会期间，总会出现无法跟上步调的时候，这时候，就要果断跳过这个地方，直接记录下一个人的发言，以免影响后面的整体记录。

7. 在记录中正确使用省略语

如使用简称或简化词语。

8. 用较为简便的写法代替复杂的写法

如：可用姓代替全名；可用缩写代替整个单词；可用一些数字和国际上通用的符号代替文字；可用音标代替生词难字等。

译　文

第二部分：相关信息

撰写会议记录的小窍门

会前

● 回顾议程。议程列出了出席会议的人员名单和会上要讨论的议题。换句话说，它列出了谁要讲什么。因此，对即将要进行的讨论和与会者了解得越多，你就能更加有效地撰写会议记录。

•制作模板。可以根据议程制作一个模板，或者列一个要讨论的主要议题的大纲。在议题之间留出足够的空间记笔记。在会议中涵盖如日期和时间、议程、与会者、休会时间、下次会议日期等所有必要的信息也是很重要的。

会中

•以自己的方式记笔记。准确的笔记应该能够描述讨论的要点和所达成的决定。记笔记的方式因人而异。只要你会后明白，记录下几个关键词即可。或者你可以使用缩写或符号帮助记笔记。

•如有必要，使用录音设备。成功记录的关键是准确地记笔记。但是，如果讲话者在热烈的讨论中说得太快或不清楚时是不可能准确记录的。使用录音设备进行记录要比会中或会后要求讲话人进行解释说明好得多。

会后

在会议之后，当一切都还清晰地印在头脑中时，有必要立刻写出会议记录的草稿。

•阅读笔记。在真正撰写会议记录之前，通读在会议期间所记录的笔记帮助回忆是很有益处的。

•使用标题，数字和项目符号。在会议上讨论的议题可能很复杂。标题、数字和项目符号是帮助建立逻辑结构的常用手段。当有人想在会议结束很久之后阅读会议记录时，这将是非常有帮助的。

•附加必要的内容。会议中分发的任何材料都应被附在会议记录中。

•修改草稿。作为写作的最后一步，为修改记录者提供最后一次纠正拼写、语法和标点符号错误的机会。然后根据普遍的五个 C 原则检查草稿。使用过去时态是有必要的，因为会议记录是记录会议中已经发生的事情。

第三部分：情境任务范例

范例 1：这是一份由李欣记录的董事会会议记录。

董事会会议记录

日期：2020 年 7 月 15 日上午 9：00

出席：吉姆·贝克

山姆·安德森

史蒂夫·尼克斯

简·韦伯斯特

迈克·史密斯

缺席：芭芭拉·怀特

上次会议记录

2020 年 7 月 2 日由安德森先生宣读并确认董事会季度会议上一次会议记录。

安德森先生的报告

1. 会议宣布开始后，董事会主席安德森先生就本季度的工作和总销售额做了一个报告。

2. 经过一阵热烈的讨论，全体董事同意下周为公司举行一次新闻发布会。

新业务

会议建议邀请澳大利亚的专家为公司所有员工进行培训。

散会

上午 11:50 散会。

秘书李欣

范例 2: 这是一份由安娜·布朗记录的正式会议记录。

绿地旅游公司

财务会议记录

2020 年 12 月 7 日星期五

皇家花园酒店

主席:爱丽丝·布莱克

出席

大卫·贝德福德

朱迪斯·布朗

祖·怀尔德

斯蒂芬·托马斯博士

列席

汤姆·亚当斯

比尔·帕奇

缺席

修·麦库恩

议程第 1 项:开会致辞

大卫·贝德福德宣读了大会议程,并欢迎每位与会者的到来。特别欢迎法律顾问斯蒂芬·托马斯博士。

议程第 2 项:确定上次会议记录

于 2020 年 7 月 23 日在皇家花园酒店召开的中期财务会议的记录。

(a)修改记录

会议记录被修改通过。

(b)产生的问题

第 16 段(上次会议记录):关于养老基金的方案。

议程第 3 项:公司财务的最新发展情况

朱迪斯·布朗根据公司的资产负债表、损益表和现金流量表,回顾了公司所存在的突出问题和未来发展趋势,并着重谈了公司退休津贴方面 220 万美金的缺口以及由此产生的影响。

议程形成决议:

(a)通过此报告内容;

(b)一旦新的财务研究报告完成,就提交到 2020 年 12 月 30 日召开的董事会上。

议程第 4 项:招聘财务主管

建议招聘一名会计师,能胜任财务控制的执行并及时向董事会和公司的管理层报告相关财务信息。

会议同意：

招聘一名全职会计师做财务主管。

议程第 5 项：其他事宜

祖·怀尔德确认将会在 2020 年下次年会前审查所有外部和内部审计员。

议程第 6 项：下次会议日期及地点

下次会议定于 2021 年 1 月 5 日上午 9 时在绿地酒店召开。

议程第 7 项：散会

会议在下午 5 点结束。

由安娜·布朗提交

Unit Seven   Be on Business

7.1   Ask and Direct the Way

Section One: Tasks

Situation 1: *Zhang Yong had just arrived at Xiamen Gaoqi International Airport. He asked a passerby where he could take a bus to the center of the city. Make a dialogue according to the situation.*

Situation 2: *Zhang Yong would go to Heaven Company for a business negotiation. He was looking for the way to that company. Make a dialogue according to the situation.*

Situation 3: *Zhang Yong was going to the shopping mall to buy some local specialties for his parents. He asked the hotel receptionist how to get there. Make a dialogue according to the situation.*

Section Two: Related Information

The History of Road Signs

Today we can see road signs everywhere, but do you know how those road signs developed over the course of time.

While driving down a busy highway, or when parking your vehicle in a parking lot, you often give a slight glance on those parking signs or road signs, little realizing their importance and necessity. [1] Have you ever wondered what the need of those signs is and how they came there in the first place? Who were the people that thought about the need of those traffic signs?

The history of road signs is very interesting. It was the Romans who made the first road sign. The Romans built massive tall columns that helped the travelers to know how far they were from Rome and what direction they should take.[2] These elevated stone towers were known as milestones and are a far cry from the modern traffic signs we come across today. We find that the road signs advanced a little during the Middle Ages[3] in European countries, there were signs put up at the intersections to point to certain cities and towns. Some of these signs also gave the distance to certain towns.

It was when the automobiles hit the road[4], that we find the use of road signs became more popular. Drivers relied on these signs to see where they were going, and how far they were from their destination. The Italian Touring Club, as the first organized group, petitioned for better road signs in 1895. International Road Congress met in Rome in 1908 to discuss road signs in Europe.

The first road signs used in the modern times were the intersection, bump, curve and railroad crossing signs. These 4 signs formed the first European road sign system. By the 1960s, different countries across the world were using international symbols to display speed limits, road conditions and other travel information for drivers.

Nowadays, there is a standard set of pictorial symbols used for the international travelers, so that they face no issues when traveling and looking for direction in the foreign lands. Today, it is common to come across electronic signs along roadways that flash words or pictures and in case of any changes, can get updated by computer instantly. These signs are very useful to convey instant information to prepare travelers to possible dangers.

Vocabulary

vehicle ['viːɪk(ə)l] *n*. 车辆，交通工具

slight [slaɪt] *adj*. 轻微的，微小的

glance [glɑːns] *n*. 浏览，一瞥

massive ['mæsɪv] *adj*. 大规模的，大块的

column ['kɔləm] *n*. 圆柱

elevate ['elɪveɪt] *vt*. 升高，举起

milestone ['maɪlstəun] *n*. 里程碑

intersection [ˌɪntə'sekʃn] *n*. 十字路口，交叉点

destination [ˌdestɪ'neɪʃn] *n*. 目的地

petition [pə'tɪʃn] *vi*. 请愿，请求

bump [bʌmp] *n*. 颠簸

curve [kɜːv] *n*. 曲线，弯道

pictorial [pɪk'tɔːrɪəl] *adj*. 绘画的，有图片的，形象的

symbol ['sɪmbl] *n*. 符号，标志，象征

update [ʌp'deɪt] *vt*. 更新

instantly ['ɪnstəntli] *adv*. 立即，马上

parking lot 停车场

be a far cry from 与……相差甚远，与……大相径庭

come across 遇到

rely on 依靠，依赖

in case 万一，一旦；如果

Notes：

1. While driving down a busy highway, or when parking your vehicle in a parking lot, you often give a slight glance on those parking signs or road signs, little realizing their importance and necessity. 当你驾车行驶在繁忙的高速公路上，或者在停车场停车时，你常常会瞥一眼那些停车标志或路标，却很少意识到它们的重要性和必要性。其中 While driving down a busy highway, or when parking your vehicle in a parking lot 为现在分词短语作时间状语。如果两个动作是完全同时发生的，多用 when 或 while 加分词这种结构。例如：Hearing the news, they all jumped with joy. (= When they heard the news, they…) 听到这个消息，他们都高兴得跳了起来；little realizing their importance and necessity 为现在分词短语作伴随状语；give a glance on…意为"瞥一眼"。

2. The Romans built massive tall columns that helped the travelers to know how far they were from Rome and what direction they should take. 罗马人建造了高大的柱子，帮助旅行者了解他们离罗马有多远，应该走什么方向。本句中主句为"The Romans built massive tall columns"；that 在句中引导定语从句，为第一层从句；"how far they were from Rome"和"what direction they should take"并列作"know"的宾语，为第二层从句。

3. Middle Ages 中世纪，约公元 476 年至公元 1453 年。

4. hit the road 指的是 appear on the road，出现在马路上。

Section Three：Situational Task Samples

Situation 1：*Li Xin wanted to visit a friend who lived in Xiamen. He asked the hotel receptionist how to get to the address of his friend.* (A：Li Xin；B：hotel receptionist；passerby[1]；D：policeman)

A：Excuse me. Could you tell me how to get to this address?

B：Let me see…18 South Lianhua Road, Siming District[2].

A：Can I walk there?

B：It's a long way from here. You'd better take No. 3 Subway Line[3] to Xianyue Mountain Station, and then take a No. 508 bus to Lianhua Middle School. It's near the address.

A：Thank you, and how can I get to the nearest subway station[4]?

B：Walk straight down the road for about ten minutes and you will see the subway station.

A：Thank you very much!

Situation 2：*Half an hour later, Li Xin arrived at Lianhua Middle School. He asked a passerby the way to his friend's address.*

A：Excuse me. I'm trying to locate this address. Could you give me some help?

C：Sorry, I'm a stranger here myself. The policeman over there may be able to help you.

A：OK, thank you all the same.

Situation 3：Li Xin asked the policeman the way to his friend's address.

A：Excuse me. Would you mind telling me the way to this address?

D：Well, you can go straight along this road and take the first turning to the left. After you cross the bridge, you will see a blue building, and the place you're looking for is right next to it.

A：Thank you very much.

D：You are welcome.

Notes

1. passerby 路人，行人
2. district 区。注意：中文地址的书写顺序为从大地点到小地点，而英文地址的书写顺序则相反；专有名词首字母要大写。
3. No. 3 Subway Line 地铁三号线，或者 Metro Line 3
4. subway station 地铁站

Section Four：Functional Sentence Bank

Ask the way（问路）

Q：How to go to someplace?（问：去某地怎么走？）

1. How can I get there/to the college? 到那里/到那所大学怎么走？
2. Which is the shortest way to the railway station? 去火车站哪条路最近？
3. Will you kindly tell me the way to the bank? 请你告诉我去银行怎么走好吗？
4. Excuse me. Could you tell me how to get to the nearest subway station?
   劳驾，能不能告诉我去最近的地铁站怎么走？
5. I'm trying to locate this address. Could you give me some help?
   我正在找这个地方，你能帮帮我吗？
6. I beg your pardon, would you mind telling me the best way to this address?
   对不起，你可以告诉我去这个地址最便捷的路吗？
7. Can you tell me which direction to get to the dining hall?
   能否告诉我，去食堂该怎么走？

Q：Where is someplace?（问：某地在哪里？）

1. Where is the exit of the supermarket? 超市的出口在哪里？
2. Is the shop south of the school? 商店是不是在学校的南面？

Q：How far is someplace?（问：去某地有多远？）

1. How far away is Renmin Road? 人民路有多远？
2. How far is it from here to the airport? 从这里到机场有多远？

3. How many miles is it to the nearest hospital? 离这里最近的医院有多少英里路？

4. Is it within walking distance? 这距离步行过去行吗？

5. Is it too far to walk? 是不是挺远，能走着去吗？

Q: How long does it take to someplace?（问：去某地要多长时间？）

1. How long does it take to get to the bus stop? 去公共汽车站要多久？

2. How long is a bus ride from the airport to your home?
   从机场乘公交车到你家要多长时间？

Q: Does this bus go to someplace?（问：这趟公交车去某地吗？）

1. Will this bus take me to the West Lake? 这路公共汽车去西湖吗？

2. Does this bus go pass the city library? 这辆公共汽车经过市图书馆吗？

3. I'm going to Disneyland. Which bus should I take?
   我要去迪士尼乐园，该乘哪辆公交车呢？

4. How do I get to the post office from here by subway? 从这里乘地铁去邮局怎么走？

Direct the way（指路）

Point out how to walk to someplace（指出步行去某地怎么走）

A. Go straight…（一直走……）

1. Go straight along this road. 沿这条路一直走。

2. Go down this street until you get to the traffic lights. 沿着这条街一直走到红绿灯那里。

3. Walk two blocks straight ahead. 往前走两个街区。

4. Walk straight down the road for about ten minutes and you'll see…
   沿着这条路走大约十分钟，你会看到……

5. Keep straight on till you come to the crossroad. ……一直走到十字路口，……

B. Turn left/right（向左/右转）

1. Turn right/left. 向左/右转。

2. Turn right/left at the traffic lights there. 在那儿的红绿路灯处往右/左转。

3. Take the first turning to the right/left. 在第一个转弯处往右/左转。
   Take the first turn on the right/left. 在第一个转弯处往右/左转。

4. Make a right/left（turn）on Taiyuan Street. 在太原街那里往右/左转。

5. Take the third street on the right. 在第三个路口处向右拐。

C. Go back…（往回走……）

1. (I'm afraid you're heading for the wrong direction.) Turn round and…
   （恐怕你走错了方向。）往回走，……

2. (After you get off the bus，) walk back two hundred meters or so…
   （下公共汽车后，）往回走 200 米左右……

3. Walk back to the corner and…往回走到拐角处，……

4. You must go back a little way…你得往回走一点儿……

D. Cross the street…（过马路……）

1. Cross the street. 过马路。

2. Cross over to the other side. 穿过马路。

3. Go through the underpass there and…穿过那里的地下通道，……

Point out how to get to a place by bus/subway（指出乘公交车/地铁怎样去某地）

A. By bus/subway（乘公共汽车/地铁）

1. Take bus number seven. 乘坐 7 路公共汽车。

2. Take a No. 2 bus to the end of the line. 乘 2 路公共汽车到底。

3. Route No. 3 takes you right there. 3 路车直达。

4. You can catch No. 10 just across the street. 你可以在马路对面乘 10 路车。

5. You can take the subway. You can also take the trolley.
   你可以乘地铁，也可以乘无轨电车。

B. How many stops to take/Where to get off the bus/subway?
   （乘公交车/地铁几站/在哪里下车?）

1. Get off at the terminal. 在终点站下车。

2. Get off at the second stop. 在第二站下车。

3. It's the fifth stop. 这是第五站。

4. It's the last stop but one. 在倒数第二站。

5. It's just four stops from here. 从这里起只有四站路。

6. Travel all the way down to the bund. 一直乘到码头。

C. Where to change the bus/subway?（在哪里换公交车/地铁?）

1. You have to take two buses to get there. 到那里要乘两辆公共汽车。

2. You'll have to change subways at least twice. 你至少要换乘两次地铁。

3. You'll have to change buses at Renmin Square. 你得在人民广场那里换乘公交车。

4. Change for the Metro Line 2 at Huaihai Road. 在淮海路换乘地铁 2 号线。

5. Change from a No. 1 trolleybus to a No. 3 subway line there.
   在那里从 1 路无轨电车换乘地铁 3 号线。

6. You'll have to get off at the shopping mall and take a No. 5 subway line.
   你得在购物中心那里下车，再换乘地铁 5 号线。

Point out the location of a place（指出某地的位置）

A. In…district，on…road…（在……区，……路）

1. It's just outside the city limits. 就在城外。

2. The college is in Queen District. 那所学院在皇后区。

3. It's the third store on your right hand side. 是右边第三个铺子。

4. It's right in the middle of the block. 就在那个街区的中间。

5. The address is 268 Hetian Street. 地址是和田街 268 号。

6. The Museum is on Hengshan Road. 博物馆在衡山路上。

B. Next to…（在……隔壁/附近）

1. The hospital is next door to the gallery. 那家医院就在美术馆隔壁。

2. You'll find it next to a supermarket. 它就在一家超市的隔壁。

3. Next door but one. 隔壁的隔壁。

4. It's right near the club. 就在俱乐部附近。

5. The bookstore is close to the underground station. 书店就在地铁站附近。

6. It's somewhere around that section. 大概就在那一带附近。

C. Around the corner（在某转角/街口处）

1. It's just around the corner. 就在转角处。

2. The building is on the next corner. 那栋楼就在下一个街角上。

3. It's on the corner of the 6th Road and He'nan Street. 在 6 号路和河南街的街口处。

4. It's at Tianjin Street and Nanjing Road. 在天津街和南京路交叉口。

D. Across the street（在马路对面）

1. It's right across the street. 就在马路对面。

2. It's directly opposite the middle school. 就在那所中学正对面。

3. It's on the other side of the street. 在马路对面。

4. It's across the street from the hotel you are staying. 就在你住的宾馆对面。

Point out the characteristics of a place（指出某地的特征）

1. There is a big statue in front of it. 门前有个大雕像。

2. It's a new red brick building. 那是一座红砖的新楼房。

3. There is a big signboard at the entrance. 入口处有一块大牌子。

4. On the left hand side，you'll see a building of English architectural design. That's the bank. 在左手边有一幢英式建筑，那就是那家银行。

5. Keep going until you see a big blue building on your right. The place you are looking for is next to it. 往前走，你会看到右面有一座蓝色的大建筑，你要找的地方就在它隔壁。

Point out the direction of a place（指出某地的方向）

1. It's due south. 在正南。

2. It's on the north side of the city. 在这座城市的北面。

3. The bus stop is south of the store. 汽车站在商店的南面。

4. The airport is northeast of the city. 机场在城市的东北面。

5. Go west. It's about 10 miles west from here. 往西走，在这里往西 10 英里左右处。

Point out the distance of a place（指出某地的距离）

A. …is not far（某地不远）

1. It's quite near here. 离这里很近。

2. It's no distance at all. 没多远。

3. It's within walking distance. 不远，可以步行过去。

4. It's only a couple of blocks from here. 离这里只有几个街区。

5. It's not far from the college. 离那所学院不远。

B. …is far（某地相当远）

1. It's far from here. 离这里很远。

2. It's a good/long way from here. 离这里挺远的。

3. It's quite a walk. 要走不少路。

4. You'll have to walk a long way. 你得走很远的路。

C. How far is someplace?（某地有多远?）

1. About 5 blocks away. 要过 5 个街区。

2. It's four streets further on. 还要再走四条马路。

3. The nearest gas station is 10 miles away. 最近的加油站离这儿有 10 英里。

4. It's more than 20 kilometers from my home to the company.
   从我家到公司有超过 20 公里的路程。

D. How long does it take to someplace? (去某地需花多少时间?)

1. It's a ten-minute ride from here. 从这里乘车去要十分钟。

2. It doesn't take long. About 5 minutes. 要不了多长时间，大约 5 分钟吧。

3. It will take about 20 minutes to walk. 步行去要花约 20 分钟。

4. It takes three hours by bike. 骑自行车去要三小时。

5. It's more than two hours' drive from here. 从这里开车去要两个多小时。

I'm lost (我迷路了)

1. I have lost my way. 我迷路了。

2. My orientation is never good. 我不会分辨方向。

3. Can you help me? I think I'm lost. 您能帮帮我吗？我迷路了。

4. Hello，officer. I can't find my way back to the hotel. Can you help me?
   警察先生，您好。我找不到回宾馆的路了，您能帮我一下吗？

I'm sorry, I don't know the way (对不起，我不认识路)

1. Sorry，I'm a stranger here myself. 对不起，我是外地人。

2. I'm afraid I'm new here myself. 对不起，我初来这里。

3. Sorry，I don't know my way around here. 对不起，这一带我不熟悉。

4. Sorry，I don't know this part of the city myself. 对不起，我对这一带不大熟悉。

You can ask someone else (你去问问别人吧)

1. I guess you'd better ask someone else. 我想你最好去问问别人。

2. Why don't you ask the policeman over there? 你为什么不去问问那边的那个警察呢？

3. The policeman over there must be able to help you. 那边的警察一定能帮到你。

4. Perhaps you could ask at the railway station. 或许你可以到火车站去问问。

I can show you the way (我可以给你带路)

1. I'm going that way myself. I'll show you the way. 我也往那边走，我会给你指路的。

2. I'm going passing it. I'll point it out to you. 我要经过那个地方，我会指给你看的。

3. I'll walk along with you if you don't mind. 你愿意的话，我可以同你一道走。

4. I'm going in that direction，anyway. 反正我也要朝那个方向走。

Section Five：Culture Tips

有趣的日本路标

日本路标的特色与其文化一样，将细致入微发挥得淋漓尽致。

中国人在日本的道路上开车行驶，一般不会有太大障碍，这里的路标大多以双语呈现，汉字加上英文，十分易懂。如果你有机会到靠近俄罗斯的地方，还会发现，路标上又体贴地加上了俄语。多国语言的路标，让游人感觉既亲切又方便。

在素有"雪国"之称的北海道，路标很多都与北海道著名的雪有关。在北海道道路两侧矗立着许多间隔相同、形式相同的红白相间箭头路标。这一排排形似路灯的箭头在日本北部地区十分常见，它们像箭一样指向地面，所指之处就是路肩。它们的作用是指示路的宽度，通常道路两侧都会有，夜间会发光。冬天的北海道，大雪纷飞的日子经常有，厚厚的积雪掩盖了道路的边缘，为了让驾驶员能够安全地行驶在道路内，这个表明道路宽度的路标就显得相当重要了。

同样的，初来北海道的驾驶员，常常会遇到前方红灯亮起却因积雪覆盖路面而找不到停止线的慌张状况。其实，细致的日本人早就考虑到了这一点，在道路旁边，驾驶者一定可以找到一个写着"停止线"的牌子。尽管这个路标的立杆可能已经被雪埋了一大半，但清晰的提示标牌，一定会坚强地露在外面。

最后，不得不说说日本的"动物路标"。与许多发达国家一样，日本也十分注重对动物的保护。在日本，如果看到"熊横断注意"的路标，那可不是闹着玩的，这意味着前面可能有熊出没。"鹿横断注意"和"狐狸横断注意"路标在日本比较常见，在高知县还有"猫横断注意"路标，而到了青蛙产卵的季节，你甚至还会看见"蛙横断注意"路标。这些形象可爱的动物路标，包含着许多温馨的含义。它们除了提醒驾驶员在行车过程中小心道路的突发情况外，更是在要求我们，不要打扰到这些大自然"原住民"的生活。

译 文

第二部分：相关信息

路标的历史

今天我们到处都可以看到路标，但是你知道那些路标是如何随着时间的推移演变和发展而来的吗？

当你驾车行驶在繁忙的高速公路上，或者在停车场停车时，你常常会瞥一眼那些停车标志或路标，却很少意识到它们的重要性和必要性。你有没有想过，那些标志有什么用，以及它们第一次是如何出现的？是谁想到人们需要那些交通标志的？

路标的历史很有趣。是罗马人创造了第一个路标。罗马人建造了高大的柱子，帮助旅行者了解他们离罗马有多远，应该走什么方向。这些高耸的石塔被称为里程碑，与我们今天遇到的现代交通标志相去甚远。我们发现，中世纪时期，欧洲国家的道路标志有一点进步，在十字路口竖立起标志指向某些城镇。其中的一些标志也标出了到达某些城镇的距离。

就是当汽车驶上马路时，我们发现路标的使用变得越来越流行。司机依靠这些标志看他们要去哪里以及离他们的目的地有多远。1895 年，意大利旅行俱乐部作为第一个有组织的团体，为修建更好的道路标志请愿。1908 年，国际道路大会在罗马举行讨论欧洲道路标志。

在现代使用的第一批路标是交叉路口、颠簸、弯道和铁路道口标志。这 4 个标志形成了首个欧洲路标体系。到了 20 世纪 60 年代，世界各地的不同国家都使用国际符号向司机们显示限速，道路状况和其他旅行信息。

　　如今，有了一套标准的图案符号可以使国际旅行者们在国外旅行和寻找方向时不会面临任何问题。今天，人们经常会在路上看到电子标志，上面有闪光的文字或图片，一旦有任何变化，可以通过电脑立即更新。这些标志传达即时信息是非常有用的，它们可以让旅行者们对可能出现的危险做好准备。

第三部分：情境任务范例

情境1：李欣想拜访一位住在厦门的朋友。他问宾馆前台人员如何到达他朋友的地址。

（A：李欣；B：宾馆前台人员；C：路人；D：警察）

A：打扰一下。你能告诉我怎么去这个地址吗？

B：让我看看……思明区莲花南路18号。

A：我可以走着去吗？

B：那里离这儿很远。你最好乘地铁3号线到仙岳山站，然后坐508路公共汽车到莲花中学。那里离这个地址很近。

A：谢谢，我怎么才能到最近的地铁站呢？

B：沿着这条路一直走大约十分钟，你就会看到地铁站。

A：非常感谢！

情境2：半小时后，李欣来到莲花中学。他询问一个路人如何去他朋友的住址。

A：打扰一下。我正在找这个地址。你能帮我一下吗？

C：对不起，我也是外地人。那边的警察也许能帮到你。

A：好的，还是要谢谢你。

情境3：李欣向警察询问如何去他朋友的住址。

A：打扰一下。您能告诉我去这个地址的路吗？

D：沿着这条路一直走，在第一个路口向左转。过桥后你会看到一幢蓝色的建筑，你要找的地方就在它旁边。

A：非常感谢。

D：不客气。

7.2　Take Public Transport

7.2.1　Take a Taxi

Section One: Tasks

Situation 1: *Sam is going to the shopping mall. He uses DiDi App. to call a taxi. Make a conversation on taking a taxi and charging the fare.*

Situation 2: *Sam is going home from the shopping mall. He stands by the road to call a taxi. Make a conversation on calling a taxi and communicating with the driver about his destination and fare.*

Situation 3: *Sam is going to Guangzhou on business. His flight will take off at 10:00 a.m. tomorrow. He needs to take a taxi to the airport before 9:00 a.m. tomorrow morning, and he needs to book a taxi today. Make a conversation on booking a taxi, taking a taxi and communicating with the driver about his destination, time and fare.*

Section Two: Related Information

Take a Taxi

If you are travelling in an English speaking country for business or pleasure, you will be likely to take a taxi.

Call a taxi. If you want to take a taxi, you should ask someone to call a taxi or just call a taxi by yourself. When the dispatch operator answers, you will hear something like "ESS Taxi. How can I help you?" or "FUL Taxi. Where are you located?" You will need to provide the address of where you are (your location) and where you are going (your destination). In some locations you don't need to call a taxi by phone. You can just wave your hand at one as it drives close to you. This is called "flagging" or "hailing" a taxi down. Stand close to the road and wave your arm out. An empty taxi will pull over for you. Many people get in the back of a taxi instead of the front passenger seat. A taxi without its light on is likely already on a taxi run for someone else.

The driver. When you get into the cab[1], you can make talks with the driver, who is always talkative and friendly. You always get useful information from the talk, such as where are the most popular restaurants. Making a small talk with a friendly taxi driver is a great way to practice your English. So don't be shy!

The fare. If you need to pick someone or something up on the way, the driver will keep the meter running even if you are not in the car. When you get off the cab, you pay the driver according to the meter. Your payment could be made by cash, credit card, debit or even foreign exchange. You could tell the driver to keep the change if you want to offer a tip[2].

Vocabulary

dispatch [dɪ'spætʃ] *vt.* 派遣；调度；　*n.* 派遣

operator [ˈɒpəreɪtə(r)] *n.* 操作员；电话接线员

location [ləʊˈkeɪʃn] *n.* 位置；场所

destination [ˌdestɪˈneɪʃn] *n.* 目的地

flag [flæg] *v.* 挥手使停下

hail [heɪl] *vt.* 打招呼

cab [kæb] *n.* 出租车

debit [ˈdebɪt] *n.* （银行账户上的）借记

meter [ˈmiːtə(r)] *n.* 仪表（计价器）；米

exchange [ɪksˈtʃeɪndʒ] *n.* 外汇；外币

pull over 靠边停车

Notes

1. get into the cab，进入出租车。taxi 在口语中常用 cab 取代。

   例：Let's take a cab to the post office. ＝ Let's take a taxi to the post office. 咱们搭出租车去邮局吧。

2. tip 指小费。在西方国家，给小费一般发生在你得到服务之后，代表了你对服务非常满意而给出的额外嘉奖，数量上一般给消费金额的 10%～20%。

Section Three：Situational Task Samples

Situation： *In this dialogue，Li Xin and Linda want to go to the airport by taxi. They called the operator to book a taxi.（A：Li Xin；B：Linda；C：Operator；D：Taxi driver）*

Book a taxi

A：How are we going to the airport?

B：Let's take a cab. [1]

A：Hello，I need to get a cab. [2]

C：OK. Give me your address.

A：Garden Hotel，8th Avenue.

C：OK. We will arrange for you as soon as possible. There is about a 15-minute wait.

A：That's fine.

Take a taxi

A：Hey! Taxi.

D：Where are you heading?

A：Capital Airport. How long is the ride from here then?

D：Well，since it's rush hour[3]，I'd say the ride would take about thirty minutes，more or less[4]. Is that okay?

B：Well，can you please speed up[5]? I'm afraid we might miss the flight.

D：I'm sorry，madam，there's a limit to the speed[6].

B：I think we are going to miss the plane.

D：I'm sorry about that. What's your flight time?

B：At 8:00.

D：Don't worry, madam. I guess we should get there no later than[7] 7:30 p. m.

B：Really? Great!

D：Here we are.

B：How much is it?

D：The meter[8] says ＄28.

B：Here is the fare.

D：Just a minute. Here's your change.

B：Keep the change. [9]

D：Thank you. Wish you a pleasant journey!

Notes

1. take a cab，搭出租车。若表示用手招一部出租车，则有下列用法：
   Let's hail a taxi. ＝ Let's hail a cab. 咱们招一部出租车吧。hail *vt.* 招呼

2. 在给出租车公司打电话订车时可以用 I need to get a cab. 或者 Can you send a cab to pick me up? pick sb. up 接某人

3. rush hour 交通高峰期；早高峰 morning rush hour 或 morning peak，晚高峰 evening rush hour 或 evening peak；早晚高峰是指人们都去上班或下班的时候，交通最为拥挤。早高峰一般是上午7、8点，晚高峰大约在6～8点。

4. more or less 多多少少；差不多；大约

5. speed up 加速；提速；slow down 减速

6. limit to the speed 限速，或者 speed limit

7. no later than 不迟于；不会晚于

8. meter 计程器；计价器

9. keep the change. 不用找钱了。意为让出租车司机保留零钱做小费。change *n.* 零钱

Section Four：Functional Expression Bank

Call for a taxi（打电话预订出租车）

1. Hello，reception desk? Can I book a taxi, please? 喂，前台吗？能给我订一辆出租车吗？

2. Hello，I'd like to book a taxi to take me to the railway station tomorrow morning.
   你好，我想订一辆出租车，明早送我去火车站。

3. Please send a taxi to this address：969 Shanghai Road.
   请派辆出租车到这个地址：上海路969号。

4. I'd like a taxi to go to the airport at 9 a. m. 我想要一辆出租车上午9点去机场。

Call a taxi on the road（在路上招呼出租车）

1. Taxi! Taxi! 出租汽车！出租汽车！

2. Hey，taxi! 喂，出租车！

3. Is this taxi taken? 这车子有人要了吗？

4. Are you engaged? 这车子有人订了吗？

5. Excuse me，are you free? 请问，这车走吗?

State destination（陈述目的地）

1. Airport return. 机场来回。

2. To the Royal Grand Hotel，please. 请去皇家大饭店。

3. Downtown shopping center，please. 请去市中心购物中心。

4. Will you give me a ride to the railway station? 你能送我去火车站吗?

5. Please take me to this address. 请送我去这个地址。

6. I haven't got the exact address. All I know is that it's behind/in front of/next to…
   我没有确切的地址，我只知道在……的后面/前面/旁边。

Ask the passenger to get on the taxi（请乘客上车）

1. Right. 行!

2. Get in，please. /Step in，please. I'll take you there. 请上车。我会把您送到那儿。
   司机如要谢绝，可用如下表达：

3. I'm sorry，I'm booked. 对不起，车子有人租了。

4. I'm engaged. 车子被人预订了。

5. I'm sorry，I'm not going that way. 对不起，我不走那条路。

Ask about arrival time（询问到达时间）

1. Could you get me to the airport by 4:00? 你能在 4 点前把我送到机场吗?

2. Do you think we can make it in half an hour? 半小时内能到吗?

3. I've got to be at the library by 10:00. Can you make it?
   我必须在 10 点到图书馆。你能赶到吗?

4. Do you think you can get me to…in an hour? 你看能不能一小时内送我到……?

Ask the driver to slow down/stop（让司机慢行/停车）

1. Slow down，please. 请慢一点儿。

2. Please park it here. 请在这里停车。

3. Just drop me here/at the end of the road/opposite the bank.
   我在这里/路的尽头/银行对面下车。

Ask about the fare（询问车费）

1. How much is it? /How much is the fare? 车费是多少钱?

2. How much/What do I owe you? 我要付你多少钱?

3. How much does the meter read? 计价器显示要收多少钱?

The driver quotes the fare（司机报出车费）

1. The fare is ＄22. 车费 22 美元。

2. The fare is shown on the meter. 车费由计价器显示。

3. It's five dollars on the meter. 计价器显示 5 美元。

4. The meter says 15 pounds. 计价器显示 15 英镑。

Pay the fare（付车费）

1. Here is the fare, and this is for you. 这是车费，这是给你的（小费）。

2. Here's 20 dollars. Keep the change. 这是 20 美元，零钱你留着吧。

3. Thanks a lot. Here. 多谢，这是车费。

4. Thank you. Here's 10 pounds. Just give me 2 pounds back, please.

   谢谢，这是 10 英镑，找我 2 英镑就行了。

5. May I have a receipt, please? 可以给我开发票吗？

Bid farewell/say goodbye（告别）

1. Thanks for the ride. 感谢您提供的接乘服务。

2. Enjoy the rest of your day. 祝您一天愉快！

3. Wish you a pleasant journey! 祝您旅途愉快！

Section Five：Culture Tips

出租车的由来

　　1907 年初春的一个夜晚，富家子弟亚伦同他的女友去纽约百老汇看歌剧。散场时，他去叫马车，问车夫要多少钱？虽然离剧场只有半里路远，车夫竟然漫天要价，比平时贵 10 倍的车钱。亚伦感到太离谱，就与车夫争执起来，结果被车夫打倒在地。亚伦伤好后，为报复马车夫，就设想利用汽车来挤垮马车。后来他请了一个修理钟表的朋友设计了一个计程仪表，并且给出租车起名 "Taxi-car"，这就是现在全世界通用的 "Taxi"（的士）的来历。1907 年 10 月 1 日，"的士" 首次出现在纽约的街头。

译　文

第二部分：相关信息

乘出租车

　　如果你去一个讲英语的国家出差或旅游，你可能会乘出租车。

　　叫出租车。如果你想坐出租车，你应该让人给你打电话订车或自己叫出租车。当接通调度员时，你会听到像 "ESS 出租车。有什么可以帮您的吗？" 或 "FUL 出租车。您在哪里？" 你需要提供你所在的地址（你的位置）和你要去的地方（你的目的地）。在一些地方你不需要打电话叫出租车。你只要朝一辆驶近的出租车挥手即可，这就是所谓的 "挥手叫" 或 "招手叫" 出租车了。站在路边，挥动你的手臂，一辆空的出租车会为你停下来。很多人坐在出租车后面的座位，而不是前面的乘客座位上。一辆没有亮灯的出租车很可能已经有人了。

　　司机。当你进入出租车，你可以与司机交谈，他总是健谈并友好的。你常常能从谈话中得到有用的信息，比如最受欢迎的餐馆在哪里。和一位友好的出租车司机闲聊是练习英语的好方法，所以不要害羞呦。

　　车费。如果你需要在路上接某个人或取某样东西，即使你不在车内，司机也会让计价器走表。当你下车时，你按计价器金额付费。你可以通过现金、信用卡、借记卡、甚至外汇进行支付。如果你想给小费，你可以告诉司机留下应找的零钱。

第三部分：情境任务范例

情境： 在这个对话中，李欣和琳达想乘坐出租车去机场。他们给接线员打电话订出租车。

（A：李欣；B：琳达；C：接线员；D：出租车司机）

订出租车

A：我们怎么去机场？

B：坐出租车吧。

A：你好，我想叫辆出租车。

C：好的，请给我您的地址。

A：第八大道，花园酒店。

C：好的，我们会尽快为您安排。请您等待 15 分钟左右。

A：好的。

乘出租车

A：嗨，出租车！

D：请问你们要去哪里？

A：首都机场。从这儿到那里需要多久？

D：哦，由于现在是交通高峰期，我想差不多要 30 分钟，行吗？

B：可不可以请您开快一点？恐怕我们会赶不上飞机。

D：抱歉，女士，有车速限制。

B：我想我们快赶不上飞机了。

D：我对此感到抱歉。你们是几点的飞机？

B：8 点。

D：别担心，女士。我想我们到达那里不会迟于 7 点 30 分的。

B：真的吗？太好了！

D：我们到了。

B：多少钱？

D：计价器显示 28 美元。

B：给您钱。

D：稍等，找您的钱。

B：不用找了。

D：谢谢，祝您旅途愉快！

7.2.2　Travel by Rail

Section One：Tasks

Situation 1：*Xiao Rui wants to take a train from Shanghai to Shenzhen for business on June 19. Make a conversation on buying a lower berth ticket at the ticket office.*

Situation 2：*Xiao Rui arrives at the station one hour before the departure time on June 19. Make conversations on going through the security check and ticket barrier.*

Situation 3：*Make conversations on getting on the train，talking to other passengers about the dining car and getting off the train.*

Section Two：Related Information

How to Take a Train

You must buy a ticket and have it checked at least twice before you board a train[1]. The following steps show you how to take a train.

1. Get to the station

Check the ticket information carefully. To avoid missing your train，you are recommended[2] to arrive at the train station at least half an hour earlier than the departure time.

2. Go through the security check to enter the station

Security check

Put your luggage，including handbags and carry-on bags，on the security scanner conveyor belt[3]. Then walk through a metal detector[4] gate to check if there are any forbidden articles on you. Unlike the security restrictions at an airport，you can take water on a train.

Look for the waiting room

After the security check，you will see some LED screens，which show current train information for the day，including each train number，terminus，departure time，and waiting room number. Check your train number on your ticket with the LED screens，and find the right waiting room. Usually，the LED screen shows train information on a cycle like this：

Train No.	Destination	Departs at	Waiting Room	Check-in Gate	State
T132	Dalian	17:57	5		waiting
K473	Kunming	16:16	9	8	checking in

Check-in

When the train is arriving，a broadcast will tell passengers to go to the ticket check gate to have your ticket checked. You are usually allowed to enter the platform approximately 5 to 10 minutes before departure. And leave enough time for queuing and waiting，as there can be a lot of people standing in line.

Bear in mind that the check-in process stops 5 minutes before the train's departure time. So you are recommended to arrive at the waiting room at least 15 minutes before the departure time.

3. Find your carriage and seat

When you are boarding the train, show your ticket to a staff member and make sure you are boarding the right train. Find the seat according to the ticket after you get on the train. Then place your baggage opposite your seat, so that you can easily keep an eye on it.

4. Get off the train

Station announcements usually come at least 10 minutes before each stop, to give passengers time to prepare to leave the train. If your destination is not the terminus of a train, you need to listen to the stop announcements carefully.

5. Get out of the station

Remember to have your ticket readily accessible as the ticket will be inspected again at the exit gate.

Vocabulary

departure　[dɪˈpɑːtʃə(r)]　n.出发；离开

luggage　[ˈlʌgɪdʒ]　n.行李

scanner　[ˈskænə]　n.扫描仪

restriction　[rɪˈstrɪkʃn]　n.限制

screen　[skriːn]　n.屏幕

cycle　[ˈsaɪkl]　n.循环；周期

broadcast　[ˈbrɔːdkɑːst]　n.广播；　v.广播；播放

platform　[ˈplætfɔːm]　n.站台

approximately　[əˈprɒksɪmətlɪ]　adv.大约

carriage　[ˈkærɪdʒ]　n.车厢

opposite　[ˈɒpəzɪt]　adj.对面的；相对的

announcement　[əˈnaʊnsmənt]　n.宣告；通告

terminus　[ˈtɜːmɪnəs]　n.终点；终点站

accessible　[əkˈsesɪbl]　adj.易接近的；可理解的；易相处的

inspect　[ɪnˈspekt]　vt.检查；检验；　vi.进行检查

take a train　乘火车

at least　至少

security check　安检

forbidden article　违禁品

departure time　发车时间

on a cycle　循环；轮回

bear in mind　牢记；记住

keep an eye on　注意；照看；留心；照管

Notes

1. board a train 上火车，还可以用 get on a train；get off a train 下火车

2. recommend sb. to do sth. 建议某人做某事；被动语态形式为 sb. be recommended to do sth.

3. security scanner conveyor belt 安全扫描仪输送带

4. metal detector 金属探测器，金属探测装置

Section Three：Situational Task Samples

Situation：*Li Xin plans to take his son Li Hao to go to Miami by train. First，he goes to the ticket office to buy tickets. Then，he takes the train to Miami with Li Hao.（A：Li Xin；B：the conductor；C：the ticket collector；D：the trainman；E：Li Hao）*

Buy tickets

A：I'd like to have some information about trains between New York and Miami.

B：There is one at 5:00 p. m. and another at 7:00 p. m.

A：How long does the trip to Miami take?

B：It takes about 30 hours.

A：Are there sleeping cars[1] and dining cars[2] on the train?

B：Yes，there are.

A：How much is a sleeper[3]?

B：$ 380 one way[4]，$ 630 round trip[5].

A：How much is a child's ticket?

B：Children under one meter in height travel free，from one meter to 1. 5 meters in height travel half fare.

A：OK，I'd like to reserve two sleepers on the 5 p. m. train to Miami for June 12，please. If possible，I would like to have lower berths[6].

B：No problem.

Take the train

At the ticket barrier

C：Ticket，please! Going to Miami?

A：Yes，here you are.

C：Thank you.

A：Which platform[7] does the 5 p. m. train go from?

C：Platform 10.

A：Thank you.

Get on the train

A：Excuse me. Is this carriage[8] No. 9?

D：Yes，it is. For Miami，up in front!

A：OK.

D：Non-passengers are requested to leave the train. The passengers take your seats, please. The train for Miami is leaving.

Talk with Li Hao

E：Where are we?

A：It's Orlando.

E：How long do we stop here?

A：Ten minutes.

E：I'm a little hungry，daddy.

A：Let's go to the restaurant car to have something to eat.

...

A：I'm a little sleepy. Wake me up half an hour before we arrive at Miami.

E：OK，daddy.

Get off the train

A：The train will be pulling in[9] at the station in a few minutes. Let's get our things ready.

E：OK. We are at last at our destination[10].

A：Wait until the train stops.

E：OK.

Notes

1. sleeping car 卧铺车厢

2. dining car 餐车，也可称为 restaurant car

3. sleeper 卧铺

4. one way 单程

5. round trip 往返票

6. lower berth 下铺；berth（船、列车等的）卧铺；middle berth 中铺；upper berth 上铺

7. platform 站台

8. carriage 火车客车车厢

9. pull in 停车

10. destination 目的地

Section Four：Functional Expression Bank

Train number（列车班次）

Inquire（询问）

1. I'd like to have some information about trains between…and…
   我想了解一些来往于……与……之间的火车情况。

2. How often do the trains leave for London? 到伦敦的火车多久一班?

3. What high-speed rails are there for New York? 到纽约的高铁有什么班次?

4. Is there a through train from…to…? ……到……有直达列车吗?

5. Which train would get me to Dover before 9：00? 我乘哪一班车可以 9 点以前到达多佛?

6. Do I have to change? 我要换乘吗？

Answer（回答）

1. There's one at 3:00 p. m. and another at 4:30 p. m. 下午 3:00 有一班，下午 4:30 还有一班。

2. There are three trains to London every day. 到伦敦的火车每天有三班。

3. It runs every four hours. 每 4 小时开一班。

4. The two morning trains are through trains, and the afternoon train is a slow train with sleeping carriage accommodation as far as Mansfield.

   上午的两班都是直达车，下午的那班是有卧铺车厢的慢车，到曼斯菲尔德。

5. There is a train for Dove leaving at 7:30 a. m. 上午 7:30 有一班开往多佛的列车。

6. You have to change at Nottingham for Brightley. 你要从诺丁汉转车到百利来。

Time of the train（列车的时间）

Inquire（询问）

1. What time does the Scotch Express leave and when does it get to Edinburgh?
   苏格兰快车什么时候开车，什么时候到爱丁堡？

2. What time does the train from Guangzhou get in/arrive?
   广州来的火车什么时候进站/到站？

3. When's the train from Hangzhou to Xi'an? 杭州来的车什么时候到达西安？

4. I want to go to Athens. When is the next train? 我要去雅典，下一班车是什么时候？

5. How long does the trip to Sydney take? 到悉尼要多久？

Answer（回答）

1. The Scotch Express leaves at half past nine in the evening and is due to arrive the next afternoon. 苏格兰快车晚上 9 点半开，第二天下午到。

2. It gets in around 3:20 p. m. 列车大约下午 3:20 到。

3. It's due in at noon/10:00 a. m. 列车中午/上午 10:00 到站。

4. The next train for Athens leaves at 2 o'clock. 下一班去雅典的车 2 点开出。

5. The journey to Sydney on the fast train takes two hours, and you don't have to change.
   乘快车去悉尼要 2 小时，不用换车。

Ticket Price（票价）

Inquire（询问）

1. How much does the ticket (to Miami) cost?（到迈阿密的）票价多少钱？

2. How much is the ticket to New York? 到纽约的票价多少钱？

3. What's the round-trip fare? 往返票多少钱？

4. How much is a child's ticket? 儿童票价多少？

5. How many days is the ticket valid? 这个票几天内有效。

Answer（回答）

1. Thirty dollars round trip. 往返票 30 美金。

2. Twenty-five fifty dollars one-way, forty round trip.
   单程 25 美元 50 美分，往返票 40 美元。

3. Children under one meter in height travel free；Children from one meter to 1.5 meters in height travel half fare. 1 米以下儿童免费；1 米到 1.5 米儿童半票。

4. The season ticket is valid for three months. 季票三个月内有效。

Buy tickets（购票）

1. Three one-way tickets to Paris，please. /Three singles to Paris，please. 买 3 张去巴黎的单程票。

2. Please give me two round-trip/return berth tickets on the 11:00 direct/non-stop train to Canberra. 我要两张 11 点去堪培拉的直达车卧铺来回票。

3. I want a second-class single to Chicago. 我要一张去芝加哥的二等单程票。

4. I wonder if my sons can go for half-price? 不知道我儿子是否能半票？

5. Give me four first-class tickets for Warsaw plus three berths. 给我四张去华沙的一等票，再加三个卧铺。

6. I'd like to reserve a sleeper on the 9a. m. train to Hamburg for June 12，please. If possible，I would like to have a lower berth. 我想在 6 月 12 日上午 9 点去汉堡的列车上预订一个卧铺。如果可能的话，我想要下铺。

Service（服务）

Inquire（询问）

1. Does the train carry a dining/restaurant car? 这车带餐车吗？

2. Are there slumber coaches on the train? 这列车上有卧铺车厢吗？

Answer（回答）

1. Yes，there is a dining car on the train. 是的，车上有餐车。

2. No，I don't believe there is. 不，我想不会有。

Get on the train（上火车）

The conductor（列车员）

1. Ticket，please! Going to Bonn? 请出示车票！去波恩吗？

2. For Konstanz，up in front! 去康斯坦茨，上车往里走！

3. Sorry to trouble you，but I must examine your tickets…thank you. 对不起，麻烦各位一下，但我得看看你们的车票……谢谢。

4. Non-passengers are requested to leave the train. 送站的人请下车。

5. Take your seats，please. The train for Dalian is leaving! 请坐到座位上去。去大连的列车就要开了。

Passenger（乘客）

1. Which platform does the 5:30 train go from? 5:30 分的列车从哪个站台出发？

2. Where is carriage No. 8? 第 8 号车厢在哪儿？

 Is this carriage No. 10? 这是第 10 号车厢吗？

3. Is this seat free/taken/vacant? 这个座位没人/有人坐/空着吗？

4. I prefer sitting here，facing the engine. 我喜欢坐在这儿，面朝车头。

 I can't sit backwards. That will make me carsick. 我反向坐不行，我会晕车的。

5. Do you mind changing places/seats with me? 你是否介意与我换一下座位？

6. Let's put our suitcases on the rack? 我们把箱子放在架子上吧。

On the journey（旅途中）

1. Where are we? 我们到哪儿了？

2. What's the name of this station? 这个车站叫什么名字？

3. What is the next station? 下一站是哪里？

4. How long do we stop here? 火车在这里停多久？

5. Please wake me up half an hour before we arrive at… 请在到达……前半小时叫醒我。

6. What time shall we arrive? 我们几点到？

7. The toilet/smoking area is at the end of this carriage. 厕所/吸烟区在这节车厢的尽头。

Get off the train（下火车）

1. We are at last at our destination. 我们总算到目的地了。

2. The train will be pulling in at the station in a few minutes. Let's get our things ready.

列车还有几分钟就要进站了，让我们收拾一下东西。

3. Wait till the train stops! 等火车停稳后再下车。

Train seats（火车座席）

hard seat　硬座	deluxe sleeper　豪华卧铺
soft seat　软座	first-class seat　一等座
hard sleeper　硬卧	second-class seat　二等座
soft sleeper　软卧	business seat　商务座

Section Five：Culture Tips

火车的由来

　　火车（指最早出现的火车蒸汽机车）通常被认为是英国人乔治·斯蒂芬森（1781—1848年）发明的。斯蒂芬森出生在一个工人家庭，8 岁当牧童，14 岁跟着父亲在煤矿当锅炉工的助手。当时英国使用蒸汽机抽水在煤矿行业已经非常普遍。为了掌握蒸汽机的构造、原理、作业和维修，没有文化的斯蒂芬森从 17 岁开始就读夜校，从小学一年级开始读起。经过几年的刻苦学习，他终于甩掉了文盲的帽子。1809 年的一天，煤矿上的一辆运煤车坏了，许多机械师都修理不好，而他修好了，于是从此被任命为工程师。与此同时，斯蒂芬森听说有人想把蒸汽机用作陆路交通的动力，制造能行走的蒸汽机，他对这一设想产生了极大的兴趣。经过几年的不懈努力，他 33 岁那年（1814 年）终于发明了一台机车。这台蒸汽机由于在前进时不断从烟囱里冒出火来，所以被人们称为火车。它能拖动 30 多吨的货物，但速度很慢，样子也难看。由于没有装上弹簧减震，开起来震动得很厉害，因此受到了许多人的嘲讽。

　　但是，斯蒂芬森并不灰心，继续研究，终于在 1825 年成功制造出世界上第一台客货运蒸汽机车。同年 9 月 27 日，这辆机车举行试车典礼。这辆机车拖着 12 节货车、7 节客车，载着 90 吨的货物和 450 名旅客，以每小时 20 多公里的速度，行驶了 12 英里。1929 年，斯蒂芬森制造了更加完善的火车。自此，火车终于得到了全世界的认可。

译　文

第二部分：相关信息

如何乘火车

你必须买票，而且在登上火车前至少要检两次票。以下步骤向您展示如何乘坐火车。

1. 到达车站

认真查看车票信息。为了避免错过火车，建议你至少比发车时间早半个小时到达火车站。

2. 通过安检进入车站

安全检查

把你的行李，包括手袋和手提袋放在安全扫描仪输送带上。然后走过一个金属探测器门检查你是否随身携带违禁物品。不像在机场的安全限制那样，你可以带水上火车。

寻找候车室

在安全检查后，你将看到一些 LED 屏幕，上面显示当天的当前列车信息，包括每辆列车的车次，终点站，发车时间和候车室号码。对着 LED 屏幕查看你车票上的车次，找到候车室。通常，LED 屏幕循环播放列车信息如下：

车次	终点站	发车时间	候车室	检票口	状态
T132	大连	17:57	5		正在候车
K473	昆明	16:16	9	8	正在检票

检票

当火车即将到达时，广播将告诉乘客们去检票口检票。通常允许在出发前约 5~10 分钟进入站台。留出足够的时间排队和等待，因为可能有很多人在排队。

请记住，在火车出发时间前 5 分钟停止检票。所以建议你在出发前至少 15 分钟到达候车室。

3. 找到车厢和座位

当你登上火车时，把你的车票出示给工作人员，并确保你登上正确的列车。上车后，根据车票找到座位。然后把你的行李放在你的座位对面，以便你可以很容易注意到它。

4. 下火车

通常至少在每次停车前 10 分钟报站，来给乘客时间准备下车。如果你的目的地不是火车终点站，你需要仔细听停车通告。

5. 出站

记得准备好你的车票，因为在出站检票口会再次检票。

第三部分：情境任务范例

情境：*李欣计划带他的儿子李浩乘火车去迈阿密。他先去售票处买票，然后和李浩一起搭乘去迈阿密的火车。（A：李欣；B：售票员；C：检票员；D：列车员；E：李浩）*

买票

A：我想了解一下来往于纽约和迈阿密之间的火车车次。

B：下午 5 点有一班，晚上 7 点有一班。

A：到迈阿密要多久？

B：大约要 30 个小时。

A：这趟列车上有卧铺车厢和餐车吗？

B：是的，有。

A：卧铺票价多少？

B：单程 380 美元，往返 630 美元.

A：儿童票多少钱？

B：1 米以下儿童免费，1 米到 1.5 米半票。

A：好的。我想在 6 月 12 日下午 5 点去迈阿密的列车上预订两个卧铺。如果可能的话，我想
要下铺。

B：没问题。

乘火车

在检票口

C：请出示车票。去迈阿密吗？

A：是的，给你。

C：谢谢。

A：下午 5 点的火车从哪个站台出发？

C：10 号站台。

A：谢谢。

上火车

A：打扰了，请问这是 9 号车厢吗？

D：是的，去迈阿密，上车往里走。

A：好的。

D：送客的人请下车。请旅客们坐到座位上去，去迈阿密的列车就要出发了。

与李浩交谈

E：我们到哪儿了？

A：奥兰多。

F：我们在这里要停多久？

A：10 分钟。

F：爸爸，我有点儿饿了。

A：咱们去餐车吃点东西吧。

……

A：我有点儿困，在到达迈阿密前半小时叫醒我。

F：好的，爸爸。

下火车

A：列车还有几分钟就要进站了，让我们收拾一下东西。

F：好的。我们总算到目的地了。

A：等火车停稳后再下车。

F：好的。

7. 2. 3 Take an Airplane

Section One: Tasks

Situation 1: *Zhang Liang is going to Guangzhou on business. He calls the air ticket office to book two first class tickets on June 18. Make a conversation on booking the air tickets.*

Situation 2: *Make a conversation on asking for help at the airport, such as how to check in, and how to pass the security check, etc.*

Situation 3: *Zhang Liang feels a little cold and thirsty on the plane. Make a conversation between Zhang Liang and the air hostess on asking for a blanket and water.*

Situation 4: *Zhang Liang is talking about the trip with his colleague Mr. Brown on the plane. Make a conversation between them.*

Section Two: Related Information

First-Time Air Travel Guide

The first-time flier may have many questions to ask about how to take an airplane. Where and how to buy an air ticket? What to do when you get to the airport? How to pass the security check? The following steps may help you to solve these problems.

Step 1: Purchase a ticket

The easiest way to buy a ticket is to search for your flight ticket online. Find an airfare search engine, then enter in your departure city, arrival city and dates, then the engine will list a range of flights that fit your criteria. Select one that suits you. When you are ready to buy a flight ticket, click on it to select and follow the purchasing instructions[1]. Usually, airlines will send you an email confirmation and e-ticket number.

Step 2: Gather photo identification

If you are traveling within your home country, you will need an ID card. If you are flying internationally, you will need a passport which is valid for six months from the date of departure.

Step 3: Ensure that your luggage meets airline requirements

Pay attention to the weight limits[2], and be sure to stay within them, or you have to pay for the overweight baggage. As for your carry-on bags, you need to pack them carefully. You are allowed to take 100 mL (or less) liquid in a single bottle which can be put into a sealable, clear plastic bag when you get on the plane. [3] Airport staff will confiscate any liquids or gels that do not adhere to their policy. [4]

Step 4: Arrive at the airport early

For your first time traveling on an airplane, allow extra time to make it through the airport and familiarize yourself with the process. To give yourself enough time, you should arrive at least two hours before a domestic flight and three hours before an international flight.

Step 5: Check in at the airline desk

Follow the signs to the check-in desk, and give your ID card to the airport employee. He will look up your reservation, print your boarding pass and collect any baggage fees for checked bags. If you have not selected seats, you can also ask the airport employee for a window or an aisle seat[5] at this time. You will be asked to place your checked bags on the scale next to the desk for weighing, and they will be tagged and placed on a conveyor to be taken to the plane. Then take your boarding pass and ID card from him or her.

Step 6: Go through security

At the security checkpoint, you will be asked to show your identification and boarding pass. Once you are at the screening machines, take off your coat or jacket, as well as your watch, mobile phone and even keys, and then place them into a plastic bin. If you take a laptop with you, place it into a separate bin, and send it down the conveyor along with your carry-on bag. Wait for an airport employee to wave you through the metal detector, and walk through. Then retrieve your items.

Step 7: Board the plane

Your boarding pass should have a gate number on it; if not, check the electronic displays to find your flight and gate number. Follow the signs to get to your gate, and have a seat until an airport employee calls for boarding. Find your seat by checking the numbers above each row after boarding.

Step 8: Collect baggage

Once your flight landed, exit the airplane and follow signs for baggage claim. Your flight number and departure city will be on an electronic display; wait until the conveyor starts moving and your bag arrives.

Vocabulary

criteria [kraɪˈtɪərɪə] n. 标准；准则（criterion 的复数）

identification [aɪˌdentɪfɪˈkeɪʃ(ə)n] n. 鉴定；识别；身份证明

passport [ˈpɑːspɔːt] n. 护照

valid [ˈvælɪd] adj. 有效的

overweight [əʊvəˈweɪt] n. 超重； adj. 超重的；过重的； vt. 使负担过重

sealable [ˈsiːləbl] adj. 可密封的；可封口的

gel [dʒel] n. 凝胶

confiscate [ˈkɒnfɪskeɪt] vt. 没收；充公

familiarize [fəˈmɪlɪəraɪz] vt. 使熟悉

scale [skeɪl] n. 秤

tag [tæg] vt. 附加；加标签于； n. 标签

checkpoint ['tʃekpɔint] *n*. 检查站；关卡

conveyor [kən'veɪə(r)] *n*. 运送者；传送带

bin [bɪn] *n*. 箱子

laptop ['læptɒp] *n*. 便携式电脑；笔记本电脑

retrieve [rɪ'triːv] *vt*. 取回

weight limit 限重

adhere to 遵循

domestic flight 国内航班

international flight 国际航班

boarding pass 登机卡；登机牌

checked bag 托运的行李

security checkpoint 安检处

electronic display 电子屏幕

Notes

1. follow the purchasing instructions 遵循购买说明

2. weight limits 限重。限重是指每个旅客被允许携带的行李重量，超出的重量则要收费。国内航班办理行李托运一般遵循：头等舱旅客是 40 千克，公务舱旅客是 30 千克，经济舱旅客是 20 千克。

3. You are allowed to take 100 mL (or less) liquid in a single bottle which can be put into a sealable, clear plastic bag when you get on the plane. 你可以用一个单独的瓶子携带不超过 100 毫升的液体上飞机，且瓶子用可封口的、透明塑料袋包装。航空公司对于液体的携带有明确的规定：乘坐从我国境内机场始发的国际、地区航班的旅客，随身携带的液态物品每件容积不能超过 100 毫升。盛放液态物品的容器，应放在最大容积不超过 1 升的、可重复封口的透明塑料袋中。每名旅客每次仅允许携带一个透明塑料袋，超出部分应托运。装液态物品的透明塑料袋须单独接受安全检查。be allowed to do…被允许做……；mL 毫升，读作 milliliter。

4. Airport staff will confiscate any liquids or gels that do not adhere to their policy. 机场工作人员将没收任何不符合他们规定的液体或凝胶。that 在句中引导定语从句。

5. window seat 靠窗的座位；aisle seat 靠过道的座位

Section Three：Situational Task Samples

Situation 1：*Li Xin came to the air ticket office to buy two air tickets from Beijing to Xiamen. Here is the dialogue between Li Xin and the booking clerk.* [1] （A：*Li Xin*；B：*Booking clerk*）

A：What flight do you have from Beijing to Xiamen today?

B：We have a nonstop flight leaving Beijing at 8:20 a. m. every day.

A：How long does the flight take?

B: The flight will take two hours.

A: What is the economy class[2] fare?

B: Economy fare from Beijing to Xiamen is ¥2,300.

A: I want two economy class tickets to Xiamen.

B: OK. China Southern Airlines Flight 702, leaving at 8:20 a.m. How would you like to pay?

A: By WeChat.

B: OK. Here are the tickets.

A: Thank you.

Situation 2: *It was the first time for Li Xin to take a plane. Miss Wang, who works at the airport, gave him some help.* (*A: Li Xin; C: Miss Wang*)

A: Excuse me. This is my first time to take a plane. How do I check in[3]?

C: May I see your ticket, please?

A: Yes. Here you are.

C: You can get a boarding pass at that counter[4]. Do you have anything to check in?

A: No, I only have a handbag.

C: Then you could wait in the departure area[5] after going through security.

A: Thank you very much.

Situation 3: *A stewardess[6] helped Li Xin to fasten the seat belt.* [7] (*A: Li Xin; D: Stewardess*)

A: Excuse me. There is something wrong with my seat belt.

D: What's the matter?

A: It won't buckle[8].

D: Let me see…You forgot to push the buckle[9].

A: I see, thank you.

(Li Xin asked the stewardess for some medicine because of air sickness.)

A: Excuse me. I'm feeling a bit airsick. Can you give me some medicine for air sickness[10]?

D: OK. Do you need anything else?

A: Yes, could you give me a cup of water?

D: OK. Here you are.

A: Thank you very much.

Situation 4: *Li Xin and his friend John are talking on an airplane.* (*A: Li Xin; E: John*)

E: Do you fasten your seat belt when you're flying?

A: Of course I do. It's the first thing I do to keep safe.

E: I rarely fasten my seat belt and I'm still fine.

A: Well, man, you'd better fasten it.

……

A: We have been flying for nearly 3 hours. When do we land?

E: We seem to be approaching[11] Xiamen.

A: We'd better put our seats upright[12]. We are going to land in a few minutes.

E: OK.

Notes

1. booking clerk 售票员
2. economy class 经济舱
3. check in 原义为"检查登记",可根据不同的语境有不同的具体意思,如这里意为"办理登机手续",下文的 check in 意为"办理行李托运手续"。
4. counter 柜台
5. departure area 候机大厅
6. stewardess (飞机上的)女服务员,空中小姐
7. fasten the seat belt 系安全带
8. buckle (用搭扣)扣紧;搭扣
9. push the buckle 拉开搭扣
10. air sickness 晕机
11. approach 靠近,接近
12. upright 直立的,竖直的

Section Four:Functional Expression Bank

Booking air tickets (订飞机票)

Forward a reservation (提出预订)

1. Hello,I'd like to make a reservation to Hong Kong, for June 12th. (打电话) 喂,我想订一张 6 月 12 日去香港的机票。
2. I'd like to have reservations for three on the 8:40 a. m. flight to Perth the day after tomorrow. 我想订三张后天飞往珀斯的上午 8:40 的航班。
3. Please book me the earliest possible flight to Berlin. 请给我订一张最早去柏林的飞机票。
4. We want four first class tickets to Chicago for Sep. 12.
   我们要四张 9 月 12 日去芝加哥的头等舱机票。

Handle a reservation (办理预订)

1. May I have your name and flight number,please? 请问你的姓名和航班号?
2. Do you want to fly first class or economy class? 你要头等舱还是经济舱?
3. One way or round trip? 单程还是往返票?
4. You have booked a Swiss Airlines Flight 289,leaving at 10:00 Sunday morning.
   你订了瑞士航空公司周日上午 10 点的 289 次航班。

Confirm a reservation (确认预订)

1. I'd like to confirm my flight. 我想确认一下我的航班。
2. I'd like to make sure my plane reservation is in order.
   我想确认我预订的机票是否已经办妥了。

Cancel the reservation (取消预订)

1. I'd like to apply for refund of my ticket. 我想要申请退票。
2. I want to give back my ticket. 我要退票。

3. How much do I have to pay for the service charge? 我要付多少手续费？

4. You have to pay a service charge of 20% of your ticket. 你得付机票价格 20% 的手续费。

Flight number（班机班次）

Inquire（询问）

1. What flights do you have from New York to Beijing the day after tomorrow?
   后天从纽约飞往北京有哪几个班次？

2. Do you fly to Chicago on Friday? 星期五你们有班机去芝加哥吗？

3. Are there any planes to Dallas on Monday? 周一有班机去达拉斯吗？

4. Do you have any direct flights to London? 你们有直飞伦敦的航班吗？

5. Which flight gets me to Boston by 10：00 a. m.？ 我乘哪班飞机能在上午 10 点前到波士顿？

6. How many flights to San Francisco do you have daily/every week?
   你们每天/每周飞往旧金山有几班航班？

Answer（回答）

1. We have a nonstop flight leaving Kennedy at 8:20 a. m.
   上午 8:20 有一趟直达班机，从肯尼迪机场起飞。

2. There is a BA Flight 185 in the morning and an AA Flight 766 in the afternoon.
   上午有英航 185 班机，下午有美航 766 班机。

3. There is a French Air Boeing-747 out of Dallas at 6:30 p. m.
   法国航空公司有一架波音 747 班机下午 6:30 分飞离达拉斯。

4. PAN AM Flight BE 532 takes off from Heathrow in the early morning, and flies direct to
   London. 泛美航空公司 BE 532 班机在上午早些时候从希思罗机场起飞，直飞伦敦。

Stopover（经停）

Inquire（询问）

1. Where would the stopovers be for BA Flight 132? 英航 132 航班中途在哪些地方停留？

2. How many hours will the stopover last? 要停几小时？

Answer（回答）

1. BA Flight 132 stops over in Tokyo and Hong Kong. 英航 132 航班在东京和香港停。

2. One hour and a half. 一个半小时。

Transfer（中转）

1. There is no direct flight to Los Angeles. You'll have a three-hour stopover in Chicago before
   continuing to Los Angeles.
   没有直飞洛杉矶的航班。你将在芝加哥停留三小时后再继续飞洛杉矶。

2. You have to change planes in San Francisco. 你得在旧金山转机。

Inquire about time（询问时间）

Inquire（询问）

1. When does the plane/flight take off? 飞机何时起飞？

2. How long does the flight take? 要飞多长时间？

3. What time does Flight CA3202 arrive/depart? CA3202 航班什么时候到/起飞?

4. When does Flight CA3202 get into Shanghai? CA3202 航班什么时间飞抵上海?

5. Will Flight CZ6409 arrive on schedule? CZ6409 航班会准点到达吗?

6. What time do I have to be at the airport? 我该什么时候到机场?

7. What time am I supposed to check in? 我应该什么时候来办理登机手续?

◆注：CA 为中国国际航空公司（Air China）的 ATA 代码；CZ 为中国南方航空股份有限公司（China Southern Airline Company Limited）的 ATA 代码。ATA 代码是国际航空运输协会 IATA（International Air Transport Association）制定的统一两位字符，主要用于航班号前。但随着航空公司越来越多，就很难保证后来成立的航空公司的英文简称又不与其他前面的航空公司重复，就开始使用相近的字母，如南航，如果按 China Southern Airline 无论是取 CS 还是 SA 都被其他航空公司占用，只好申请使用发音相近的 CZ 了。

Answer（回答）

1. The flight will take off at 11:20 a.m. 这架班机上午 11：20 起飞。

2. The flight will take 6 hours. 这次飞行要 6 小时。

3. Flight CA3202 departs at 6:10 p.m. and arrives at 8:45 p.m.
   CA3202 航班下午 6：10 起飞，晚上 8：45 到达。

4. The time of arrival is 3:55 p.m. 抵达时间为下午 3：55。

5. Due to the weather, the flight will be delayed for one hour.
   由于天气原因，航班将延迟 1 小时抵达。

6. You will have to be at the airport by 9:20 at the latest. 你最迟 9:20 必须到机场。

7. The check-in time is 2:00 p.m. 办理登机手续的时间是下午两点。
   You have to check in no later than 2:40 p.m. 你办理登机手续的时间不得迟于下午 2:40。

Ticket price（机票价格）

Inquire（询问）

1. How much/What is the fare to London? 到伦敦多少钱?

2. How much is the round trip? 往返票多少钱?

3. What is the economy/business/first class fare from…to…?
   从……到……的经济舱/商务舱/头等舱多少钱?

4. What is the lowest fare from…to…? 从……到……的最低票价是多少?

Answer（回答）

1. One way is $350. /It's $350 one way. 单程票 350 美元。

2. Round trip is $550. /It's $550 round trip. 往返票 550 美元。

3. Economy fare round trip from Moscow to Paris is $860 during the peak/off season.
   从莫斯科到巴黎经济舱往返票在旺/淡季是 860 美元。

4. The lowest fare from…to…is… 从……到……的最低票价是……

Discount/Special tickets（特价/特殊机票）

1. I'd like some information about the special plane fares to Tokyo.
   我想知道关于去东京的特价机票情况。

2. Excuse me. Is there any stand-by seat available on your flight to London?

飞往伦敦的班机有没有临时出售的机票？

Check-in（办理登机手续）

Passenger（乘客）

1. Where will the customs procedure take place? 海关手续在哪里办理？

2. Now that our baggage and passports have been examined，let's get our boarding cards and have the baggage checked.

既然我们的行李和护照都已经检验过了，咱们就去拿登机牌并托运行李吧。

3. Could you tell me where to check in for Flight 529 to Sydney?

您能告诉我飞往悉尼的 529 次航班在哪里办理登机手续吗？

4. Is the right counter for Flight BA 267 to London?

英航飞往伦敦的 267 次航班是在这儿办手续吗？

Airport service personnel（机场服务人员）

1. I'll just change your ticket. 我来给您换票。

2. Do you want a window seat or an aisle seat? 您要靠窗，还是靠过道的座位？

3. Your flight will be boarding at Gate C5 at 9：55. 您的航班 9：55 分在 C5 登机口登机。

4. Do you have baggage to check in? 您有行李要托运吗？

5. I'm sorry，but only one carry-on is allowed. 对不起，随身只准携带一件行李。

6. The free allowance for baggage is 20 kilos. 免费行李限额是 20 公斤。

7. Your bags are 15 kilos overweight. You are allowed only 20 kilos of baggage.

您的行李超重 15 公斤，限额只有 20 公斤。

Go through the security check（通过安全检查）

1. Put all your carry-on baggage on the belt，please.

请把所有随身携带的行李放到传送带上。

2. Would you please put your watch，keys and other metal articles into the box? Now walk through the gate，please.

请您把手表、钥匙和其他金属物品放入这个盒子里。现在，请通过这道门。

3. Just walk through the metal detector…fine，thank you for your corporation.

请通过金属探测器……好，谢谢您的合作。

4. Do you have any metal objects on you? 您是否携带了金属物品？

5. Now step through again，…fine，thank you. Here's your necklace.

再走过去，……好，谢谢，这是您的项链。

Board the plane（登机）

1. What's your seat number，madam? 女士，您的座位号是多少？

My seat is 18D. 我的座位是 18 排 D 座。

2. Please place your bag under your seat. 请把您的包放在座位下面。

3. Excuse me，sir，but are those bags on the overhead luggage rack yours?

请原谅，先生，那些放在行李架上的包是您的吗？

Take-off（起飞）

1. The plane is taking off. Please fasten your seat belt.

　飞机就要起飞了，请系好您的安全带。

2. Put the back of your seat in an upright position. 把座位靠背放到垂直的位置。

On the flight（在飞行途中）

1. The forecast says the weather is fine，and we are expecting a smooth flight all the way.

　预报的天气很好，我们可望全程平稳飞行。

2. Could I have a blanket for my son，please? 请问能给我儿子拿条毯子吗？

3. I'm feeling a bit airsick. 我觉得有点儿晕机。

4. I feel like vomiting. 我觉得想吐。

5. Please give me a paper bag. 请给我一个纸袋。

6. I don't feel well. Can you give me a glass of water? 我感到不舒服，能给我一杯水吗？

7. Could you give me some medicine for air sickness? 能给我点儿晕机药吗？

Landing（降落）

1. We seem to approaching Beijing. 我们好像快要飞抵北京了。

2. We have been flying for 3 hours. When are we due to land?

　我们已经飞行了整整3个小时。我们该在什么时候降落。

3. The plane is landing down. 飞机正在降落。

4. We'd better put our seats upright. We're going to land in a minute.

　我们最好把座椅靠背调直。马上就要降落了。

Airport traffic（机场交通车）

Inquire（询问）

1. Is there an airport bus to the city? 去市内有机场交通车吗？

2. What time is the next bus? 下一班车什么时候开？

Answer（回答）

1. There is a bus from here every half an hour or so. The bus stop is right over there.

　每隔半小时左右有一班交通车，车站就在那儿。

2. There is an airport bus that goes into the city every hour on the hour.

　每小时整点有一班机场交通车开往市里。

Section Five：Culture Tips

飞机的由来

　　千百年来，人类为实现遨游太空的理想，不知做了多少次冒险的尝试。1896年8月12日，德国滑翔机专家奥托·利连撒尔在经过两千多次滑翔之后，失事殒命。这个消息传到美国俄亥俄州的代顿城，引起了自行车修理工莱特兄弟（威尔伯·莱特和奥维尔·莱特）的极大关注。这两位没有受过高等教育的年轻人，经过刻苦自学钻研和无数次模型试验，在总结前人经验的基础上，终于在1903年秋制造了世界上第一架动力飞机"飞行者号"。这是一架用轻质木料做骨架，蒙上帆布的较简陋的双翼飞机，它靠一台12马力的汽油内燃机推动螺旋桨，有活动的方向舵操纵升降和左右盘旋，驾驶者能俯卧在下层主翼的正中进行操纵。1903 年 12 月 17 日上午 10 时 35 分，"飞行者号"由奥维尔·莱特驾驶，在一个沙丘上做了首次飞行。尽管只飞了 35 米远（时间为 12 秒），然而这是人类历史上第一次成功的动力载人飞行。以后，经过科学家们无数次的改进，终于有了现代飞机。

译　文

第二部分：相关信息

第一次乘飞机旅行指南

首次乘坐飞机的人可能会问很多关于如何乘坐飞机的问题。在哪里和怎样买机票？当到达机场时该做什么？如何通过安全检查？以下步骤可以帮助你解决这些问题。

步骤 1：买票

最简单的购票方式是在网上搜索机票。找到一个机票搜索引擎，输入你的出发城市、到达城市和日期，然后，该引擎将列出一系列符合你标准的航班。选择一个适合你的航班。当你准备购买机票时，单击它选择并遵循购票说明进行购买。通常，航空公司会向你发送一封确认的电子邮件和电子机票号码。

步骤 2：采集照片身份证明

如果你在国内旅行，你需要一张身份证。如果你乘坐国际航班，你将需要一张护照，有效期为自离境之日起六个月。

步骤 3：确保您的行李符合航空公司的要求

注意限重，一定不能超重，否则你得付超重行李费。至于你的随身行李，你需要仔细打包。你可以用一个单独的瓶子携带不超过 100 毫升的液体上飞机，且瓶子用可封口的、透明塑料袋包装。机场工作人员将没收任何不符合他们规定的液体或凝胶。

步骤 4：提前到达机场

第一次乘坐飞机，给自己留出多余的时间通过机场，并熟悉这个过程。为了给自己足够的时间，乘坐国内航班至少要提前两个小时到达，国际航班则要提前三小时。

步骤 5：在航空公司的柜台办理登机手续

按照指示标志到检票台，并将你的身份证交给工作人员。他将查看你的预订，打印登机牌，并收取托运行李的费用。如果你没有选择座位，这个时候你也可以要求工作人员给你选择窗口或过道座位。你将被要求将你托运的行李放在桌子旁边的秤上称重，它们将被贴上标签并放到传送带上，送上飞机。然后你可以从他或她那儿领取登机牌和身份证。

步骤 6：通过安检

在安检处，你将被要求出示身份证和登机牌。一旦你站在检测机前，脱下你的外套或夹克，连同你的手表、电话甚至钥匙，然后把它们放入一个塑料箱内。如果你随身携带笔记本电脑，把它放进一个单独的箱子里，然后把它连同你的随身行李一起放到传送带上。等待一个工作人员通过金属探测器对你进行检查，并走过。然后取回你的物品。

步骤 7：登机

你的登机牌上应该有登机口号码；如果没有，请查看电子显示屏，找到你的航班号和登机口号码。按照指示标志到达你的登机口，并找个位置坐下，直到工作人员要求登机。登机后通过检查每排座位上方的号码找到你的座位。

步骤8：取行李

一旦你的航班降落，下了飞机，要遵循标识认领行李。你的航班号和出发城市将显示在一个电子显示屏上；等到传送带开始移动，你的行李就到了。

第三部分：情境任务范例

情境1： 李欣来到售票处购买两张从北京到厦门的机票。这是李欣和售票员的对话。（A：李欣；B：售票员）

A：从北京到厦门今天有哪些航班？

B：每天上午8:20我们有从北京起飞的直达班机。

A：要飞多长时间？

B：需要两个小时。

A：经济舱的票价是多少？

B：从北京到厦门的经济舱票价是2,300元。

A：我想要两张去厦门的经济舱机票。

B：好的。中国南方航空公司702航班，将在早上8:20起飞。请问您怎样付款？

A：微信支付。

B：好的。这是您的票。

A：谢谢。

情境2： 李欣是第一次乘飞机，机场工作人员王小姐给了他一些帮助。（A：李欣；C：王小姐）

A：不好意思，这是我第一次坐飞机。我该怎么登机呢？

C：我能看一下您的机票吗？

A：好的，给你。

C：您可以到那个柜台去取登机牌。您有什么需要托运的吗？

A：没有，我只有一个手提包。

C：那么安检之后您可以在候机大厅等候上机了。

A：非常感谢。

情境3： 一位空姐/机上乘务员帮助李欣系好安全带。（A：李欣；D：空姐）

A：打扰一下，我的安全带好像出了点儿问题。

D：怎么了？

A：扣不上了。

D：我帮您看一下……您忘了拉开这个搭扣了。

A：哦，谢谢。

（李欣问空姐/机上乘务员要晕机药。）

A：对不起。我有点儿晕机。你能给我一些晕机药吗？

D：好的。您还要点儿别的吗？

A：是的，你能给我一杯水吗？

D：好的。给你。

A：非常感谢。

情境 4：李欣和他的朋友约翰在飞机上交谈。（A：李欣；E：约翰）

E：你坐飞机系安全带吗？

A：当然了，安全第一啊。

E：我很少系，也没出什么事啊。

A：老兄，你最好还是系上吧。

······

A：我们已经飞了将近 3 个小时了。我们该在什么时候着陆？

E：我们似乎快到厦门了。

A：我们最好把座位竖起来。我们将在几分钟后着陆。

E：好的。

7.3   Stay in a Hotel

Section One: Tasks

Situation 1: *Wang Jian is going to be on business in Shenzhen. He plans to live in Home Inn Hotel and is making a reservation by telephone. Make a dialogue according to the situation.*

Situation 2: *Wang Jian arrived at the Home Inn Hotel he reserved in Shenzhen. He is checking in at the reception desk. Make a dialogue according to the situation.*

Situation 3: *Wang Jian found that the air-conditioner doesn't work, so he called the receptionist. Make a dialogue according to the situation.*

Situation 4: *Wang Jian planned to check out, so he called the receptionist first and then came to the reception desk to settle the bill. Make a dialogue according to the situation.*

Section Two: Related Information

Different Types of Star Hotels

The hospitality industry offers a variety of hotels ranging from one-star to five-star and super deluxe hotels to cater to the different preferences of travelers. Here's an overview of what's on offer in the different star-rated hotels so you can choose the right hotel for your next holiday.

One-star hotels

These hotels offer basic bedding and bathroom facilities. The furniture, decor, etc. may not be of high quality, but is mostly comfortable. Arrangements for meals may or may not be included, but if they are, this could be restricted to breakfast only. And remember in one-star hotels you won't have bell-boys[1] or hotel staff available for carrying your luggage.

Two-star hotels

The extra star here is for a proper reception desk and some amount of staff presence. Breakfast could be complimentary, but you will need to pay for other meals. Because of the limited staff, there won't be room service. Two-star hotels are suitable for people with limited budgets who are travelling with their families and need a safe place to stay.

Three-star hotels

These are better furnished and have restaurants where you could have your meals. Other amenities could include a TV set in the room, direct dial telephone, some room service, etc. Three-star hotels are mostly good for business travellers who are travelling for a short period on business. They are generally part of a large chain and have branches in more than one location.

Four-star hotels

The premium variety of hotels starts from here. You can expect larger rooms, better decor, more amenities, better services like availability of porters, 24-hour room service, laundry, and multi-cuisine restaurants, etc. Four-star hotels are mostly used by corporate travellers where the company pays for the stay.

Five-star hotels

In a five-star hotel, you can enjoy breakfast served in bed, shoes polished, clothes washed and facilities for getting almost everything done without even lifting a finger. Other facilities include huge lobbies, round-the-clock room service[2], swimming pools, gyms, sauna, beauty salons, badminton/tennis courts··· the list is endless. The staff in these hotels mostly comprised by graduates majored in hotel management from the best schools, are well-trained in customer service, crisis management, etc. The five-star hotel clienteles[3] always include big names from the fields of entertainment, business, and sports, and of course, the well-heeled[4] crowd.

Five-star deluxe hotels

The so-called deluxe/luxury hotels which mainly cater to the movers and shakers of the world always have a private balcony, personal masseur, king-sized beds[5], etc. The most well-known brands belonging to this category include the Taj, Hilton, Leela Palace[6], etc.

Nowadays there are some that claim to be seven-star hotels. The Burj Al Arab Hotel in Dubai[7] is one such super deluxe hotel. The 54-storey beach-side hotel boasts of ferrying its customers in Rolls Royce cars[8], transporting guests to the airport by helicopter and lots more.

Vocabulary

hospitality [ˌhɔspɪ'tæləti] *n*. 殷勤好客；招待；款待

deluxe [də'lʌks] *adj*. 豪华的；高级的

overview ['əuvəvjuː] *n*. 概述

facility [fə'sɪləti] *n*. 设备

decor ['deɪkɔː(r)] *n*. 装饰风格；布置；装饰

complimentary [ˌkɔmplɪ'mentrɪ] *adj*. 赠送的；赞美的

budget ['bʌdʒɪt] *n*. 预算

furnish ['fɜːnɪʃ] *vt*. 陈设；布置；装修（房屋）

premium ['priːmiəm] *adj*. 优质的；高昂的

amenity [ə'miːnəti] *n*. （环境等的）舒适；便利设施

porter ['pɔːtə(r)] *n*. 门童；搬运工人

cuisine　[kwɪˈziːn]　*n.* 菜肴

polish　[ˈpɔlɪʃ]　*v.* 润色；擦光

sauna　[ˈsɔːnə]　*n.* 桑拿浴；桑拿房

badminton　[ˈbædmɪntən]　*n.* 羽毛球；羽毛球运动

comprise　[kəmˈpraɪz]　*vt.* 包含；由……组成

clientele　[ˌkliːənˈtel]　*n.* 顾客；客户

heel　[hiːl]　*n.* 脚后跟

balcony　[ˈbælkəni]　*n.* 阳台

masseur　[mæˈsɜː(r)]　*n.* 男按摩师

ferry　[ˈferi]　*vt.* 渡运，运送；*vi.* 摆渡

range from…to…　范围从……到……

cater to　面向；供应伙食；迎合

be of high quality　质量高

boast of　夸耀；吹嘘

Notes

1. bell-boy 酒店服务员，也可称为 bell-man

2. round-the-clock room service 24 小时客房服务；round-the-clock 时钟走一圈，指代任何时间

3. clientele（企业、商店、专业人士等为之提供服务的）主顾，委托人；client：（律师等专业人士的）委托人，当事人，或者买东西、服务的顾客，客人。二者的主要区别是，前者通常用得比较夸张、正式，或者说使用者一般属于上流社会；而后者则使用较随意。

4. well-heeled　有钱的；富有的

5. king-sized bed　特大号的床

6. Taj，Hilton，Leela Palace　泰姬酒店，希尔顿酒店，莉拉宫

7. The Burj Al Arab Hotel in Dubai　迪拜的帆船酒店

8. Rolls Royce cars 劳斯莱斯汽车

Section Three：Situational Task Samples

Situation 1：*Li Xin is going to be on business in Qingdao. He plans to live in Holiday Inn* [1] *and is making a reservation by telephone.*（*A*：*Receptionist* [2] *of the hotel*；*B*：*Li Xin*）

A：Holiday Inn，what can I do for you?

B：I'd like to make a reservation for the night of June 1st.

A：What kind of room would you like?

B：Single room [3] with air-conditioning.

A：Let me check. Sorry，we have no single room available here. How about a standard room?

B：Well，how much is it?

A：380 yuan a night，including breakfast.

B：OK.

A：May I have your name，please?

B：Li Xin.

A：When will you arrive?

B：Around 3 o'clock that afternoon.

A：OK，we'll keep the room for you until 6 p. m.

B：OK，thank you!

A：You are welcome.

Situation 2：*Li Xin arrived at the Holiday Inn Hotel he reserved in Qingdao. He is checking in at the reception desk.*（*B*：*Li Xin*；*C*：*The receptionist*）

C：Good afternoon. Can I help you?

B：Good afternoon. I booked a room last week. My name is Li Xin.

C：Would you excuse me for a minute while I check our list?

B：OK.

C：Our reservation record shows that you want a standard room. Is that correct?

B：Yes.

C：We have a nice room for you. It's number 320. Could you just complete the form，please?

B：OK.

C：We require a deposit⁴ of 500 yuan.

B：Do you accept traveller's check⁵?

C：Yes，we do.

C：Would you like to order some room service?

B：Yes，I'd like a wake-up call at 6 o'clock tomorrow morning.

C：OK. Is there anything else?

B：By the way，I'm expecting a package from Yantai. Please inform me if it arrives.

C：No problem. We'll inform you as soon as it arrives. Let me call a bell-boy to take your bags up for you.

B：No，thank you. I only have one bag. I can manage it myself.

C：Enjoy your stay. Dinner is served from six o'clock till ten. The dining room is down there，through the door on the right.

B：Thank you very much.

C：You're welcome.

Situation 3：*Li Xin found that there was something wrong with the facilities，so he called the receptionist.*（*B*：*Li Xin*；*C*：*The receptionist*）

C：Good evening，sir. What can I do for you?

B：There is no hot water in my room. Besides，I don't think the air-conditioner works.

C：I'm sorry，sir. I will call the Engineering Department immediately. We will see to it.

B：I hope you can fix it quickly. You know it is really hard for me to go to sleep in such a hot room.

C：We will do our best. Do you mind to sit in our mini-bar for a while? We can offer you a free cold drink.

B：That's fine.

C：Sorry for the trouble.

B：It doesn't matter.

Situation 4：*Li Xin planned to check out* [6] *, so he came to the reception desk to settle the bill.*（*B：Li Xin；C：The receptionist*）

B：I want to check out. My name is Li Xin，Room 320.

C：Here is your bill. The total including tax for one day is 540 yuan.

B：Can I pay by credit card?

C：Certainly. Your card，please?

B：Here you are.

C：Thank you. Please sign your name right here. OK，here is your receipt. Please keep it.

B：Thank you. I really enjoy my stay here.

C：I am glad to hear that. We look forward to serving you again.

Notes

1. Holiday Inn 假日酒店

2. receptionist 前台服务人员；reception desk 前台

3. single room 单人房。常见的酒店房型还有 double room 双人房；standard room 标准间

4. deposit 押金，保证金

5. traveller's check 旅行支票

6. check out 退房结账，办理离店手续。通知服务员核查该房内原有物件和饮品小食是否齐全，是否损坏弄脏和客人是否遗下物件。也要留意客人是否由房间内打出付费电话，在酒店内的饭店及消费场所是否签单消费，总结无误扣除应收款项收回押金单据，退回余款和单据给客人，也不要忘记说一声多谢，请他下次再来光顾，并祝客人一路顺风。

check in 指办理入住登记手续，是要给客人填写入住表格，内容包括：姓名、性别、国籍、居住地、身份证（外国人护照）号码、联络电话、入住日期和天数。客人支付押金及酒店给回押金单据等。然后前台服务人员将酒店房间门钥匙交给客人。

Section Four：Functional Expression Bank

Reserve a room（预订房间）

Guests（客人预订）

1. I would like a room for two on Sunday. 我想订一个周日的双人房间。

2. I'd like to make reservations for the nights of June 1st and 2nd.
   我想预订 6 月 1 日和 2 日两晚的房间。

3. Can I book a double room from 12th of July to 20th of October.

我可以预订从 7 月 12 日到 10 月 20 日的一个双人间吗？

4. Please reserve me a suite of two rooms for 10 days beginning from tomorrow.

请给我订一间两室的套房，从明天开始，用 10 天。

5. Would you reserve a room in the name of Anna Steward? A single room for two nights.

你以安娜·斯图尔特的名字订一间房好吗？一个单人间，住两个晚上。

6. I booked a standard room three days ago. I'm Kate Winn.

我三天前订了一个标准间，我叫凯特·温英。

7. My name is John. I have a reservation here for a family room with a spare bed.

我叫约翰，我在这里订了一个家庭房，外加一张床。

Receptionist（酒店前台）

1. Would you excuse me for a minute while I check our list?

请稍等片刻让我查一下订单好吗？

2. Could you give me your initial? 可以告诉我您姓名的首字母吗？

3. Yes，we have your reservation right here，Mr. Brown.

对的，布朗先生，我们这里有您的预订。

4. Our reservation record shows that you want a standard room. Is that correct?

我们的预订登记上写着，您要一个标准间，对吗？

5. Yes，we have a nice room for you. It's number 219. Now will you please register?

对的，我们为您准备了一个好房间，是 219。请登记好吗？

Introduction of available rooms（介绍可提供的客房情况）

1. It's a suite room，facing the sea. 是一个面向大海的套间。

2. The room commands a good view of the mountain. 从那个房间可以望见很美的山景。

3. We can let you have a double room on the fourth floor. It's a valley-view room with bath.

我们可以在四楼提供一间双人房，有浴室，望出去是山谷。

4. You can have a room with either a queen- or a king-size bed.

你可以有一个房间，内有一张大号或特大号床。

5. I'm afraid some of you will have to double up because there aren't enough rooms.

房间不够了，恐怕你们有几位只能两人合住一间了。

Guests' specific room requirements（客人提出具体的住房要求）

1. I want a single room with bath，with an ocean view，if possible.

我要一个带浴室的单人间，可能的话，面对大海的。

2. I'd prefer a room overlooking the lake. 我想要一间俯瞰湖泊的房间。

3. Do you have a room with a waterbed? 有没有带水床的房间？

Talk about the room price（谈论房价）

Guests（客人）

1. How much is a presidential suite? 一间总统套房要多少钱？

2. How much do you charge for the room? 这间房要多少钱？

3. Does that include breakfast?（这个价钱）包含早餐吗？

4. Does that include tax? （这个价钱）包含税金吗？

5. Do you give discount rate for a week or more? 住一周以上是否可以打折？

Receptionist（酒店前台）

1. The singles range from ＄35 to ＄65 per night. 单间每夜从 35～65 美元。

2. It's ＄30 for a single and ＄45 for a double. 单人间 30 美元，双人间 45 美元。

3. ＄45 a night，including two meals：breakfast and dinner. 45 美元一夜，包括早晚两餐。

4. The room is ＄50 a night. The tax is extra. 这房间是 50 美元一晚，税金另算。

5. We give 10% discount for one week，15% for two weeks and over.
   住满一周价格优惠 10%，住两周或两周以上的优惠 15%。

Check-in（办理住宿登记）

1. Would you fill out/in the registration form，please? Here is a pen.
   请填写住宿登记表好吗？这里有笔。

2. Would you please complete this registration card? 填一下住宿登记卡好吗？

3. Here is a pen. Could you sign your name，please? 这里有笔，请您签个字好吗？

4. We require a deposit of ＄100. 我们要求支付 100 美元的保证金（押金）。
   I'm afraid we have to ask for a deposit of ＄300.
   恐怕我们得要求支付 300 美元的保证金（押金）。

5. We'll have to ask you to pay in advance. 我们要求预先支付。

6. We hope you'll have a pleasant stay here. 希望您在这里过得愉快。

7. I'll call the bell-boy to show you to your room. 我来叫行李员带您去房间。

8. The bell-man will take your bags up for you. 行李员会把您的行李送上去的。

Introduce service items（介绍服务项目）

1. If you need anything，please ring us. 需要什么，请给我们打电话。

2. If you have any laundry，just leave it in the laundry bag over there.
   如果有要洗的衣服，请放在那边的洗衣袋里。

3. The hotel telephone operator will call you if you ask for a wake-up call for the time you
   want. 酒店电话接线员可以根据您需要的时间，随时叫醒您。

4. The hotel provides various kinds of entertainment in the evening.
   晚间酒店提供各种各样的娱乐活动。

5. Our hotel has facilities for business meetings and conventions.
   我们酒店提供商务会议所需的设施。

6. There are reception rooms for meetings on every floor. 每个楼层都有供开会使用的接待室。

Ask the receptionist for help（要求前台接待员代办事情）
Guests（客人）

1. I'm expecting a package from London. Please inform me if it arrives.
   我在等一个伦敦来的邮包，到了请通知我。

2. We're going out for a walk. If anyone comes to visit，please ask him to wait.
   我们出去散散步，如果有人来访，请让他稍等。

3. Put in a call for me at 7：00 tomorrow morning. 请于明早 7 点钟叫我。

Receptionist（酒店前台）

1. A Mr. White has called to see you. 一位怀特先生来找过您。

2. There's a message left by a lady half an hour ago. 半小时前有一位女士给您留了言。

3. Mrs. Stone，you have a letter and a fax. 斯通太太，您有一封信和一份传真。

Guests' complaint（客人投诉）

1. I'd like to talk to the manager. 我想找经理说话。

2. Will you call the manager for me? 请帮我叫一下经理好吗?

3. My room is too noisy. I wonder if I can change it for a quiet one，please.
   我那房间太吵了，能否给我换一间安静一点的。

4. I think I need another blanket. It was a bit chilly last night.
   我想我需要一条毯子，昨天夜里有点儿冷。

5. The bathroom light in my room doesn't work. Could you have somebody come and fix it?
   我房间的浴室灯坏了，能不能找人来修一下。

Check-out（结账）

Guests（客人）

1. I want to check out. My name is…Room 502. 我要结账，我的名字是……502 号房间。

2. Can I have my bill now? I'm leaving in half an hour.
   现在可以给我账单吗? 我半个小时后要走。

3. I'd like to pay my bill now. I'm checking out at 11：40. 我现在想结账，我准备 11：40 走。

4. I'd like to settle the bill in advance so that we won't feel rushed tomorrow morning.
   我希望提前结好账，这样明天早上就不用太匆忙了。

5. Will you make out two separate bills for me? You see，I pay for my meals and my company pays for the room. 请你把账分开算好吗? 我自己负责餐费，公司替我付房费。

6. Will you please send me a porter to carry my baggage downstairs?
   请你为我叫一个服务员帮我把行李搬到楼下，好吗?

Receptionist（酒店前台）

1. Check-out time/The checking out time is 12：00 a. m. You will be charged for a full day if you don't check out before noon.
   结账时间是中午十二点，如果您十二点之前不结账，您得再付一整天的房费。

2. Here's your bill. The total including tax for the four days is $ 516.
   这是您的账单，四天包括税金总共是 516 美元。

3. Your bill comes to $ 339. You can pay with cash or traveler's check or with a credit card. 总计是 339 美元，您可以用现金或旅行支票或信用卡进行支付。

Room types（酒店基本房型）

standard room 标准房   business room 商务房

superior room 高级房   mountain-view room 山景房

deluxe room 豪华房   city-view room 市景房

lake-view room 湖景房

ocean-view room 海景房

river-view room 江景房

executive room 行政房

special promotion 特价房

twin room 双床房

queen room 大床房

single room 单人间

double room 双人间

triple room 三人间

family room 家庭房

suite 套房

superior suite 高级套房

deluxe suite 豪华套房

business suite 商务套房

executive suite 行政套房

presidential suite 总统套房

Section Five：Culture Tips

酒店的起源与发展

酒店起源于古代，随着商品经济的出现，因为商人的旅行导致了酒店最早的雏形——客栈的产生。

我国酒店业的发展

我国是世界上最早出现酒店的国家之一。殷商时代的驿站，就是最早的外出住宿设施。周王朝时出现的馆舍由专人管理，供各种官客沿途食宿。其中"侯馆"的规模比较大，相当于现在的宾馆或高级招待所，而当时接待一般旅客的旅馆泛称为"逆旅"。秦汉、魏晋时代，也都有专门提供食宿和服务的设施。到了唐代，随着经济和对外贸易的发展，人口的增长，使酒店业有了较快的发展。当时首都长安等大城市有不同等级和性质的酒店供各阶层人士居住，还有专门接待外宾的"四方馆"等。明清时代北京设有"会同馆"，以接待外国使臣和国内各兄弟民族的代表。现代酒店在我国的出现，只不过是近百年的事。这些酒店，在南方称为大酒店，在北方称为大饭店，是专为帝国主义官商和达官贵人服务的。

西方酒店业的发展

西方大约在古希腊和罗马时代就已存在了酒店的雏形——客栈，但直到19世纪才开始大规模兴起。国外酒店业从最早的驿站、客栈、旅店到现代化的大酒店、国际连锁酒店公司，大体经历了四个发展时期。

1.客栈时期：这是酒店最早的雏形。

2.大酒店时期：在19世纪的欧洲，随着上流社会极为奢侈生活方式的蔓延，专为王室、贵族、大资产阶级服务的豪华酒店应运而生。

3.商务酒店时期：到了20世纪初期，随着世界经济的发展，新市场的开辟，导致了商务旅游的急剧增长。商务酒店的特点是提供完善的设备和设施，进行优良服务，使旅游者感到舒适、方便、清洁、安全，而价格便宜合理。美国人斯塔特勒在布法罗建造的一家有300间客房的"斯塔特勒酒店"。该酒店应用科学的管理方法，实现了成本低、效益高的经济效果。此酒店的出现标志着酒店业进入了一个新的历史时期。

4.新型酒店时期：新型酒店时期也称酒店联号（连锁酒店）阶段。美国是世界上实行酒店连锁管理最早、最大和最多的国家。

译　文

第二部分：相关信息

不同类型的星级酒店

　　酒店业提供了各种各样的酒店，从一星级到五星级和超豪华酒店，以满足不同喜好的旅客。这是一篇关于不同的星级酒店提供什么服务的概述，以便你可以为下次的假期选择合适的酒店。

一星级的酒店

　　这些酒店提供基本的床上用品和卫浴设施。家具、装饰等可能质量不高，但大多舒适。膳食安排可能会或可能不会包括在内，但如果包含，可能也仅限于早餐。而且请记住，在一星级酒店不会有服务员或酒店工作人员帮你搬运行李。

二星级的酒店

　　这里额外的一颗星是由于有一个正式的接待台和一些员工。早餐可能是免费的，但你需要支付其他膳食。由于工作人员有限，所以没有客房服务。两星级酒店是适合那些预算有限的与家人一起旅行，并需要一个安全的地方住的人。

三星级的酒店

　　这里的家具更好，并且有供您就餐的餐厅。其他便利设施包括房间内的电视机，直拨电话，一些客房服务等。三星级酒店大多适合商务旅行者短期出差居住。它们通常是一个大型连锁酒店的一部分，并在多个地点都有分店。

四星级的酒店

　　从四星级酒店开始就是优质酒店。你可以期待较大的房间，更好的装修，更加舒适的环境，更好的服务。如搬运服务，24 小时客房服务，洗衣服务和各色菜式的餐厅等。四星级酒店主要接待那些由公司支付住宿费的人员。

五星级的酒店

　　在五星级酒店里，你可以享受在床上吃早餐服务，擦鞋服务，洗衣服务，以及甚至不需要动手指头就可将几乎一切工作都做好的服务。其他服务设施包括巨大的大厅，24 小时客房服务、游泳池、健身房、桑拿、美容美发沙龙、羽毛球或网球场……无穷无尽的项目。这些酒店的工作人员主要由从最好的学校毕业的酒店管理专业的毕业生组成。他们在客户服务、危机管理等方面接受过良好的培训。五星级酒店的主顾包括娱乐、商业和体育界的明星大腕，当然也有富人群体。

五星级豪华酒店

　　所谓的豪华酒店主要面向国际名流们，通常拥有私人阳台、私人按摩师、特大号的床等。属于这一类最知名的品牌酒店包括泰姬酒店、希尔顿酒店、莉拉宫等。

　　如今有一些自称是七星级的酒店。迪拜的帆船酒店就是这样一家超级豪华的酒店。这家 54 层楼的海滩边的酒店宣称拥有运送客户的劳斯莱斯汽车，运送客人去机场的直升机以及更多的服务。

第三部分：情境任务范例

情境 1：李欣将要去青岛出差，他打算住在假日酒店。他正在打电话预订房间。（A：酒店

前台接待员；B：李欣)

A：这里是假日酒店，有什么能为您服务的吗？

B：我想预订 6 月 1 日晚上的房间。

A：您想要什么房型？

B：带空调的单人间。

A：让我查查。对不起，没有单人间了。标准间可以吗？

B：那要多少钱呢？

A：一晚 380 元，含早餐。

B：好的。

A：能告诉我您的名字吗？

B：李欣。

A：您什么时候到？

B：那天下午 3 点左右。

A：好的，我们会为您保留房间到晚上 6 点。

B：好的，谢谢你！

A：不客气。

情境 2：*李欣到达了他预订的青岛的这家假日酒店，他正在前台办理入住登记。（B：李欣；C：前台接待员)*

C：下午好，有什么能帮到您吗？

B：下午好，我上周订了一间房。我叫李欣。

C：请稍等片刻让我查一下单子好吗？

B：好的。

C：我们的预订登记上写着，您要一个标准间，对吗？

B：是的。

C：我们为您准备了一个好房间，是 320 房间。请填表登记好吗？

B：好的。

C：我们要求支付 500 元的保证金。

B：你们接受旅行支票吗？

C：是的，我们接受。

C：您要不要订客房服务？

B：是的。请明天早上 6 点钟提供叫醒服务。

C：好的。还需要其他服务吗？

B：顺便说一下，我在等一个烟台来的包裹，到了请通知我。

C：没问题。包裹一到我们就通知您。我叫个服务员把您的行李送上去。

B：不用，谢谢。我就一个包。我自己就行了。

C：祝您住宿愉快。晚餐从六点钟开始一直到十点。餐厅就在那儿，穿过门向右转。

B：非常感谢。

C：不客气。

情境 3：*李欣发现房间设备有些问题，于是他给前台接待员打了个电话。（B：李欣；C：*

前台接待员）

C：先生，晚上好。有什么我能帮忙的吗？

B：房间里没有热水，而且，空调好像也坏了。

C：对不起，先生，我现在就给工程部打电话。我们会尽快处理此事的。

B：我希望你们能尽快修理好，要知道，在这么热的房间里是很难睡着的。

C：我们会尽力的。您介意到我们的迷你酒吧坐一会儿吗？您可以尝一尝我们为您准备的免费冷饮。

B：好吧。

C：对给您带来的麻烦深表歉意。

B：没关系。

情境 4：李欣打算退房，于是他来到前台结账。（B：李欣；C：前台接待员）

B：我要结账，我的名字是李欣，320 房间。

C：这是您的账单，一天包括税金总共是 540 元。

B：我能用信用卡支付吗？

C：当然。请把您的卡给我，好吗？

B：给你。

C：谢谢，请在这里签名。好了，这是您的收据，请拿好。

B：谢谢你，我在贵酒店住得很愉快。

C：很高兴您这样说，希望有机会再为您服务。

7. 4　Business Negotiation

Section One: Tasks

Situation 1: *Susan, purchasing manager of TEK Company, is in business negotiation with Mr. Zhang, the representative of XYZ Company. As the representative of her company, Susan wants to order 1,000 mobile phones from XYZ Company. Make a dialogue on the price discussion with Mr. Zhang.*

Situation 2: *Make a dialogue on the discussion of terms of payment according to situation 1.*

Situation 3: *Make a dialogue on the discussion of shipment according to situation 1.*

Situation 4: *Make a dialogue on the sales confirmation according to situation 1.*

Section Two: Related Information

How to Negotiate in Business

Business is negotiation. You will negotiate to buy, to sell, to conclude contracts with suppliers, to fix the staff salaries and so on. What is more, you have to negotiate with regulators, banks and insurances. It means that the business life is a permanent negotiation with other people who are defending their own interests. [1]

Pre-negotiation

Before you decide to negotiate, it is a good idea to prepare. What is it exactly that you want to negotiate? You should carefully study your file, take notes, and then set out your objective[2]. What is involved? Know your extremes: how much extra can you afford to give to reach an agreement?

Know what your opponent is trying to achieve by their negotiation. This is useful information that could be used to your benefit and may well be used to reach a final agreement.

Negotiating

It is important that you approach the other party directly. The appointment should be made in person, writing or by phone, which will allow you to set the agenda in advance. [3]

Therefore, it's time to negotiate and you've prepared well. What else must you have? Two things: confidence and power. Confidence comes from knowing your business, your product as well as its worth, and being able to communicate these well with the other party. Your power will come from your ability to influence. It is always important that you keep the negotiation in your control[4]: this can mean within your price range, your delivery time or your profit margin.

When negotiating, aim as high as you feel necessary in order to gain the best deal for yourself.

Make sure that you remain flexible throughout the negotiation in case the opponent decides to change the direction of the agreement. This is where your preparation comes to good use: knowing your limits and the other party's needs. If you're a quick thinker then you've got an advantage. You'll need to turn it around quickly if things start to go against you without putting your objectives at risk. [5]

Vocabulary

negotiate [nɪ'ɡəʊʃieɪt] *vi.* 谈判，协商，交涉；　*vt.* 谈判达成

negotiation [nɪ,ɡəʊʃi'eɪʃn] *n.* 协商，谈判

supplier [sə'plaɪə(r)] *n.* 供应商

regulator ['reɡjuleɪtə(r)] *n.* 调整者，监管者

permanent ['pɜːmənənt] *adj.* 永久（性）的，永恒的，不变的

extreme [ɪk'striːm] *adj.* 极端的，极限的

opponent [ə'pəʊnənt] *n.* 对手；敌手；反对者

flexible ['fleksəbl] *adj.* 灵活的；柔韧的

negotiate with sb 与某人进行谈判/交涉/协商

conclude contract with sb. 与某人订立合同

what is more 此外，另外

reach an agreement 达成协议

profit margin 利润率

in case 以防，万一，免得

Notes

1. It means that the business life is a permanent negotiation with other people who are defending their own interests. 这意味着，商业活动永远是为了维护自己利益与其他人进行的交涉。这里 who 引导限制性定语从句，修饰先行词 other people；negotiate with sb. 与某人进行交涉。

2. set out your objective 设定你的目标；set out one's objective 设定某人的目标

3. It is important that you approach the other party directly. The appointment should be made in person, writing or by phone, which will allow you to set the agenda in advance. 很重要的一点是，你应该直接约见对方。亲自或书面或电话预约，这样可以让你提前确定日程。make an appointment to do 预约/约定做某事；in person 亲自，亲身；set the agenda 制订日程；in advance 提前，事先；that 在句中引导主语从句。

4. keep the negotiation in your control 使得谈判在你的控制之下；keep sth. in one's control 使得某物在某人的控制之下

5. You'll need to turn it around quickly if things start to go against you without putting your objectives at risk. 如果事情开始不利于你的目标，你就需要迅速扭转局势。turn around 用法很多，可以意为"（使）转身，（使）好转，改变意见，使变得完全不同"，此处指"扭转局势"；go against 意为"违背"，此处指"朝着不利于你的方向发展"；put sth. at

risk 把某物置于危险之中；without 是介词，后面若跟动词，则用动名词形式。

Section Three: Situational Task Samples

Situation: *James Brown Co. Ltd. wants to order some chinaware from ABC Trade Company. They are in business negotiation on this matter.（A: The seller Li Xin, sales manager in ABC Trade Company; B: The buyer Miss Cai, the representative of James Brown Co. Ltd.）*

Meet each other for the first time

A: Good morning, Miss Cai. This is the first time that I've had the pleasure of meeting you in person.

B: Good morning, Mr. Li. Nice to meet you, too.

Discussion on price

A: I hope we can settle the price for our chinaware through your visit.

B: I think so. We came here to talk to you about our requirements of HX Series chinaware. Have you got the catalogues for this line?

A: We've specially made out a price-list which covers those most popular items on your market. Here you are.

B: Oh, it's very considerate of you. If you excuse me, I'll go over your price-list right now.

A: Take your time, Miss Cai.

B: Mr. Li, after going over your price-list and catalogues, we are interested in No. HX1005 and No. HX1328 products, but we found that your prices are much higher than those offered by other suppliers. It would be impossible for us to push any sales at such high prices[1].

A: I'm sorry to hear that. You must know that the cost of production has risen a great deal in recent years while our prices of chinaware basically remain unchanged. To be frank, our commodities have always come up to our export standard[2] and the packages are excellent designed and printed. So our products are moderately priced.

B: I'm afraid I can't agree with you in this respect. I know that your products are attractive in design, but I wish to point out[3] that your offers are higher than some other suppliers´ quotations. I've received the offers from your competitors in other countries and your price is not competitive in this market.

A: Miss Cai, as you may know, our products which are of high quality have found a good market in many countries. So you must take quality into consideration[4], too.

B: I agree with what you say, but the price difference should not be so large. If you want to get the order, you'll have to lower the price. If you are prepared to cut down your prices by 8%[5], we might come to terms.

A: 8%? I'm afraid you are asking too much. Actually, we have never given such low price. For friendship's sake[6] we may exceptionally consider reducing the price by 5%[7]. This is the highest reduction we can afford.

B：OK. I accept. We want to order 800 sets of No. HX1005 and 550 sets of No. HX1328.

A：OK.

Discussion on terms of payment[8]

B：Now, let's talk about the terms of payment. Would you accept D/P[9]? I hope it will be acceptable to you.

A：The term of payment we usually adopt is sight L/C[10].

B：But I think it would be beneficial to both of us to adopt more flexible payment terms such as D/P term.

A：Payment by L/C is our usual practice of doing business with all customers for such commodities. I'm sorry，we can't accept D/P terms.

B：All right.

Discussion on shipment

B：Well，as for shipment，the sooner，the better. When is the shipment to be made?

A：The Shipment is to be made before or on October 30，2018.

B：We have to point out that the goods are not allowed to be shipped by partial shipment[11].

A：OK. By the way，where are the ports of shipment and destination?

B：Tianjin and Toronto.

Confirmation

A：I'm glad we have brought this transaction to a successful conclusion and hope this will be the forerunner of other business in the future.

B：All right. I accept your offer of 800 sets of HX1005 at the price of USD 28 per set，and 550 sets of HX1328 at the price of USD 16 per set. Shipment is to be made no later than October 30，2018 after receipt of L/C and not allowed to be shipped by partial shipment. [12] The ports of shipment and destination are from Tianjin to Toronto. The payment term is by L/C at sight.

A：That's right. I will get the Sales Confirmation ready tomorrow for your signature. Would it be convenient for you to come again tomorrow morning?

B：OK. We expect to find a good market for your goods and hope to place further orders with you in the near future. See you tomorrow morning.

A：See you.

Notes

1. push any sales at such high prices 以如此高的价格推销任何商品。push sales 推销；at … price 以……价格

2. come up to our export standard 达到我们出口的标准

3. point out 指出

4. take…into consideration 把……考虑进去

5. cut down your prices by 8% 降价 8%；by 指下降幅度

6. for friendship's sake 出于友谊，由于友谊的缘故，也可替换为 for the sake of friendship。sake 为名词，缘故；for the sake of…由于……的缘故

7. reducing the price by 5% 降价 5%，用法同 Notes 5。

8. terms of payment 付款方式

9. D/P（documents against payment）付款交单：经济贸易交易中付款方式的一种。是出口人的交单以进口人的付款为条件，即出口人将汇票连同货运单据交给银行托收时，指示银行只有在进口人付清货款时，才能交出货运单据。按支付时间的不同，付款交单又分为即期付款交单（D/P sight）和远期付款交单（D/P after sight）。

10. L/C（Letter of Credit）信用证，是指开证银行应申请人（买方）的要求并按其指示向受益人开立的载有一定金额的、在一定的期限内凭符合规定的单据付款的书面保证文件。信用证是国际贸易中最主要、最常用的支付方式。Sight L/C 即期信用证，指开证行或付款行收到符合信用证条款的跟单汇票或装运单据后，立即履行付款义务的信用证。

11. partial shipment 分批装运

12. I accept your offer of 800 sets of HX1005 at the price of USD 28 per set, and 550 sets of HX1328 at the price of USD 16 per set. Shipment is to be made no later than October 30, 2018 after receipt of L/C and not allowed to be shipped by partial shipment. HX1005 以每套 28 美元的价格我方订货 80 套，HX1328 以每套 16 美元的价格供货，我方订购 550 套。收到信用证后不迟于 2018 年 10 月 30 日装船，不允许分批装运。no later than 不迟于……

Section Four：Functional Expression Bank

Meet someone for the first time（初次见面）

1. We know you through our correspondence，Mr. Black. I'm glad to meet you. 通过信件来往我们已经认识了，布莱克先生。很高兴见到您。

2. This is the first time that I've had the pleasure of meeting you in person.［正式］初次当面见到您，十分荣幸。

3. I was assigned to negotiate business with you. 公司指派我和您具体洽谈业务。

Explain the purpose of one's visit（说明来意）

1. We are very interested in your software. 我们对贵公司的软件很感兴趣。

2. I wish to find out the possibilities of importing some of your oil-drilling equipment. 我想了解一下进口你们的某些采油设备的可能性。

3. The purpose of my coming here is to inquire about possibilities of establishing trade relations with your corporation.
［正式］我到贵公司来的目的是想探寻与贵公司建立贸易关系的可能性。

The scope of business（介绍经营范围）

1. We are suppliers of machine tools of various types. 我们是各类机床的供货商。

2. Our company deals in computers and mobile phones. 本公司经销电脑和手机。

3. We are distributors with business branches in major cities in Canada.
   我们是经销商，在加拿大大城市里都有分销商/分公司/分店。

4. We have been in this business for more than 30 years. 我们做这一行生意已经三十多年了。

Request and provide catalogs and samples（索取与提供商品目录和样品）

1. Have you got the catalog for this line? 你们有这方面的目录吗？

2. Would it be possible for me to have a closer look at your samples?
   ［委婉］能不能让我仔细看一下你的样品。

3. There might be a few of your models we'd be interested in, if I could go over your latest
   catalogs. ［委婉］要是我能看一下你们最新的商品目录，或许有我们感兴趣的样式。

4. Here are the latest catalogs and brochure. 这些是最近出的目录和产品手册。

5. We have brought with us a series of catalogs for our latest models.
   我们带来了一套最新的产品目录。

6. This is the sample. Apart from that，there is also a brochure.
   这是样品，另外还有一本产品手册。

Inquiry（询价）

1. We are thinking of placing an order for H5001. May I know the price?
   ［委婉］我们考虑订购 H5001 型，可以告诉我价格吗？

2. Would you let me have some idea of the price? ［委婉］能否给我介绍一下价格？

3. If your prices are favorable，I can place the order right away.
   如果你的价格优惠，我可以马上订货。

Quote price（报价）

1. Here are our latest price sheets. 这是我方最新的价格单。

2. I'm sure you'll find our price most favorable. 你肯定会发现我们的价格很优惠。

3. You will see that our price is highly competitive. 你会发现我方价格是很有竞争力的。

4. Our prices compare favorably with those offered by other manufacturers.
   同其他制造商比较，我们的价格很优惠。

Dispute on price（价格争议）

The buyer bargain（买方还价）

1. It is difficult for us to sell the goods，as your price is so high.
   你们的价格那么高，我们很难销售。

2. At present the supply of this commodity exceeds the demand. 目前这种商品供大于求。

3. Your price is 20% higher than that of last year. 你方的价格比去年高出 20%。

4. Your price is higher than some of the quotations we've received from other sources.
   你们的价格比我们从别处所得的报价高。

The seller insists on the original price（卖方坚持原价）

1. It's impossible for us to lower our price. 我们不可能降价。

2. That's almost cost price. 这差不多是成本价了。

3. You should take quality into consideration. 你应该考虑质量。

4. Our products are of high quality. 我们的产品质量高。

5. The cost of production has been skyrocketing in recent years. 近年来生产成本猛涨。

6. Our price is reasonable compared with that in the international market.
与国际市场价格相比，我们的价格是合理的。

7. This is our rock bottom price. No further concession can be made in this respect.
这是我们的最低价格。这方面我们不能再让步了。

Bilateral Compromise（双方妥协）

1. In order to get the business done，we're quite willing to make some concessions.
为了成交，我们很愿意做些让步。

2. If your order is large enough，we'll consider giving you some discount.
如果你们订货量大，我们可以考虑打个折扣。

3. Well，in order to encourage further business，we are prepared to cut our price by 3%.
好吧，为了促进进一步交易，我们准备降价 3%。

4. In order to conclude the transaction，we accept your price.
为了达成交易，我们接受你方的价格。

5. All right，we agree to conclude the transaction at the price of ＄450 per ton.
好吧，我们同意以每吨 450 美元的价格成交。

Order goods（订货）

Buyer（买方）

1. We want to order 600 cases. 我们想订 600 箱。

2. We'd like to place an order with your corporation for 500 TV sets.
［委婉］我们愿意向贵公司订购 500 台电视机。

3. As for this product，we'll take as many as you have in stock.
这个产品，有多少存货我们就买多少。

4. We'd like to increase the order for this product by 3,000 pieces?
［委婉］这种产品我们增订 3,000 台。

Seller（卖方）

1. As for this commodity，we can assure you of our regular supply.
这种商品，我们可以向你们保证常规的供应。

2. I think we are able to supply you with no more than 500 cases this month，and we'll let
you know when new supplies are available.
我想我们这个月最多只能向你们提供 500 箱，新货一到我们就通知你们。

3. I'm afraid we are not able to supply as much as you required.
我们恐怕无法满足你们要求的数量。

Terms of payment（付款方式）

1. Would you explain specifically your proposition about the terms of payment?
［委婉］请具体解释一下你们关于付款方式的建议好吗？

2. For large orders, we insist on payment by L/C. 对于大额订货，我们坚持以信用证付款。

3. We would prefer you to pay for your imports in U. S. dollars.

　　[委婉] 我们希望你们最好用美元支付进口货款。

4. We hope you'll agree to our request for installment payment for our present transaction.

　　我们希望你方同意我方关于目前这笔交易的分期付款要求。

Sign a contract（签合同）

1. We'll draft the contract and bring it over to you tomorrow afternoon.

　　我们将起草合同，明天下午送到你处。

2. The contract is ready. Would you mind reading it through?

　　合同已经准备好，您是否要过目？

3. It contains basically all we have agreed upon during our negotiation.

　　这份合同基本上把我们谈判达成一致的内容都写进去了。

4. Please sign your name here. 请您在这里签字。

5. The contract is in duplicate, one for each party. 本合同一式两份，双方各保存一份。

6. Now we are getting somewhere. I think a little celebration is called for.

　　现在我们有一些进展了，该小小地庆祝一下。

Section Five：Culture Tips

商务洽谈中拒绝的技巧

　　拒绝是商务洽谈中一项极难掌握且极其有用的语言技巧。拒绝的语言技巧可谓丰富多彩，最常用的有：

1. 赞赏婉拒法

　　商务洽谈中，当想要拒绝对方所提的要求或条件时，不仅要考虑理由的充分合理性，而且要尽量照顾对方的心情和自尊，所谓"责人要思其堪受"，要极力避免对抗心理的产生。最佳的选择是，赞赏加拒绝，即以赞赏的先入效应来稀释拒绝的负效应，先从对手的观点态度中找出某些非实质性的"积极点"，给对方适度的赞赏，摆出对对手的理解与尊重。然后，再就双方看法不一致的实质性内容进行阐述，达到委婉地拒绝对手的要求的目的。例如：

　　"是的，您能理解为什么事情会那样，但说实话……"

　　"是的，您在那件事上当然是正确的，但是另一方面……"

　　"您没错，您能这样说，假如我站在您的位置上，我也会这样说，但……"

2. 反问婉拒法

　　对方也许会对我方提出一些不切实际的指责或完全自利的无理要求。这种情况下，拍案而起，以尖刻的口气回击对方，并非是一种良策，甚至会中对方的"激将"之计。最好的方法是抓住对方的破绽，层层设问，环环相扣，令其无法招架，继而收回其无理要求或不切实际的指责。例如，"按此协议执行，本公司的1,500万元资金在两年内岂不'颗粒无收'吗？第三年的情况又能怎样？本公司投入资金1,500万元在两年内毫无收益，第三年情况一定能好转吗？本公司投入资金的合理利润问题将如何解决？请帮我想想办法，我很希望本公司的1,500万元资金在两年内也获得与贵方同样的30%的毛利。我方的要求过分吗？

有劳指教。"

3. 暗示拒绝法

如果对方提出的意见和要求不好回答或不值得回答，或者正面拒绝可能引起不必要的争论。这种情况下，最佳的方法是，以幽默、说笑、答非所问等形式，向对方暗示拒绝。例如"先生，您开的这个价让我怎么说好呢？如果真有这个好价钱，请您通知我，我会带上老婆孩子一块儿去买的。"

4. 强调客观拒绝法

如果对方提出的要求超过了我方所能接受的限度，而运用其他方法无法摆脱对方的纠缠时，不妨使用强调客观原因拒绝法，把对方的要求分解为若干个由于客观原因无法解决的方面，通过对"个体"的拒绝达到对"全体"的拒绝。例如，"本公司已有了一条规定：凡与合同以外的公司订货，均需领导班子集体讨论。不巧的是，另外两位经理出差去了，实在抱歉，我们今后如需再订合同，会与贵方取得联系的。"

5. 寻找借口拒绝法

当洽谈对手自恃在人际关系上的某些优势而提出过分要求时，若碍于情面不宜直接拒绝对方，可尝试以自己的权力限制、政策限制等为借口，先告诉对方事情决定于某一关键环节，而这一环节是自己无法突破的，然后，表示愿意尽最大的努力尝试突破它——这里的尝试，双方都明白是一张"空头支票"，然而却可以达到避免双方关系紧张的良效。例如，"好吧，您的要求我完全理解，只是这笔交易金额太大，要经总经理批准。这样吧，您先请回，我一定尽量向总经理转达您的意见。一有消息，我会即刻跟您联系，好吗？"

6. 允诺补偿拒绝法

商务洽谈中，对于对方的要求，如果己方不太愿意接受，最好不要用果断拒绝的方式，以免引发各种不良后果，丧失可能获得成功的机会。这种情况下，为了平衡对方因遭拒绝而造成的心理失衡，应力求在心理需求上或物质利益上对对方作稍微的补偿，以对对方要求外的让步求得对对方要求的拒绝。例如，"这样大的降价我实在无权决定了。这样吧，价格不再升降了，我给你们每台复印机都多配一盒碳粉，好吗？"

7. 自陈感觉拒绝法

为了保持融洽、和谐的洽谈气氛，双方都宜持克制的态度。若对方在洽谈中，玩弄各种计谋时，我方不宜严词抗议，而应通过陈述自己的感觉与愿望，来澄清事实，维护自身的权益。例如，"交货的保证条件这样写，怎么我总感到它与两天前的一致意见不尽相同呢？"这样，不仅含蓄地揭露了对手在语言上所玩弄的"技巧"，而且让对手难以否认，从而达到否决对方意见的目的。

译　文

第二部分：相关信息

如何进行商务谈判

商务即谈判。你在与供应商进行购买、出售、订立合同时，确定员工的工资等时候都会谈判。此外，你必须与监管机构、银行、保险公司进行谈判。这意味着，商业活动永远是为了维护自己利益与其他人进行的交涉。

谈判前

在你决定谈判之前得做好准备。你的谈判内容到底是什么？你应该仔细研究文件，做笔记，然后设定你的目标。了解谈判都包含哪些内容？知道你的底线：你能另外付出多少以达成最终的协议？

了解你的对手试图通过谈判要达成什么。这是对你有利的信息，而且可以被很好地利用以达成最终的协议。

谈判

很重要的一点是，你应该直接约见对方。亲自或书面或电话预约，这样可以让你提前确定日程。

所以，到了谈判之时你已经做好了充分的准备。你还必须具备什么？两件事：自信和力量。信心来自于了解你的生意，你的产品以及它的价值，并能够很好地就这些内容与另一方进行沟通。你的力量源于你的影响力。使得谈判始终在你的控制下这一点很重要：这会意味着将谈判控制在你所能接受的价格、交货时间和利润率范围内。

当谈判时，将目标定得尽可能高，以便为自己获取最大的利益。

确保你在谈判中保持灵活，以防对方决定改变协议的方向。这就是你的准备得到充分利用的地方：知道自己的底限和对方的需求。如果你思维敏捷，那么你就已经具备了优势。如果事情开始不利于你的目标，你就需要迅速扭转局势。

第三部分：情境任务范例

情境： 詹姆斯·布朗有限公司想从 ABC 贸易公司订购一些瓷器。他们正在就这件事进行商务谈判。（A：卖方 ABC 贸易公司销售经理李欣；B：买方詹姆斯布朗有限公司的代表蔡小姐）

初次见面

A：早上好，蔡小姐。初次当面见到您，十分荣幸。

B：早上好，李先生。见到您也很高兴。

讨论价格

A：我希望通过您的来访，我们可以解决我们的瓷器价格。

B：我也是这样想的。我们来谈谈我们对 HX 系列瓷器的要求。你们有这方面的价格目录吗？

A：我们特地制定了一份价格单，上面列出了你们市场上最受欢迎的商品。给您。

B：哦，您考虑得真周到。请原谅，我马上看一下你们的价目表。

A：蔡小姐，您慢慢看。

B：李先生，看了你们的价格表和商品目录，我们对货号为 HX1005 和 HX1328 的商品感兴趣，但我们发现你们的价格比其他供货商高太多了。我们不可能以如此高的价格推销任何商品。

A：听到这个消息我很遗憾。您要知道，生产成本大大上升，而近几年我们的瓷器价格基本上保持不变。坦率地说，我们的商品一直达到出口标准，并且包装的设计和印刷也很棒。所以我们的产品定价适中。

B：恐怕在这方面我不能同意您的观点。我知道你们的产品在设计上很有吸引力，但我想指出你们的报价比其他一些供货商的报价高。我已经收到了来自其他国家你们竞争对手的报价，而你们的价格在这个市场上没有竞争力。

A：蔡小姐，您可能知道，我们的产品质量很高，在许多国家都有很好的市场。所以您必须也要考虑到质量。

B：我同意您所说的，但价格差异不应该这么大。如果您想得到这个订单，就必须降低价格。如果你们准备降价 8%，我们可能会达成协议。

A：8%？恐怕您要求的太多了。事实上，我们从来没有给过这么低的价格。为了友谊，我们可以破例考虑降价 5%。这是我们能承受得起的最高降价。

B：好的，我接受。我想订购 800 套 HX1005 和 550 套 HX1328。

A：好的。

讨论付款方式

B：现在我们来谈谈付款方式吧。你们接受付款交单吗？我希望您会接受。

A：我们通常采用的付款方式是即期信用证。

B：但我认为可以采用更灵活的付款方式，如付款交单这种方式对我们双方都是有利的。

A：信用证付款是我们与所有客户进行此类商品交易的惯常做法。对不起，我们不能接受付款交单这种方式。

B：好吧。

讨论装运

B：嗯，至于装运，越早越好。什么时候装运？

A：2018 年 10 月 30 日前或当日装运。

B：我们得指出货物不允许分批装运。

A：好。顺便问一下，装运港和目的港分别是哪里？

B：天津和多伦多。

确认

A：很高兴我们这次交易圆满成功，希望这将是今后开展其他业务的良好开端。

B：好的。HX1005 以每套 28 美元的价格供货，我方订购 800 套；HX1328 以每套 16 美元的价格供货，我方订购 550 套。收到信用证后货物不迟于 2018 年 10 月 30 日装船，不允许分批装运。装运港和目的港是从天津到多伦多。付款方式是即期信用证支付。

A：是的。我明天将准备好销售确认书，以便您签字。您明天早上再来一下方便吗？

B：好的。我们希望能为贵公司的商品找到一个好的市场，并希望在不久的将来与你们进一步订货。明天早上见。

A：再见。

Unit Eight Reception

8.1 Invitation

Section One: Tasks

Situation 1: *Wang Qi is inviting Liu Yang to his birthday party next Friday evening. Liu Yang can't accept the invitation for some reasons. Make a dialogue between them.*

Situation 2: *Zhao Yu, manager of MON Company, wants to invite Mr. Yao, manager of DSS Company, to attend the tenth anniversary ceremony of MON Company. Write an invitation card to Mr. Yao for Zhao Yu.*

Situation 3: *Mr. Smith wants to invite Dr. Brown to a dinner party in his house at half past six, May 8th. Write an invitation letter to Dr. Brown for Mr. Smith.*

Section Two: Related Information

How to Write an Invitation Letter

An invitation letter serves the purpose of inviting a guest to a party, event or celebration while conveying more information than a traditional invitation card. It serves two purposes: one is to invite the individual to the event, and the other one is to ensure that the person receiving the letter is going to attend.

There are two tenses used within the invitation letter, the present and the future.[1] The present tense conveys information about the event and the future tense ensures the guest is going to attend.

Business Invitation Letter

A business invitation letter is a formal way to invite peers and clients to events which are being hosted by the company. The professional invitation should be written in a formal tone[2].

The introduction allows the hosts to introduce themselves, as well as the organization they represent.

Next, in the body of the letter[3] it is important to outline all of the information about the event. The date and time should be included as well as the theme and purpose for the event. At this point, a date should be mentioned by which guests should provide their reply, and it may also contain any information regarding special roles played at the event, attire and items required for the guest to bring, etc.

Then the appreciation for the guest to attend the party should be shown. Stating that you look forward to seeing the individual at the event is necessary, and a handed signature should be included in the conclusion.

Friendly Invitation Letter

A friendly invitation letter is similar to a business letter but contains less formal speech. Friendly invitation letters are used for a variety of reasons from engagement parties[4], baby showers[5] and housewarming parties to wedding invitations.

Nowadays, invitation letters are used as an alternative to traditional invitations. They allow the host to convey different messages through the tone of the letter. An invitation letter allows the host to convey additional information that can't be expressed in a traditional invitation card. For example, memories of the past can be shared with close friends and family members.

Vocabulary

invitation [ˌɪnvɪ'teɪʃn] n. 邀请；请柬

celebration [ˌselɪ'breɪʃn] n. 庆祝；庆祝会（仪式）

convey [kən'veɪ] vt. 表达；传达，传递

individual [ˌɪndɪ'vɪdʒuəl] n. 个人；个体；adj. 个人的；个别的；独特的

tense [tens] n. 时态

formal ['fɔːml] adj. 正式的

peer [pɪə(r)] n. 同辈，同等的人；同伴

professional [prə'feʃənl] adj. 专业的；职业的

host [həʊst] n. 主人，东道主；节目主持人

outline ['aʊtlaɪn] vt. 概述，略述；画轮廓

theme [θiːm] n. 主题

regarding [rɪ'gɑːdɪŋ] prep. 关于；至于；就……而论

attire [ə'taɪə(r)] n. 服装，衣服

appreciation [əˌpriːʃi'eɪʃn] n. 感谢，欣赏

salutation [ˌsælju'teɪʃn] n. 称呼

signature ['sɪgnətʃə(r)] n. 签名，署名

engagement [ɪn'geɪdʒmənt] n. 约定，约会；订婚，婚约

housewarming ['haʊzwɔːmɪŋ] n. 乔迁庆宴

alternative ［ɔːlˈtɜːnətɪv］ *adj.* 替代的；*n.* 可供选择的事物

additional ［əˈdɪʃənl］ *adj.* 额外的，附加的；另外的

invitation card 请柬

look forward to doing 期待做某事

be similar to… 与……相似

a variety of… 各种各样的……

Notes

1. present tense 现在时态；future tense 将来时态
2. in a formal tone 以正式的语气/口吻。formal 正式的，反义词为 informal 非正式的
3. in the body of the letter 在书信的主体部分，body 原意指身体，此处指正文或主体。
4. engagement party 订婚仪式
5. baby shower 给准妈妈的一场"物浴"和"灵浴"。在美国各式各样的派对当中，baby shower 当属最温馨可爱的一种。名为 baby shower，却不是给婴儿沐浴，而是在婴儿预产期的前一两个月内，准妈妈的女性好友将准妈妈的女朋友们、女同事们召集起来，共同把祝福、忠告、礼物连同幽默洒向准妈妈，为的是帮助她做好物质和精神上的双重准备。

Section Three：Situational Task Samples

1. Oral invitation

Situation：Li Xin is inviting his important client Mr. Hoffman to dinner. The following are three kinds of responses of Mr. Hoffman. They are accepting the invitation，declining the invitation[1] and canceling or postponing the invitation.（A：Li Xin；B：Mr. Hoffman）

（1）Accept the invitation

A：Mr. Hoffman, may I invite you to have dinner in my house next Thursday?

B：Yes, thank you very much. I'd be delighted to. When shall I arrive?

A：How about half past six?

B：OK. I'll be there on time[2].

（2）Decline the invitation

A：Mr. Hoffman, I'd like to invite you to attend the opening ceremony[3] of our company.

B：That's very kind of you, but I'm afraid I can't manage it. My mother had an accident last week, so I have to take care of her.

A：I'm sorry to hear that. I hope she will get well soon.

B：Thank you.

（3）Cancel or postpone the invitation

A：Mr. Hoffman，I'm sorry to tell you that I can't have dinner with you next Thursday, because I will have an important meeting that evening.

B：What a pity!

A：Yes，maybe we can make it some other time. How about next Tuesday?

B: OK. I'll just be free on Tuesday.

A: Then see you on Tuesday evening.

B: See you.

2. Invitation cards[4]

Dr. and Mrs. John Smith invited Li Xin to have dinner in their house. The following are the examples of the invitation cards on offering an invitation, accepting and declining the invitation.

(1) Offer an invitation

Dr. and Mrs. John Smith

request the pleasure of

Mr. Li Xin's

company at dinner on Sunday, the twenty-third of March

at seven p. m.

Dover House, Ipswich, Massachusetts

R. S. V. P.[5]

(2) Accept the invitation

Mr. Li Xin

accepts with pleasure

Dr. and Mrs. John Smith's

kind invitation to dinner on Sunday,

the twenty-third of March

at seven p. m.

Dover House, Ipswich, Massachusetts

(3) Decline the invitation

Mr. Li Xin

regrets that a previous engagement[6] prevents his accepting

Dr. and Mrs. John Smith's

kind invitation to dinner on Sunday,

the twenty-third of March

at seven p. m.

Dover House, Ipswich, Massachusetts

3. Invitation letters

Mrs. Black invited Li Xin to have dinner with her family next Monday evening, August 10th, at six p. m.. The following are the examples of invitation letters on offering an invitation, accepting the invitation and declining the invitation.

(1) Offer an invitation

Dear Li Xin,

We should be so happy to have you come to dinner with us in my house next Monday evening, August 10th, at six p. m.. We are inviting a few other members of your class, and are looking forward to knowing you all a little better.

Sincerely yours，
Jane Black

(2) Accept the invitation

Dear Mrs. Black，

    I shall look forward with pleasure to coming to dinner with you and Mr. Black next Monday evening，August 10th，at six p. m. . It is very kind of you to ask me.

Sincerely yours，
Li Xin

(3) Decline the invitation

Dear Mrs. Black，

    I regret very much that I am not able to accept your kind invitation to dinner with you next Monday evening，August 10th，as I am already engaged for that evening. I am very sorry to miss this chance of being with you and Mr. Black in your home.

Sincerely yours，
Li Xin

Notes

1. They are accepting the invitation，declining and canceling or postponing the invitation. 它们是接受邀请、拒绝邀请和取消或推迟邀请。"accepting the invitation"，"declining the invitation" 和 "canceling or postponing the invitation" 是动名词短语作表语。

2. on time 按时，准时；in time 及时

3. opening ceremony 开业典礼

4. invitation card 请柬

5. R. S. V. P. 是法语 "Répondez, s'il vous plait" 的缩写，意思是："Reply, if you please"，中文意为："请赐回示/请赐复"。亦可用下列词句：接到正式请柬后应尽可能在 24 小时内予以答复。如果不能赴宴，须明确说明原因，以便女主人可以有时间另作安排。

6. previous engagement 事先的约定

Section Four：Functional Expression Bank

Offer an invitation(提出邀请　正式→非正式)

1. Could we have the honor of your presence at the meeting? 能否请您光临本次会议?

    There is a reception this evening. Your attendance is welcome. 今晚有个招待会，欢迎您光临。

    May I invite you to dinner next Sunday? 下星期日我可以请您吃饭吗?

    I was wondering if you'd like to see a movie with us Monday evening.

    我想知道您是否愿意在星期一晚上和我们一起去看电影。

Could you please come to…? 您能否光临……?

2. I would like to invite you to see a movie Friday evening. 我想请你星期五晚上去看电影。

Would you like/care to do…? 你要不要……?

Would you be interested in doing…? 有兴趣干……吗?

Won't you come in and have a cup of tea? 请进来喝杯茶好吗?

You will stay to dinner, won't you? 你留下来吃饭,好吗?

3. Why don't you come around and have supper with us after the interview?
你面试以后顺便到我们这里来吃晚饭好吗?

You must come and stay with us for the weekend. 你一定要来和我们一起过周末。

4. How/What about going shopping this evening? 晚上去购物怎么样?

Hey, d' you fancy a bite (to eat) this evening? 喂,想不想今晚去吃一顿?

("d' you" 意为 "would you",为口语化说法)

【注】朋友分手时说 "Drop over sometime." / "We'll have to get together soon." 等,不能理解为邀请,而是表示亲善、友好的客气话。(drop over 顺便拜访)

Accept an invitation（接受邀请　正式→非正式）

1. Thank you for the kind invitation. That would give me the greatest pleasure.
感谢您的友好邀请,那将使我荣幸之至。

2. That would be wonderful/nice. 那将太好了。

Thank you. That's really very kind of you. 谢谢你。你真是太客气了。

Yes, thank you very much. I'd be delighted to. 非常感谢你。我很高兴去。

Thank you. I'd love/like to. 谢谢,我很愿意。

Yes, that would be marvelous. 行,好极了。

3. I'll take you upon that. 我将接受您的邀请。

Sounds great. 这主意真棒。

Yes, great/fantastic. 行,好/妙极了。

【注】接受别人的邀请,不能只说一声:"Thank you."因为 Thank you 不能表示你是否接受。如果接受,则应该加上:I'd love to. /That's kind of you. 或者再重复一下对方所约的时间,如:I should be delighted to. Tomorrow evening at half past six.

Decline an invitation（拒绝邀请　正式→非正式）

1. Much to my regret I wouldn't be able to accept your invitation owning to a previous engagement. 很遗憾,因为有约在先,不能接受您的邀请。

Well, that's very kind of you, but I'm afraid I have already arranged/promised to…
噢,您太客气了。可是我已安排/答应……

What a pity, I would have loved to come. 太遗憾了,我真的很想去。

2. I wish I could, but Mr. Brown is coming Wednesday evening.
我真希望我能去,可布朗先生星期三晚上要来。

That's very kind of you, but I'm afraid I can't manage it.
你太客气了,但恐怕我来不了。

Well…I'd like to, but I'm not sure I have time. 嗯……我倒是很想去,就是怕没有时间。

I'd love to，but I've got something else on. 我倒是很想去，只是我手头另有事。

No，it's already late. I must go home，but thank you all the same.

不，已经很晚了，我必须回家去。不过，我还是要谢谢你。

3. No，thanks. 不了，谢谢。

【注】（1）通常来说，表示你确实不能接受邀请，最好是加上你谢绝的理由。只说一声"I'll not come."'No，I can't."是非常不礼貌的。

（2）如果对别人的邀请，不能立即做出肯定或否定的答复，可以这样说：

I can't say for sure. It depends if I can spare the time. Can I let you know this afternoon?

我不确定，这要看我是否能抽出时间。我今天下午告诉你好吗？

But I think I may have to work that evening. Could I let you know tomorrow?

但我想我那天晚上可能要工作，我明天告诉你好吗？

That sounds very nice but I'm not sure if I can. 听起来很不错，但我不确定我是否能去。

（3）如果需经和别人商量后才能决定，可以这样说：

But I'm not sure whether my husband is free then. Can I call you back?

但我不确定我丈夫是否有空，我给你回电话好吗？

Thank you very much，but I have to check with/have a word with my wife and call you again. 非常感谢，但我必须和我的妻子确定一下，再打电话给你。

Well，just let me ask Alice. I'll call you tomorrow and let you know for sure.

好吧，让我问问爱丽丝。我明天给你打电话告诉你确切信息。

Invite to dinner or lunch（邀请参加宴会或便餐）

1. May I have the pleasure of your company at dinner next Tuesday?

［正式］下周二宴会，可否赏光？

2. Our manager has sent me over to say that he wishes the pleasure of your company at a dinner party tomorrow evening.

［正式］我们经理派我来告诉您，他希望您能赏光出席明晚的宴会。

3. Our manager would like to invite you to a dinner party this evening at Beijing Restaurant. Here is the invitation card.

［委婉］今晚我们经理想请您去北京饭店吃饭。这是给您的请柬。

4. May I invite you to my house for dinner this evening?

［委婉］可以请您今晚来敝舍用餐吗？

5. I'd like you to come to our dinner party very much.

［委婉］我很想请您来参加我们的宴会。

6. We're having one or two people round for dinner next Sunday. We'd be glad if you could come.［委婉］下周日我们请一两个人来我家吃饭，如果您能来，我们会很高兴的。

7. Hey，Tom. What do you say we go out for lunch together today? My treat.

喂，汤姆。今天一起出去吃午饭怎么样？我请客。

8. Let's have dinner together at Jinshan Barbecue Restaurant. It's on me.

我们一起去金山烧烤店吃晚饭吧。我请客/付账。

9. Why don't you come round for a meal one evening next week?

你下星期哪个晚上过来吃顿饭好吗？

10. Please stay for lunch. 请留下吃午饭吧。

【注】关于邀请别人到饭店吃饭，英美人的习惯与我们有所不同。如果邀请者说：Let me treat you to coffee. 我请你喝咖啡吧。/I'd like to take you to the steak house for dinner. 我想带你去牛排屋吃晚饭。这表明由邀约者付费。如果邀约者说：Let's go to get a beer. 咱们喝杯啤酒去吧。/ Want a cup of coffee? 想喝杯咖啡吗？/How about going out to lunch Thursday? 这周四出去吃午饭怎么样？以上这些情况饭钱并不由邀约者支付，一般是各付各的账。

Invite to ceremonies，meetings，celebrations（邀请参加典礼、会议、庆祝会）

1. We should be very grateful if you could come to…and give us a talk on…on June 12th, Thursday.
   ［正式/书面］如果您能于 6 月 12 日（星期四）来……作个题为……的报告，我们将十分感激。

2. I hope you will honor us with your presence at the celebration.
   ［正式］望您能大驾光临这次庆祝会。

3. Would you do me the pleasure of attending our wedding anniversary?
   ［正式］您能赏光，参加我们的结婚纪念吗？

4. I'd like you to attend our graduation ceremony. ［委婉］我想邀请你参加我们的毕业典礼。

5. I'd like you to a farewell party for Anna Steward on Sunday. ［委婉］我想邀请你参加周日为安娜·斯图尔特举行的欢送会。

6. Dr. Porter，we're having a conference and we'd like to have you join us very much and give us your views. Do you think you could manage?
   ［委婉］波特博士，我们准备举行一次会议，我们很想请您参加并发表意见，您能来吗？

7. How would you like to come to a small get-together at Bill's house?
   ［委婉］你是否愿意来比尔家参加一次小小的聚会？

8. We're having a party this weekend. Will you join us?
   这个周末我们要举行一次聚会，你能来参加吗？

Section Five：Culture Tips

拜访礼仪

应邀去朋友家中做客，务必要准时。不守时是失礼的。一般性拜访可送小礼物，若赴家宴，可再丰厚些。礼物应交给女主人，并说"我希望你能喜欢"等客套话，不要说"小意思，不成敬意""东西不好，请笑纳"等中国人送礼时常爱讲的话。这类话会让外国人觉得你看不起他们，明知道东西不好还要送给他们，轻则被认为待人不诚，重则被认为有嘲讽蔑视的含义。正确的说法应该是："嗨，这是我精心为你挑选的礼物，希望你能喜欢。"

一般来说，美国人不随便送礼，但遇到节日、生日、婚礼或探视病人时，送礼还是免不了的。美国人最喜欢在圣诞节赠送礼物。此外，美国人认为单数是吉利的，有时送三个梨也不感到菲薄，不同于中国人讲究成双成对。

美国人收到礼物一定会马上打开，当着送礼人的面欣赏或品尝礼物并立即向送礼者道谢。不同于中国人总是把礼物放在一边，等客人走后，再看礼物。这在西方，会令送礼物的人感到难堪，因为他会觉得自己精心挑选的礼物并没让主人太在意。

在外国人家中，不要对他们的摆设大加评论，也不要随意欣赏某件物品，那样会导致主人一定要将你极为赞赏的物品送给你，引起尴尬。

如主人家养有猫、狗等宠物，要对它们友好，外国人是十分珍爱宠物的。

美国人办事讲究效率，重视有计划地安排自己的时间，绝不希望有人突然来拜访。因此，要拜访他们，事先预约是必不可少的。

译　文

第二部分：相关信息

如何写邀请信

邀请信的目的是邀请客人参加聚会、活动或庆典，然而传递的信息比传统的请柬要多。它有两个目的：一是邀请个人参加活动，二是确保收信人能够参加。

在邀请信中使用的时态有两种：现在时和将来时。现在时态传递有关事件的信息，而将来时态以确保客人将出席。

商务邀请函

商务邀请函是一种正式的邀请同行和客户参加公司即将举办的活动的方式。这种专业的邀请函应采用正式的语气书写。

介绍部分用作主办方自我介绍以及介绍他们所代表的组织。

接下来，在邀请函的主体部分列出活动的所有信息是很重要的。应包含活动的日期、时间以及主题和目的。在这一点上，应提及客人应给予答复的截止日期。它也可能包含，如客人在活动中所要扮演的特殊角色，客人需要带来的服装和物品等任何的信息。

然后，应该感谢客人前来参加聚会。说明你期待在活动中看到这个人是很有必要的，结尾应包含手写签名。

友好邀请信

友好邀请信和商业信函类似，但语言上没那么正式。友好邀请信可用于各种各样的情况，从订婚仪式、给准妈妈的"物浴"和"灵浴"、乔迁聚会到婚礼邀请应有尽有。

如今，邀请信可替代传统请柬的作用。它们可使主人通过信的语气传递不同的信息。邀请信可以使主人传达在传统的请柬中无法表达的附加信息。例如，可以与亲密的朋友和家人分享对往事的回忆。

第三部分：情境任务范例

1. 口头邀请

情境：李欣在邀请他的重要客人霍夫曼先生吃晚餐。下面的对话是霍夫曼先生的三种答复。它们分别是：接受邀请，拒绝邀请和取消或推迟邀请。（A：李欣；B：霍夫曼先生）

（1）接受邀请

A：霍夫曼先生，下周四可以请您到我家里吃晚饭吗？

B：可以，非常感谢你，我很愿意去。我什么时候到合适呢？

A：六点半怎么样？

B：好的，我会准时到的。

（2）拒绝邀请

A：霍夫曼先生，望您能参加我们公司的开业典礼。

B：你太客气了，但恐怕我来不了。我妈妈上周出车祸了，所以我得照顾她。

A：我很抱歉听到这个消息，希望她能早日康复。

B：谢谢你。

（3）取消或推迟邀请

A：霍夫曼先生，很遗憾地告诉您下周四我不能和您一起吃晚餐了，因为我那天晚上将有一个重要的会议。

B：太遗憾了！

A：是啊，也许我们能换个时间。下周二如何？

B：好的。我周二正好有空。

A：那就周二晚上见了。

B：再见。

2. 请柬

约翰·史密斯博士和夫人邀请李欣到他们家吃饭，以下是关于发出邀请、接受邀请以及拒绝邀请的请柬范例。

（1）发出邀请

李欣先生：

谨定于 3 月 23 日星期日下午七时在马萨诸塞州的伊普斯威奇镇多佛宅邸设宴，敬请光临。请赐复。

约翰·史密斯博士夫妇　敬上

请赐回示

（2）接受邀请

约翰·史密斯博士夫妇：

李欣愉快地接受约翰·史密斯博士夫妇于 3 月 23 日星期日下午七时在马萨诸塞州伊普斯威奇镇多佛宅邸的晚宴，不胜荣幸之至。

李欣　谨复

（3）拒绝邀请

约翰·史密斯博士夫妇：

承蒙邀请于 3 月 23 日星期日下午七时前往马萨诸塞州的伊普斯威奇镇多佛宅邸赴会，现因事前有约，不能从命，甚歉。

李欣　谨复

3. 邀请信

布莱克夫人邀请李欣下周一即 8 月 10 日晚上六时与她家人共进晚餐，以下是关于发出邀请、接受邀请以及拒绝邀请的邀请信范例。

(1) 发出邀请

亲爱的李欣：

我们很希望你能在 8 月 10 日，下周一晚上六点到舍下来和我们共进晚餐，我们还邀请了你班上的几位同学，希望借此机会彼此多熟悉一下。

您真诚的

简·布莱克

(2) 接受邀请

亲爱的布莱克太太：

我将高兴地期待着 8 月 10 日，下周一晚上六点，与您和布莱克先生共进晚餐。我很感激您的盛情邀请。

您真诚的

李欣

(3) 拒绝邀请

亲爱的布莱克太太：

我非常抱歉不能在 8 月 10 日，即下周一晚上六点，与你们共进晚餐，因为我那晚已经有约了。错失与您和布莱克先生在府上相聚的机会，我感到非常遗憾。

您真诚的

李欣

8.2 Welcome and Farewell

8.2.1 Welcome

Section One：Tasks

Situation 1：*Professor Smith is going to MTM Company to make a report. Jack, the administrative assistant, comes to the hotel to pick him up. Make a dialogue according to the situation.*

Situation 2：*Make a speech on welcoming the new employee Lily.*

Situation 3：*Make a speech on welcoming the Canadian cooperators on behalf of MTM Company.*

Section Two：Related Information

How to Give a Welcome Speech?

What is a welcome speech? It is a short and brief speech that is used during various events, of both business and personal nature, to either introduce the event or in some situations to introduce a person and welcome him or her. [1] An important thing to be kept in mind about a welcome speech is that it should be informative, polite, and positive. [2]

Given below are some tips on how to give welcome speeches.

State the objectives. Welcome speeches at general should be brief. It is important to state the objectives or the purpose of the activity at the beginning.

Welcome the audience. Chief guests of the formal function[3] should be welcomed first, other important guests on the dais should be the second, the guests on the front row should be the third, and then everybody down the stage in the hall.

Welcome expression. A variety of expressions should be used during the speech to make it livelier; but at the same time it should not be overdone. Most importantly, a sincere and confident approach from the speaker will create a feeling of unity and reflect hospitality from the host.

Introduce another speaker. If there is going to be another speaker at the event after you, then it is important that you introduce him or her before concluding your speech. [4]

Control the time. Maximum duration[5] of welcome speech can be three to four minutes. If it is extended beyond that, the guests may feel bored.

Vocabulary

informative [ɪnˈfɔːmətɪv] *adj.* 提供信息的；增长见闻的
objective [əbˈdʒektɪv] *n.* 目的；目标

audience ['ɔːdiəns] n. 观众；听众

dais ['deɪs] n. 台；讲台

overdo [ˌəʊvə'duː] vt. 做得过分；夸张

approach [ə'prəʊtʃ] n. 方法；途径

maximum ['mæksɪməm] adj. 最大值的；最大量的

duration [djuˈreɪʃn] n. 持续的时间；期间

welcome speech 欢迎词；欢迎辞

keep in mind 记住

Notes

1. It is a short and brief speech that is used during various events, of both business and personal nature, to either introduce the event or in some situations to introduce a person and welcome him or her. 它是一个简短的演讲，用于各种场合，既可以是商务的，也可以是私人性质的，内容要么介绍某个事件，要么在某些情况下介绍某人，并表示欢迎。either…or… 要么……要么……；that 引导定语从句，在从句中作主语，修饰先行词 speech。

2. An important thing to be kept in mind about a welcome speech is that it should be informative, polite and positive. 关于欢迎辞，我们要记住的一件重要事情是：它应该是传递信息的，礼貌的和积极的。that 在句中引导表语从句；to be kept in mind 动词不定式作后置定语修饰 an important thing。

3. formal function 正式场合

4. If there is going to be another speaker at the event after you, then it is important that you introduce him or her before concluding your speech. 如果活动中在你之后还有另一个演讲者，那么在结束你的演讲之前介绍他或她是很重要的。…it is important that…为 "it is＋形容词＋that从句"，it 是形式主语，that 从句是真正主语。

5. maximum duration 最长时间

Section Three：Situational Task Samples

Situation 1：*Li Xin, the Sales Manager of ABC International Trade Limited Company, came to the airport to pick up*[1] *his client Miss Wood. The following dialogue is between Li Xin and Miss Wood.*（*A：Li Xin；B：Miss Wood*）

A：Excuse me, are you Miss Wood from New York?

B：Yes, Jenny Wood. You are…

A：I'm Li Xin from ABC International Trade Limited Company[2]. Please call me Bill, that's my English name.

B：Hi, Bill. It's very nice to meet you. Just call me Jenny.

A：I'm very glad to meet you, too. My car is in the underground parking lot[3]. Let me help you with your bags.

B：Thank you very much.

A：Did you have a pleasant trip?

B：It's very wonderful.

A：My boss has been having a meeting the whole day. Could you go to the hotel and have a rest today? I'll pick you up at 9:00 tomorrow morning.

B：That'll be fine.

Situation 2：*Anne*，*the Executive Director*，*welcomes new employee Carol.*

Carol joins us today as an administrative assistant[4]. She graduated from Fudan University where she majored in administrative management. Carol is known to many of you already，as she has been working with us for three months as an intern[5]. Carol is also an amateur fitness instructor [6]. If anyone has questions about body management，you can consult her. Welcome back，Carol!

Situation 3：*Sun Hui*，*on behalf of Mr. Zhou*，*the President of PJ Vocational &Technical College* [7]，*received a delegation* [8] *from the German AHK* [9] *and delivered a welcome speech* [10] *to the German guests before the beginning of the banquet* [11].

Good evening!

Today we are especially glad and happy to receive the delegation from the German AHK. On behalf of the President of our college，Mr. Zhou，I want to extend a warm welcome and fraternal greeting[12] to you and thank you for joining us tonight. The purpose of this reception is，of course，to express our appreciation[13] for the friendly cooperation you have shown us over the years… I hope all of you have a pleasant and unforgettable[14] evening!

Notes

1. pick up sb. 接某人

2. ABC International Trade Limited Company ABC 国际有限公司

3. underground parking lot 地下停车场

4. administrative assistant 行政助理

5. intern 实习生

6. amateur fitness instructor 业余健身教练；amateur *adj.* 业余的；fitness *n.* 健康，健壮 instructor *n.* 教练，导师

7. PJ Vocational & Technical College PJ 职业技术学院

8. delegation 代表团

9. German AHK 德国工商大会

10. deliver a welcome speech 致欢迎辞

11. banquet 宴会

12. extend a warm welcome and fraternal greeting 表示热烈的欢迎和友好的问候

13. express our appreciation 表达我们的感谢

14. unforgettable 难忘的

Section Four：Functional Expression Bank

Expressing welcome（表示欢迎）

Formal occasions（正式场合）

1. Welcome to our company. 欢迎光临我们公司。

2. I am pleased to be able to welcome you to our company. 我很高兴能欢迎你来我们公司。

3. Welcome to China/Beijing/Shanghai，Mr. Smith. We are very pleased that you could come to visit our company.

   欢迎您到中国/北京/上海来，史密斯先生。很高兴您能来访问我们公司。

4. Gentlemen，it's a great honor to have you in Beijing/Shanghai.

   先生们，能在北京/上海接待你们深感荣幸。

5. I'd like to thank you for coming. 我要谢谢你的到来。

6. May I take this opportunity to thank you for coming. 我愿借此机会感谢您的光临。

7. I'm…from…. I've come on behalf of our company to welcome you.

   我是来自……（公司）的……，我代表我们公司欢迎您。

8. Professor Brown，I'm very happy to welcome you and the members of your delegation to our company. 布朗教授，非常高兴您和您的代表团成员访问我公司，欢迎。

Informal occasions（非正式场合）

1. Welcome to be here. 欢迎光临。

2. Welcome back，Jack. It's nice to have you back. 欢迎归来，杰克。很高兴你回来了。

3. I'm so glad to see you again，Mrs. Black. 很高兴再次见到您，布莱克太太。

4. I'm glad you're here to stay. Did you have a pleasant trip?

   很高兴您能在此逗留。您旅途愉快吗？

5. I'm glad you could all get here. 我很高兴你们都能来。

6. I'm glad to see so many people here. 我很高兴看到这么多人在这里。

7. It's great to be back here. 很高兴回到这里。

8. Hello again everybody. Thank you for being on time/making the effort to come today. 向大家再次问好。谢谢你们准时到来/今天能过来。

The opening remarks of welcome speech（欢迎辞的开场白）

1. Please allow me to give a word of welcome to our guests. 请允许我向客人们致欢迎辞。

2. I wish to extend a warm welcome to you who have come from all parts of the world to attend this congress. 我想对从全世界各地来参加会议的代表们，表示热烈的欢迎。

3. It's a great honor and privilege to greet you as delegates from all over the world to the International Congress of Art.

   能够欢迎各位来自世界各地的代表们参加本次国际艺术学会，我深感荣幸。

4. It gives me great pleasure on behalf of our company to extend a warm welcome to the members of Canadian delegation who have been invited to our country by our company.

   我很荣幸代表本公司，向应邀前来访问我国的加国代表团表示热烈的欢迎。

5. It is a great cause of joy for me to be allowed the opportunity of extending my heartiest welcome to our distinguished guests from various companies on the occasion of our

opening ceremony. 我很高兴有机会在开幕式上，向来自各公司的贵宾们致以热烈的欢迎。

6. It is with great pleasure that I extend a warm welcome to the delegation from the XYZ Company, led by Mr. White.

我以极其愉快的心情在这里向以怀特先生为首的 XYZ 公司代表团表示热烈的欢迎。

The concluding remarks of welcome（欢迎辞的结束语）

1. I should like to end these words of welcome with an earnest prayer for the great success of this convention/negotiation. 我真诚地预祝会议/洽谈成功，并以此来结束我的欢迎辞。

2. In conclusion, I offer to this convention my best wishes for success and to the participants a happy and meaningful stay in this country.

最后，我预祝会议成功，并祝与会者在此度过愉快而有意义的时光。

Section Five：Culture Tips

欢迎礼仪

迎接客人要有周到的安排，应注意以下事项：

1. 对前来访问、洽谈业务、参加会议的外国、外地客人，应先了解对方到达的车次、航班，安排与客人身份、职务相当的人员前去迎接。若因某种原因，相应身份的主人不能前往，前去迎接的主人应向客人做出礼貌的解释。

2. 主人到车站、机场去迎接客人，应提前到达并恭候客人的到来，绝不能迟到，让客人久等。若迎接来迟，必定会给客人留下不好的印象，事后无论怎样解释，都无法消除这种失职和不守信用的印象。因此在迎接工作中，工作人员必须准确掌握来宾乘坐的飞机（车、船）抵达的时间，在客人抵达之前到达迎接地点等候客人，并备好专用车辆接送客人到达下榻之处。

3. 接到客人后，应首先问候"一路辛苦了""欢迎您来到我们公司"等。然后向对方做自我介绍，如果有名片，可送予对方。注意送名片的礼仪：当你与长者、尊者交换名片时，双手递上，身体可微微前倾，说一句"请多关照"。你想得到对方名片时，可以用请求的口吻说："如果您方便的话，能否留张名片给我？"作为接名片的人，双手接过名片后，应仔细地看一遍，千万不要看也不看就放入口袋，也不要顺手往桌上扔。

4. 主人应提前为客人安排好住宿，帮客人办理好一切手续并将客人领进房间，同时向客人介绍住处的服务、设施，将活动的计划、日程安排交代给客人，并把准备好的地图或旅游图、名胜古迹等介绍材料交给客人。

5. 将客人送到住地后，主人不要立即离去，应陪客人稍作停留，热情交谈。谈话内容要让客人感到满意，比如客人参与活动的背景资料、当地风土人情、有特点的自然景观、特产、物价等。考虑到客人一路旅途劳累，主人不宜久留，让客人早些休息。分手时将下次联系的时间、地点、方式等告诉客人。

6. 在迎送工作中，还应注意陪车的礼仪。迎接客人抵达、欢送客人以及一些外事访问活动时，一般应当安排人员陪车，起到接待和引路的作用。在陪车中，工作人员应注意的主要是上下车的顺序和坐车时的位置安排。在顺序上，掌握"后上先下"的原则。"后上先下"的礼节体现了主客有序的礼仪，客人为重，客人为尊。在乘车的位置上，应掌握"以右为尊"的原则。按西方的礼俗，右为大，左为小。两人同行，右者为尊；三人并行中者为尊。宴席上，主人的右座为尊贵宾客的位置。同样，在陪车时，应请客人从右侧门上车，坐于右座，主人或公关人员从左侧门上车，坐于左侧，翻译坐在司机旁边的座位上。如果车内后排座位需要坐三人，则顺序是：中间为大，右边为次，左边为再次，前排为最小。但是如果客人上车后，坐到了主人左侧座位上，则应主随客便，不必再请客人挪动位置。

译　文

第二部分：相关信息

如何致欢迎辞

什么是欢迎辞？它是一个简短的演讲，用于各种场合，既可以是商务的，也可以是个人性质的。内容要么介绍某个事件，要么在某些情况下介绍某人，并表示欢迎。关于欢迎辞，我们要记住的一件重要事情是：它应该具有信息性、礼貌性和积极性。

以下是一些关于如何致欢迎辞的提示。

陈述目的。欢迎辞一般应简短。开始的时候就陈述活动的目的是很重要的。

欢迎观众。在正式场合应首先欢迎主要客人，其次是台下台上的其他重要客人，然后是坐在台下第一排的客人们，最后是大厅里的所有人。

欢迎表达。为了使演讲更加生动，应该使用多种表达，但同时也不宜过度使用。最重要的是，演讲者真诚而自信的方式将会在观众中产生一种凝聚力，并反映主办方的好客之情。

介绍另一位演讲者。如果活动中在你之后还有另一个演讲者，那么在结束你的演讲之前介绍他或她是很重要的。

控制时间。欢迎辞最多持续3~4分钟，如果超时了客人可能会觉得无聊。

第三部分：情境任务范例

情境1：ABC国际贸易有限公司的销售经理李欣来机场接他的客户伍德小姐。下面是他们之间的对话。（A：李欣；B：伍德小姐）

A：打扰一下，您是来自纽约的伍德小姐吗？

B：是的，珍妮·伍德。你是……

A：我是ABC国际贸易有限公司的李欣。请叫我比尔，那是我的英文名。

B：您好，比尔。认识您很高兴。叫我珍妮就好。

A：认识您也很高兴。我的车在地下停车场。让我来帮您提包吧。

B：非常感谢。

A：您旅途愉快吗？

B：很棒。

A：我的老板今天一直在开会。您能先回宾馆休息吗？明早九点我来酒店接您。

B：好的。

情境2：安妮作为行政主管，欢迎新员工卡罗尔。

卡罗尔今天加入我们公司担任行政助理。她毕业于复旦大学，主修行政管理。卡罗尔曾经在公司进行了为期三个月的实习，因此我相信我们中的许多人已经非常熟悉她了。卡罗尔也是一名业余健美教练。如果大家有关于形体管理方面的问题，可以咨询她。欢迎回来，卡罗尔！

情境 3： 孙慧代表 PJ 职业技术学院周院长接待来自德国 AHK 的一个代表团，并在宴会前向德国客人致欢迎辞。

晚上好！

今天，我们特别高兴能够接待来自德国 AHK 的代表团。我代表我们学院的周院长向诸位表示热烈的欢迎和友好的问候，感谢大家光临今天晚上的招待会。此次招待会的目的当然是为了感谢这些年来贵方的友好合作……希望大家都度过一个愉快、难忘的夜晚！

8.2.2 Farewell

Section One: Tasks

Situation 1: *Anne is saying goodbye to Jenny after having dinner at Jenney's house. Make a dialogue according to the situation.*

Situation 2: *Anne comes to the airport to see her client Mr. Reagan off. Make a dialogue according to the situation.*

Situation 3: *Anne is going to move to another city with her parents. Mr. Smith, the manager of her department, is going to hold a farewell party for her. Make two farewell speeches as Mr. Smith and Anne respectively. Assuming that you are her department manager, holding a farewell party for her, and giving her a farewell speech; Anne will also make a farewell speech at the party.*

Section Two: Related Information

Farewell Speech[1]

A farewell speech or farewell address is a speech given by an individual who is leaving a position or place, such as farewell speeches for graduations, retirements or departures from certain job or club. Sometimes a farewell speech could also be given by a colleague, manager or a boss.

Farewell speeches mark significant departures. They are much more than a casual "see you later" and a mumbled "thanks for everything". Then what message should be included in a farewell speech?

Try to think of what you have done while at the place you're leaving, and summarize it from the beginning to the end. It's good to take some time to reflect on what you've gained at this place and what you'll miss. At the end of your farewell speech, you should offer sincere wishes to others who remain work there.

Well, how to deliver a farewell speech? First, you can open it with a fun icebreaker, such as a joke or a great witticism, which could grab the audience's attention right away.[2] Second, keep the speech brief. You might have a lot to say, but this speech is not the time to get into minute details about it. Remember that people likely need to get back to work, or have other things they'd like to do with their time. Third, speak with confidence. Many people get nervous when speaking in front of a crowd. There are plenty of tricks to help yourself battle nerves if you need to. Make sure to practice your speech many times; then, prepare yourself for standing in front of a group.[3]

Vocabulary

farewell [feə'wel] *n.* 告别，辞别，再见

address [ə'dres] *n.* 演讲，致辞，地址

individual [ˌɪndɪ'vɪdʒuəl] *n.* 个人，个体　*adj.* 个人的，个别的，独特的

significant [sɪgˈnɪfɪk(ə)nt] *adj.* 重大的，有意义的

casual [ˈkæʒjʊəl] *adj.* 随便的，非正式的，临时的

mumble [ˈmʌmb(ə)l] *n.* 含糊的话，咕噜；*vi.* 含糊地说话 *vt.* 含糊地说，抿着嘴嚼

summarize [ˈsʌməraɪz] *vt.* 总结，概述 *vi.* 做总结，做概括

icebreaker [ˈaɪsbreɪkə] *n.* 缓和拘谨气氛（或打破僵局）的事物（或行为举止）

witticism [ˈwɪtɪsɪzəm] *n.* 妙语；名言；俏皮话

trick [trɪk] *n.* 窍门，花招

nerves [nɜːvz] *n.* 神经紧张

reflect on 回忆，仔细想

get into minute detail 不厌其详

plenty of 许多，大量的，充足的

Notes

1. farewell speech 告别演说，告别演讲

2. First，you can open it with a fun icebreaker，such as a joke or a great witticism，which could grab the audience's attention right away. 首先，你可以用一个有趣的开场白来打破僵局，比如一个笑话或者一句很棒的名言，这样就可以立刻吸引住观众的注意力。Icebreaker 名词，意为"打破僵局的话语或事物"。在本句话中我们采用了翻译技巧中的词性转换法，如本句中将英语中的名词词性转变为汉语中的动词词性，"用……打破僵局"，这是翻译中一种很常见的手法。grab one's attention 吸引某人的注意力；right away 马上，立即

3. Make sure to practice your speech many times；then，prepare yourself for standing in front of a group. 务必多次练习演讲，并站在一群人面前做好准备。make sure 确保，务必；prepare sb. for (doing) sth. 使某人为……做好准备

Section Three：Situational Task Samples

Situation 1：*After dinner at Li Xin's house，Mr. Smith stood up and said goodbye.*（*A：Mr. Smith；B：Li Xin*）

A：Thank you for the wonderful dinner and thank you for all your help during my stay here.

B：It has been a great pleasure working with you.

A：We have to say goodbye now.

B：Oh，can't you stay a little longer?

A：That's really nice of you，but I really can't.

B：Well，it's too bad that you have to go.

A：Thank you again for your warm reception and hospitality.

B：It's my pleasure. We hope you will visit Shanghai again.

A：Certainly. I'd be glad to.

B：Please give my best regards to your family.

A：I will. Thank you very much. Goodbye.

B：Goodbye.

Situation 2: *Li Xin saw Mr. Smith off*[1] *at the airport.* (A: *Mr. Smith*; B: *Li Xin*)

A: It's very kind of you to see me off at the airport.

B: I'll miss you. I hope we'll keep in touch.

A: Sure. Before saying goodbye, I'd like to say it has been a very pleasant and productive trip[2] for me. Your company has left me a very good impression[3], and I am deeply moved by[4] your hospitality. I think our cooperation will be a very successful one.

B: Thank you very much, Mr. Smith. You are playing a very important part in[5] the cooperation. We hope we can hear from[6] you soon.

A: Of course you will.

B: Please let me know if I can be of any help[7] while you are in China.

A: It's a deal. [8]

B: It sounds like they're boarding now. So have a good trip!

A: I'll see you later.

B: Or maybe sooner!

A: Goodbye!

B: Goodbye!

Situation 3: *Li Xin will go to Harvard University to study further. Here are two farewell speeches which are given by the manager of Financial Department , Mr. Hall and the other one from Li Xin.*

Farewell speech for Li Xin from Mr. Hall

Good evening, everyone!

I am sure all of us know Mr. Li Xin in the Financial Department. He has always been an outstanding employee and it is impossible for anyone not to have heard of him yet. Fortunately for him and unfortunately for us, Li Xin has chosen to move out of the city to study further. And I, as the head of the Financial Department, would like to say a few words to him before he leaves.

Li Xin joined our company as an intern[9], right out of college. Though our company was a little hesitant to hire[10] him for lacking of working experience, we also saw true potential in him. A highly passionate boy, Li Xin has greatly contributed to the improvement and development of the Financial Department.

I, on behalf of[11] everyone here, wish you all the luck with your life ahead. We hope to see you shining brighter and achieve what you truly deserve.

Farewell Speech from Li Xin

Good evening, everyone!

Thank you for this wonderful farewell party that has been hosted for me. I am truly moved by this gesture, and if I knew sooner that I was so valued here, I may have reconsidered moving on!

Jokes apart, I want everyone here to know that this place is the reason why I have become the person I am today. I have learned everything that I needed to learn, things that college never prepared me enough for, from this wonderful job.

I want to thank our company, particularly my mentor[12], Mr. Hall, for giving me the space to grow, for allowing me to make my own decisions, and then learning from my own mistakes. Your guidance and faith in me has carved a special place in my life, and you will always be remembered.

As I move on to a different world with different opportunities, I can only say that I would never have been able to do this if I hadn't got my first opportunity here. I will always cherish[13] everything this company has given me. Thank you everyone!

Notes

1. see sb. off 为某人送行
2. a pleasant and productive trip 一次愉快的、收获颇丰的旅行
3. leave sb. a good impression 给某人留下好印象
4. be deeply moved by… 被……深深地感动
5. play an important part in… 在……中发挥重要作用
6. hear from sb. 收到某人的来信
7. be of any help 有所帮助
8. It's a deal. 一言为定；就这么说定了。
9. intern 实习生
10. be hesitant to do… 做……犹豫不决
11. on behalf of 代表
12. mentor 导师，指导者，良师益友
13. cherish 珍惜

Section Four：Functional Expression Bank

Saying goodbye（辞行）

1. I'd like to say goodbye to everyone.［委婉］我要向诸位辞行。
2. I've come to say goodbye. I'm flying home on Friday afternoon.
   我是来辞行的，我周五下午要乘飞机回家。
3. I'm calling to say goodbye. 我打电话向你告别。
4. I must thank you for your kind hospitality. 我一定要感谢你们的款待。
5. Everything I've seen here has left a deep impression on me.
   我在此所见的一切都让我印象深刻。
6. I'll never forget the three wonderful weeks in London.
   我将永远不会忘记在伦敦度过的美妙的三周。
7. I shall miss you very much. 我会很想你们的。
8. We'll feel sorry at this moment of parting. 在这临别的时刻，我们都感到依依不舍。

Looking forward to your next visit（欢迎再次光临）

1. (Please) come again.（请）您再来。

2. Thank you so much for coming. Hope you'll come again. 感谢光临，欢迎再来。

3. Hope you'll visit Beijing more often. 欢迎您以后多来北京。

4. Hope to see you again next year. 希望明年再见到你。

5. Remember to look me up if you're ever in Shanghai. 要是你来上海的话，别忘了来找我。

6. Next time you are in Chengdu, look me up. 你下次来成都时，来找我。

Telling each other to take good care of himself/herself （互道珍重）

1. Take care (of yourself)！请（您）多保重！

2. Be careful of your health. 注意你的健康。/请多保重。

3. Look after yourself. 保重。

4. Take good care of yourself, please. 请多多保重。

Hope to keep in touch （希望保持联系）

1. Call me later. 稍后给我打电话。

2. Give me a call sometime. /Call me sometime. 有空给我打电话。

3. Hope we'll keep in touch. ［非正式］希望我们会保持联系。

4. I really enjoyed meeting you, and let's keep in touch. 认识你真高兴，我们要保持联系。

5. Take care of yourself and don't forget to keep in touch. 多多保重，别忘了保持联系。

6. Can you tell me how I can get in touch with you, and what's your email address?
   我怎么能够和你联系呢？还有你的电子邮箱地址？

We'll meet some other day （后会有期）

1. See you (later). 再见。/回头见。

2. I'll be seeing you. 后会有期。

3. I hope I can see you again. 希望还能再见。

4. Well, perhaps we can get together another time. 也许我们下次还会再见的。

5. I shall miss all of you. Let's get together soon. 我会想念你们的，后会有期。

Seeing guests off and expressing wishes （送行及表达祝愿）

1. Oh, I'm very sorry to hear that you're leaving us.
   哦，听说你要离开我们，我真是舍不得。

2. We're going to miss you, Mr. Smith. 我们会想你的，史密斯先生。

3. It has been a real pleasure having you with us. You're a fine scholar. You'll go far.
   和你在一起真是愉快。你是一名优秀的学者。你将前途无量。

4. Mr. Hoffman wanted to come to see you off, too, but on account of some business he had to attend. He wishes you a bon voyage.
   ［正式］本来霍夫曼先生也要来给你们送行的，因为临时有事来不了了。他祝你们一路平安。

5. It's a pleasure to come to see you off. I wish you a pleasant trip home.
   ［正式］很高兴为你们送行。祝你们回程旅途愉快。

6. Send us a message as soon as you arrive, please. 请您一到达就给我们发信息。

7. I wish you a pleasant journey/trip. 祝你旅途愉快。
   Goodbye and happy landing. 再见，祝你愉快抵达。

8. Everything goes smoothly. /Bon voyage. /Enjoy your trip. /Have a good trip.

一路顺风。

9. Everything goes well. 万事如意。

Thanks for seeing off（答谢送行）

1. It's so kind of you to come to see me off. 你来送行，真是太感谢。

   It's very kind of you to come all the way to see me off. 你远道而来为我送行，我很感激。

   It's so nice of you to take the trouble to see me off. 谢谢你不辞辛劳来为我送行。

2. Thank you for the help you've rendered me during my stay here.

   〔正式〕感谢您在我逗留期间所给予的帮助。

3. I'll never forget the hospitality I've received during my stay here.

   〔正式〕我当铭记在此逗留期间受到的盛情款待。

4. I don't know how I can ever thank you enough. 我不知怎么感谢你们才好。

5. I'll think of you often and I'll write to you as often as I can.

   我会经常想念你们，并尽量多写信。

6. I look forward to seeing you in my country. 我期望着在我国与你见面。

7. Well，goodbye，everyone，and thank you again for everything.

   那么，大家再见了，再次谢谢你们所做的一切。

Section Five：Culture Tips

送别礼仪

　　招待客人后，作为主人，应该礼貌地送别客人。如果是外国客人，更应该把客人送到酒店的门口以表示东道主的体贴。如有需要，给客人叫一辆出租车就更显周到了。

　　如果我们所接待的外宾是一次比较正式的到访，那么招待这些从国外特地来访的客人，就应该有周全的计划。送别的环节里应该包含饯别宴。宴会内容必须考虑客人的需求和禁忌，事先做好安排，使对方感到自己备受重视，进而加深宾主之间的友谊。

　　对一般家庭到访的客人就不用那么麻烦了，但主人应该至少要送客人到房屋门口，或电梯口。然后与客人一一握手道别，注意不要握完手就马上转身离去，而应该目送客人远去。另外，中西方文化差异甚大，中国人表达情感的方式相对内敛。所以，如果你和老外送别，举止不妨洒脱奔放一些，不要吝于拥抱，否则老外会觉得你是"冷血动物"。

　　送别的环节里，有时候还包含赠送礼物。礼物的选择是一门艺术，可选择具有民族特色的工艺品，如中国人司空见惯的风筝、笛子、剪纸、筷子、脸谱、书画、茶叶等，一旦到了外国友人手里，往往会备受青睐，身价倍增。礼物不在贵重而在于合适，有时送太贵重的礼品反而会使受礼者不安。对于外国人来说，把客人来访期间的活动照片精选汇集成册，在送别时作为礼物送给对方也是很好的礼物。这种礼物既表达了对客人的友好和尊重，又富有纪念意义。

译　　文

第二部分：相关信息

告别演讲

　　告别演讲或告别演说是一个人打算离开某一职位或地方所发表的讲话。如毕业典礼、退休或离开某些工作或俱乐部的告别演讲。有时候，也可能是某位同事、经理或老板发表告别演讲。

　　告别演讲标志着重要的离开。它们不仅仅是一个随意的"再见"和一个嗬嗬的"谢谢你所做的一切"。那么在告别演讲中应该包含什么信息呢？

　　试着想想你在即将离开的地方做了些什么，然后从头到尾地总结一下。最好花点时间回顾一下你在这个地方得到了什么，以及你会错过什么。在你的告别演讲结尾，你应该向仍留在那里工作的人们表示真诚的祝愿。

　　那么，如何发表告别演讲呢？首先，你可以用一个有趣的开场白来打破僵局，比如一个笑话或者一句很棒的名言，这样就可以立刻吸引住观众的注意力。其次，演讲要简短。你可能有很多话要说，但是这个演讲并不是详细讨论的时候。请记住，人们可能需要回去工作，或者愿意用自己的时间去做其他事情。第三，自信地讲话。在一群人面前说话时，许多人会感到紧张。如果需要的话，有很多技巧可以帮助你战胜紧张。务必多次练习演讲，并为站在一群人面前做好准备。

第三部分：情境任务范例

情境1： 在李欣家吃过晚餐后，史密斯先生起身告别。（A：史密斯先生；B：李欣）

A：谢谢您请我吃这顿丰盛的晚餐，也非常感谢我待在这儿期间您对我的帮助。

B：和您一起工作非常愉快。

A：现在我们该说再见了。

B：哦，您不能再待一会儿吗？

A：真谢谢您的好意，但是我真的不能再耽搁了。

B：好吧，真是太遗憾了。

A：再次感谢您的热情款待。

B：这是我的荣幸。希望您再到上海来。

A：那当然，我很乐意。

B：请向您全家转达我衷心的问候。

A：我会的，非常感谢，再见！

B：再见！

情境2： 李欣在机场为史密斯先生送行。（A：史密斯先生；B：李欣）

A：非常感谢您来机场送我。

B：我会想念您的，希望我们能保持联系。

A：那当然。在再见之前，我想说于我而言，这是一次愉快的、收获颇丰的旅行。贵公司给我留下了非常好的印象，我被你们的热情友好深深地感动了。我想我们的合作将会非常成功。

B：非常感谢您，史密斯先生。在此次合作当中，您的作用举足轻重。我们希望能够尽快得到您的回复。

A：当然会的。

B：您在中国期间，如果有什么我能帮得上忙的就找我。

A：一言为定。

B：好像要登机了，那么祝您一路顺风！

A：我们还会再见的。

B：也许更早！

A：再见！

B：再见！

情境 3： 李欣将赴哈佛大学深造。下面两篇分别是财务部经理霍尔先生为他做的告别演说以及李欣自己的告别辞。

霍尔先生为李欣致告别辞

各位晚上好！

我相信我们大家都知道我们财务部的李欣先生。他一直是一名出色的员工，任何人都不可能没听说过他。李欣已经选择了离开这座城市去进一步深造，这对他来说是幸运的，对于我们来说是不幸的。作为财务部门的负责人，我想在他离开之前对他说几句话。

李欣在刚刚大学毕业时作为一名实习生加入了我们公司。当时由于他缺乏工作经验，我们公司在雇佣他时有点儿犹豫，但是我们也看到了他身上真正的潜力。李欣是一个充满激情的男孩，为财务部门的进步和发展做出了很大的贡献。

在此，我代表在座的各位，祝你前程似锦。我们希望看到你更加出色的表现，并实现你真正的价值。

李欣的告别演讲

大家晚上好！

感谢各位为我举办的这次很棒的告别会。我真的很感动，如果我早点儿知道我在这里这么受重视，我可能会重新考虑是否要继续深造！

开个玩笑，我想让大家知道，是这个地方成就了如今的我。在这份极好的工作中，我学到了我需要学习的一切，这些是我在大学从未学到的。

我要感谢我们的公司，尤其是我的导师，霍尔先生，是您给了我成长的空间，是您让我自己做出决定，从自己的错误中学习。您对我的指导、给予我的信心在我生命中已经留下特殊的烙印，我将永远铭记。

当我走向一个拥有不同机遇的另一个领域时，我只能说如果没有在这里获得的第一次机会，我就永远无法取得如今的成就。我会永远珍惜公司给我的一切。谢谢大家！

8.3 Shopping

Section One: Tasks

Situation 1: One day, Bill came to a shop to buy a sweater. The shop assistant offered him some help on selecting the sweater. Make a dialogue and act it out with your partner.

Situation 2: Bill bargained with the shop assistant and finally got the sweater at a reasonable price. Make a dialogue and act it out with your partner.

Section Two: Related Information

Online Shopping

Online shopping is a form of electronic commerce which allows consumers to buy goods or services directly from a seller over the Internet with a web browser.[1] Consumers find a product of interest by visiting the website of the retailer directly or by searching among vendors with a shopping search engine, which displays the availability and pricing at different e-retailers.[2] By 2016, customers can shop online with a range of different computers and devices, including desktop computers, laptops, tablet computers and smart phones.

When a customer buys products or services in an online shop, the process is called business-to-consumer (B2C) online shopping[3]. When an online store enables businesses to buy from other businesses, the process is called business-to-business (B2B) online shopping[4]. A typical online store enables the customer to browse the firm's range of products and services, view photos or videos of the products, along with information about the product specifications, features and prices.

Online stores usually enable shoppers to use "search" function to find specific brands or items. Online customers must have access to the Internet and a valid method of payment in order to complete a transaction, such as a credit card, or a service such as PayPal[5]. For physical products (e.g., paperback books or clothes), the e-retailer ships the products to the customer; for digital products, such as digital audio files of songs or software, the e-retailer typically sends the file to the customer over the Internet. The largest of these online retailing corporations are Alibaba, Amazon and eBay.[6]

Vocabulary

commerce ['kɔmɜːs] *n.* 商务；商业；贸易
browser ['brauzə(r)] *n.* 浏览器

retailer ['ri:teɪlə(r)] *n*.零售商

vendor ['vendə(r)] *n*.卖主；摊贩

availability [ə,veɪlə'bɪlətɪ] *n*.有效；有益；可利用性；可得到的东西（或人）

laptop ['læptɒp] *n*.便携式电脑；笔记本电脑

smartphone [sma:t fəʊn] *n*.智能手机

typical ['tɪpɪkl] *adj*.典型的；特有的或特别的

specification [,spesɪfɪ'keɪʃn] *n*.规格；说明书

feature ['fi:tʃə(r)] *n*.特征；特点

brand [brænd] *n*.牌子；商标

access ['ækses] *n*.入口；出口；接近；进入；*vt*.接近；进入；使用；接近；获取

valid ['vælɪd] *adj*.有效的

search engine 搜索引擎

tablet computer 平板电脑

e-retailer 电子零售商

digital audio file 数字音频文件

Notes

1. Online shopping is a form of electronic commerce which allows consumers to buy goods or services directly from a seller over the Internet with a web browser. 在线购物是电子商务的一种形式，它可以让消费者使用网络浏览器通过互联网从卖家直接购买商品或服务。a form of…一种……形式；electronic commerce 电子商务；allow sb. to do sth. 允许某人做某事；which 引导定语从句，先行词为 electronic commerce。

2. Consumers find a product of interest by visiting the website of the retailer directly or by searching among vendors with a shopping search engine, which displays the availability and pricing at different e-retailers. 消费者通过直接访问零售商的网站或通过使用购物搜索引擎在供应商之间搜索来找到感兴趣的产品，这种搜索引擎显示相同产品在不同的电子零售商处的供货情况以及定价。by 指通过某种方式，为介词，后面接动名词；visit the website 访问网址/网站；which 引导非限定性定语从句，先行词为 a shopping search engine。

3. business-to-consumer（B2C）online shopping 企业对消费者（B2C）在线购物

4. business-to-business（B2B）online shopping 企业对企业（B2B）在线购物

5. PayPal 贝宝，是美国 eBay 公司的全资子公司。1998 年建立，是一个总部在美国加利福尼亚州圣荷西市的因特网服务商，允许在使用电子邮件标识身份的用户之间转移资金，这种方式取代了传统的邮寄支票或者汇款的方法。PayPal 也和一些电子商务网站合作，成为它们的货款支付方式之一；但是用这种支付方式转账时，PayPal 要收取一定金额的手续费。

6. Alibaba，Amazon and eBay 三大购物网站：阿里巴巴、亚马逊和易贝。

Section Three：Situational Task Samples

Situation：*One day，Li Xin came to a shop to buy a jacket. The following dialogues are between Li Xin and the shop assistant.*（*A：Shop Assistant；B：Li Xin*）

A: Good morning. Can I help you?

B: Good morning. I'm looking for a new jacket.

A: Our jackets are over there next to coats and accessories[1]. We are having a sale this week. Everything is thirty percent off[2].

B: I like this jacket. Can I try it on?

A: Of course. The fitting rooms are over there.

B: Thanks.

...

B: Do you have the same thing in a darker shade? This one is rather showy on me. Perhaps you can show me something plainer.

A: Is this what you are looking for?

B: Is a bigger size available? This one is too small for me.

A: Let me check… I'm afraid we don't have any of this size on hand. It will be soon in stock[3], I believe. If you leave your phone number, I'll ring you.

B: Don't be so troublesome. Do you have any other styles?

A: Yes, perhaps you could try this one. It's lighter and warmer.

B: How much is it?

A: It's 160 dollars.

B: May I try it on?

A: Of course.

B: Look, there is a flaw[4] in this jacket. One of the threads is in different color.

A: I'll bring you another one. I'll be right back, sir… I'm afraid this is the only one we have.

B: Well, can you give a discount[5]?

A: I'm sorry. We can't give a discount. It's a sale price already.

B: Do you give a discount if I pay by cash?

A: OK. I'll give you a five percent discount[6] if you pay in cash.

B: OK. I'll take it.

A: Do you need anything else?

B: No, thanks.

A: Let me wrap it up for you.

B: Never mind wrapping it up. Just put it in a bag. How much should I pay you?

A: 152 dollars.

B: Here you are.

A: Thank you. Goodbye.

B: Bye.

Notes

1. accessories *n.* 配饰；是 accessory 的复数形式

2. thirty percent off 降价 30%，或打七折

3. be in stock 有存货

4. flaw n. 缺陷，瑕疵

5. give a discount 打折

6. five percent discount 九五折

Section Four：Functional Expression Bank

Greet the customers（向顾客打招呼）

1. May I help you?［委婉］您买什么？

2. What can I do for you? 我能为您做什么？

3. Is there anything I can do for you? 有没有我能为您做的事情？

State and inquire shopping intention（陈述与询问购物意图）

State shopping intention（陈述一般购物意图）

1. I would like a woman's raincoat, large size.［委婉］我想要一件女式雨衣，大号的。

2. I want to buy/am looking for some souvenirs of Disneyland, please.
［委婉］我想买几件迪士尼乐园的纪念品。

3. Get me a roll of tape and a bottle of glue, also some staples for the stapler.
给我拿一卷胶带，一瓶胶水，还有订书机用的订书钉。

4. I'd like to look at sports clothes. Something is very "in". 我想看看运动服，要很时髦的那种。

5. Would you show me some sweaters that are light and warm?
［委婉］让我看看质地轻而保暖的毛衣好吗？

6. I need a briefcase. Can you show me some? 我要一个公文包，能让我看几种吗？

7. May I see that blue pair of slippers?［委婉］可以让我看看那双蓝色的拖鞋吗？

Ask for certain commodity（询问是否有某种商品）

1. Do you sell coverlets? /Have you got coverlets to sell? /Have you got any coverlets?
你们卖不卖床罩？

2. I'd like to get a shirt like this. Can you get one in my size?
我想要一件这样的衬衫，能拿一件尺寸适合我的吗？

Ask the salesperson to recommend the goods（请店员推荐商品）

1. What kind of toy would you recommend for a baby just about to celebrate its first
birthday?［委婉］给快过一周岁生日的娃娃买玩具，你推荐买什么？

2. I'd like to pick up something for this sunburn. Could you recommend something?
［委婉］我想买一种能治晒斑的产品，能介绍一下吗？

The salesperson recommends the goods（店员推荐）

1. We have a wide selection of T-shirts. Let me show you. 我们有许多种 T 恤衫，我给您看看。

2. We are having a sale on sandals this week. Everything is forty-five percent off.
这星期我们凉鞋大甩卖，全部降价 45%（打五五折）。

3. We have a full range of sizes and colors. You can choose from the rack on your right.
我们有各种规格和颜色的，您可以从右边的架子上挑选。

4. Let me show you some samples of various qualities. 我来给您看看各种不同质地的样品吧。

5. Is this what you are looking for? 这是不是您想要的？

Select goods（挑选商品）

Color and style（关于颜色和式样）

1. Do you have this kind of socks in darker brown? 有没有偏深棕色一点儿的这种袜子？

2. Do you have the same thing in a lighter shade? 有没有同款的，但颜色略浅一点儿的？

3. I like the style，but I don't care for the color. I want something brighter in color.
   我喜欢这个式样，但不喜欢这种颜色，我想要颜色鲜艳一点儿的。

4. It's rather showy. Perhaps you can show me something plainer.
   有点儿太艳了，或许还是让我看看比较素雅一些的吧。

5. I'm afraid it's a bit too fancy for me. 恐怕对我来说有点儿太花哨了。

6. I want something with national design. 我想要一些有民族设计的东西。

Specification and size（关于规格和尺寸）

1. Do you have the same thing in a smaller size? 同样的有没有小一些的？

2. I like this one，but the size is wrong. 我喜欢这一款，但尺码不对。

3. Please give me the king size. 请给我特大号的。

4. Well，actually I wanted something slightly larger. 唉，实际上我是想要稍微再大一点儿的。

Ask for something cheaper（询问是否有更便宜的商品）

1. Don't you have something in a lower price range? 有没有价格低一档的货？

2. Have you anything that doesn't cost so much? 有没有不用花这么多钱的？

Request for trial or trial run（要求试穿或试用）

1. May I try it on? ［委婉］可以试穿一下吗？

2. I'd like to try on this pair of jeans. Where's the fitting room?
   我想试一下这条牛仔裤。试衣间在哪里？

3. Can you show me how it works? 能给我示范一下怎么用吗？

4. Can you give a demonstration? I want to make sure it works smoothly and without any
   noise. 能展示给我看看吗？我想确定它运转自如而且无噪声。

Asking the price and bargaining（问价、讨价还价）

A customer asks the price（顾客问价）

1. What does it cost? 什么价钱？

2. How much a piece, please? 请问多少钱一件？

3. How much do you charge for the washing machine? 这台洗衣机多少钱？

4. Is this on sale? 这是不是降价的（商品）？
   Is this a sale item? 这是降价的货吗？

The salesperson tells the price of the goods（店员告知商品价格）

1. These are twenty dollars each. 每件12美元。

2. It's 80 cents per piece. 每个80美分。

3. It sells at ＄3 a bottle. 每瓶卖3美元。

4. The regular price is ＄65 a pair. 原价是 65 美元一双。

Customer's response to the price（顾客对价格的反应）

1. The price is a bit too high. 价格有点儿太高了。

2. That's rather expensive，isn't it? 相当贵，不是吗？

3. That's more than I want to pay. 高出我的预算了。

4. That seems reasonable. 价格是公道的。

5. Oh，that's a good price. 哦，价格不错。

Counter-offer（顾客还价）

1. Can you give a discount? 可以打个折扣吗？

2. Can you cut down the price a bit? 可以便宜一点儿吗？

3. Do you give a discount if I pay by cash? 如果我付现金，是不是可以打折扣？

4. Can you sell it for ＄28? I can give you no more than that. 28 美元卖不卖？再多我就不要了。

The salesperson explains not to accept counter-offer（店员说明不能接受还价）

1. We have only one price. 我们这里不还价。

2. We can't give any discounts. 我们这里不打折。

3. We can't give a discount. It's a sale price already. 我们不打折，这已经降过价了。

4. We only sell at the fixed price. /Our price is fixed.
   我们买东西价格是固定的。/我们价格是固定的。

5. The computer is sold under authorized price. It's the same for every shop in Beijing.
   这电脑是统一定价，北京所有店都是一样的价格。

The salesperson agrees to offer a discount.（店员同意打折扣）

1. All right. We'll offer you a special discount of 5%.
   好吧，我们给您特别优惠，打个 95 折吧。

2. OK. I'll give you a 15% discount if you pay in cash.
   好吧，如果您付现金，我就给您打 85 折。

3. It all comes to ten dollars forty cents，but I'll make it ten dollars. OK?
   总计 10 美元 40 美分，就付 10 美元吧，怎么样？

To buy or not to buy（买或不买）

Decide to buy（决定买）

1. That's just what I've been looking for. I'll take it. 那正是我想要的，我买了。

2. This suits me very well. 这东西正合我意。

3. I think this one will do. 我看这个就行了。

4. This is the very thing I need. 这正是我需要的东西。

5. I'll have this pair then. 那么我就要这一双了。

Decide not to buy（决定不买）

1. I'm sorry, but it isn't what I want. 对不起，这不是我想要的。

2. That's not what I'm looking for. Sorry to have troubled you.
   那个不是我想要的，对不起，麻烦你了。

Packing（包装）

The salesperson asks about packing（店员询问关于包装的要求）

1. Let me wrap it up for you. 让我帮您包好。

2. Shall I wrap them together or separately? 要包在一起，还是分开包装？

3. Do you wish to have it wrapped up as a gift? 您希望把它作为礼物包装吗？

Customer's request for packing（顾客提出包装要求）

1. Please wrap my purchases together. 请把我所买的东西都包在一起。

2. Never mind wrapping it up. Just put it in a box. 不用包起来，装在一个盒子里就行了。

3. Can you gift-wrap it for me? 可以帮我把它作为礼品包装起来吗？

4. Put them in a gift box and put on a ribbon，please. 请装在一个礼品盒子里并扎根丝带。

Payment and collection（付款、收款）

Checkout（结账）

1. How much is it all altogether? 总共多少钱？

2. How much do they come to in all? 这些加在一起一共多少钱？

3. What does that come to? 总共多少钱？

4. How much should I pay you? 我该付你多少钱？

Payment（付款）

1. Do you accept traveler's checks? 你们收旅行支票吗？

2. I wonder if I could pay by credit-card.［委婉］不知能不能用信用卡付款？

3. I have the exact amount here. 我的钱正好（不用找了）。

4. Well，here's a ten. 嗯，这是一张 10 元的钞票。

5. Sorry，I happen to have no small change with me. 对不起，我恰巧没有零钱。

Collection（收款）

1. I'm afraid we don't accept checks. 对不起，我们不收支票。

2. You can pay by check or credit card，but you can have a discount for cash. 您可以用支票或信用卡付款，但付现金可以打折。

3. Do you want to pay by cash or credit card? 您是付现金还是刷信用卡？

Will this be cash or credit card? 现金，还是刷信用卡？

Section Five：Culture Tips

黑色星期五（美国商场的圣诞促销）

关于"黑色星期五"的由来有多种说法，第一种就是指黑压压的一片人在感恩节后的星期五去商场排长队购物。

较普遍的是第二种说法：由于这一天是感恩节（11月的第四个星期四）后开业的第一天，之后就是美国传统而盛大的圣诞节，人们通常由此开始圣诞节大采购。美国的商场每年这一时间都会推出大量的打折和优惠活动，以在年底进行最后一次大规模的促销。而传统上用不同颜色的墨水记账，红色表示亏损，即赤字，黑色表示盈利。由于很多商店都会顾客盈门并有大额进账，所以把这个星期五叫作黑色星期五，用以表示这一天期待会有盈利。

第三种说法是：因为商店的打折活动一般都在感恩节结束的午夜（即周五零点）开始，想买便宜货的人必须摸着黑冲到商场排队买便宜货，这也可以视为是"黑色星期五"的一个来历。这种行为有个非常形象的叫法，即 Early Bird（早起的鸟儿）。

每年 11 月和 12 月本就是美国的传统购物旺季，"黑色星期五"更是美国人一年中购物最疯狂的日子。而商店的员工则使用"黑色星期五"这一名字来自嘲，表示这一天会忙得要死。而一些抗议消费至上主义的团体也特意选择这一天为"不消费日"。

在"黑色星期五"这天，绝大多数商店都会在清晨五、六点钟就开门，有的甚至更早。商家更会提前在报纸上刊登广告，发放优惠券，对商品大幅降价等吸引顾客。很多消费者把这一天看作准备圣诞礼物或买便宜货的黄金时间，由于降价商品数量有限，很多热门商店（如沃尔玛）门前在前一天晚上就会排起长队。而商店开门的那一刻也有时会由于过于拥挤和激烈争抢而酿成踩踏事件。

由于各商家要到最后一刻才公布自己的降价商品清单，并把这看作商业秘密，而网络上往往在几个星期前就出现了从各个渠道搞到的降价信息，从而也会引发一些法律纠纷。

尽管"黑色星期五"购物活动开展得热火朝天，但这种火热似乎却折射出另一种意义上的萧条。有评论称，"黑色星期五"的火热正是因为很多人平时都不敢花钱买东西，都等着感恩节之后开启降价折扣商品的"购物季"再出手。

一些商家（如 Best Buy）为了避免黑色带来的负面意义与联想，通常会使用"绿色星期五"的叫法，这里的绿色指的是美元钞票的颜色。

译　文

第二部分：相关信息

在线购物

在线购物是电子商务的一种形式，它可以让消费者使用网络浏览器通过互联网从卖家直接购买商品或服务。消费者通过直接访问零售商的网站或通过使用购物搜索引擎在供应商之间搜索来找到感兴趣的产品，这种搜索引擎显示相同产品在不同的电子零售商处的供货情况以及定价。截至 2016 年，顾客可以使用一系列不同的计算机和设备进行网上购物，包括台式电脑、笔记本电脑、平板电脑和智能手机。

当顾客在网络商店购买产品或服务时，该过程称为企业对消费者（B2C）在线购物。当一家网络商店使得一个企业能够向另一个企业购买商品时，该过程被称为企业对企业（B2B）在线购物。典型的网络商店使顾客能够浏览公司的产品和服务范围，查看产品的照片或视频，以及关于产品规格、特点和价格的信息。

网络商店通常能够让购物者使用"搜索"功能找到特定的品牌或商品。在线顾客必须接通互联网并拥有有效的支付方式以完成交易，例如信用卡或诸如贝宝类的服务。对于实体产品（例如平装书或衣服），电子零售商将产品运送给客户；对于数字产品，例如歌曲的数字音频文件或软件，电子零售商通常通过互联网将文件发送给顾客。这些在线零售公司中最大的是阿里巴巴、亚马逊和易贝。

第三部分：情境任务范例

情境：一天，李欣来到商店买一件夹克衫。以下是李欣和售货员的对话。（A：售货员；B：李欣）

A：早上好，我能帮您吗？

B：早上好，我想买一件新夹克衫。

A：我们的夹克衫在那边，在大衣和饰品旁边。我们这周大减价，所有商品打七折。

B：我喜欢这件夹克，我可以试试吗？

A：当然可以，试衣间在那边。

B：谢谢。

……

B：同样的款式有没有颜色略深一点儿的？这件我穿有点儿太艳了，或许还是让我看看比较素雅一点儿的吧。

A：这件是不是您想要的？

B：有没有大一号的，这件我穿太小了。

A：让我看看，恐怕我们目前没有这个号的了，我相信很快会进货的。如果您留下电话号码，货到时我会打电话通知您的。

B：别那么麻烦了，有没有其他款式的夹克衫？

A：是的，也许您可以试试这件。这件更轻、更暖和。

B：这件多少钱？

A：160 美元。

B：我可以试穿一下吗？

A：当然了。

B：看，这件夹克衫上面有个瑕疵，有一根线颜色不一样。

A：我再给您拿另外一件来。先生，我马上就回来……恐怕这是我们仅有的一件了。

B：可以打个折吗？

A：对不起，我们不能打折，这已经降过价了。

B：如果我用现金付款是不是可以打折呢？

A：好吧，如果您用现金付款，我就给您打个 95 折吧。

B：好的，我买了。

A：您还需要点儿别的什么吗？

B：不用了，谢谢。

A：让我帮您包好。

B：不用包起来，装一只袋子里就可以了。我该付你多少钱？

A：152 美元。

B：给你。

A：谢谢您，再见。

B：再见。

8. 4　Having Dinner

8. 4. 1　Entertain Friends at Home

Section One：Tasks

Situation 1：Zhang Jun and his wife invite Mr. and Mrs. Brown to have dinner in their house. He greets and welcomes the guests at the door, and then asks them to enter the living room. Make a dialogue according to the situation.

Situation 2：During the dinner, Zhang Jun and his wife invite the guests to drink and eat. Then as the host, Zhang Jun also proposes a toast. Make a dialogue according to the situation.

Situation 3：After dinner, the Browns thank them for their kind invitation and then leave. Make a dialogue according to the situation.

Section Two：Related Information

How to be a Polite Guest

Some British and American people like inviting friends for a meal at home. Dinner parties usually start between 7 and 8 p. m. and end at about 11 p. m. Ask your hosts what time you should arrive. It's polite to bring flowers, chocolates or a bottle of wine as a gift.

Usually the evening starts with drinks and snacks. If you want to be extra polite, say how much you like the room, or the pictures on the wall. But remember—it's not polite to ask how much things cost.

In many families, the husband sits at one end of the table and the wife sits at the other. They eat with their guests.

You'll probably start the meal with soup, and then you'll have meat or fish with vegetables, and then dessert, followed by coffee or tea. It's polite to finish everything on your plate and to take more if you want it.

Did you enjoy the evening? Call your hosts the next day, or write them a short "thank you" letter. British and American people like to say "thank you, thanks, thank you very much" all the time!

Vocabulary

snack ［snæk］*n.* 小吃

extra ［'ekstrə］*adv.* 特别地；非常　*adj.* 额外的；附加的

dessert [di'zɜ:t] *n*.餐后甜点；甜点心

as a gift　作为礼物

start with　从……开始

at the end of…　在……的尽头/一端

all the time　始终；一直

Section Three：Situational Task Samples

Situation：*Li Xin and his wife Liu Qian invited their American friend Jane and Sam to have dinner in their house last Friday evening.*（*A*：*Li Xin*；*B*：*Jane*；*C*：*Sam*；*D*：*Liu Qian*）

Welcome the guests

A：Come in，Jane. It's good to see you. Oh，Sam，thank you for your port[1]！

B：Hi，Li Xin.

C：You have a really nice house！

A：Thank you. Come on in，please. Let me take your coats. Please take seats. Help yourselves to some fruit.

B：Thank you.

Seat the guests at the table

A：Jane，Sam，the table is set. Let's go to the dining-room.

C：OK.

B：Qian，let me help you.

D：Oh，no，thanks，my dear. I have almost finished cooking. I'll be right there. You take a seat first.

A：Jane，down here，beside Sam.

B：OK. Thank you.

During the dinner

D：Jane，would you try our rice wine？

B：No，thanks. I'm not used to strong drinks. It'll go to my head.

D：You can rest assured[2] you won't get drunk.

B：I'll just try a drop then.

A：Sam，which do you prefer，brandy or Moutai？

C：I'm trying to stay away from drinking. Doctor's prescription，as a matter of fact.

A：Come on，be a sport[3]. A little drink is good for your health.

C：Then I'll drink a little bit of Moutai. I hear it's the best liquor in the world.

A：OK. Let me fill your glass. I propose a toast to our friendship.

B/C：To friendship！

D：Cheers！ …I hope you like Chinese food. I've cooked some typical Chinese dishes for you today.

A：Just help yourselves to whatever you like. I hope the dishes are to your taste.

B：I like them. They're done just to my taste.

D：Let me help you to some fried diced chicken with peanuts[4].

B：Thank you. It's very delicious. What a wonderful cook you are!

A：Jane，try some cold dishes. This is preserved egg[5].

B：No，thanks，I just don't feel like it. I'll try some sour beans[6].

D：Your plate is almost empty. Help yourself to some more fish.

C：I'm afraid I've had more than enough. All the dishes this evening are well cooked. I need a good appetite[7] to enjoy Chinese hospitality.

D：I'm glad you enjoy it.

After the dinner

D：Why don't you make yourselves comfortable in the lounge[8] while I get something to drink?

A：OK. Let's go…Try some of our home-made cakes.

B：Thank you. They taste great.

D：Who would like coffee or tea?

C：Coffee，and I'll take black coffee[9].

B：Tea，please.

D：Here you are.

B：Thank you. That was a great meal. You must have spent a lot of time preparing it.

D：It's nothing but a home-cooked Chinese meal. I'm glad you enjoy it.

Take a leave（Half an hour after dinner）

B：We really had a nice evening，but it's late. We've got to leave now.

D：Could you stay a little more while[10]?

B：I'm going to attend an opening ceremony at nine tomorrow morning. I must get up early.

D：Well，I'm sorry you can't stay any longer. Thank you for visiting us.

C：It's very nice staying with you tonight.

A：Drop in[11] again when you're free. You're always welcome.

C：Thank you very much. I will. Good night.

D：Take care. Good night.

Notes

1. port 波特酒，产自葡萄牙

2. rest assured 放心，确信无疑

3. be a sport 爽快点，够朋友一点

4. fried diced chicken with peanuts 宫保鸡丁。fried 油炸的；diced 切成丁的，切成小块的；peanut 花生。当英语里没有某一事物的名称时我们要根据该事物的特征做解释性说明，即采取意译的翻译方法，宫保鸡丁这道菜我们就通过对食材和烹制方法的描述做了解释性翻译。

5. preserved egg 皮蛋

6. sour beans 酸豆角

7. appetite 胃口，食欲

8. lounge 客厅，前厅

9. black coffee 不加牛奶（或奶油和糖）的咖啡，清咖啡

10. stay a little while 稍微待一会儿；stay a little more while 再多待一会儿

11. drop in 顺便拜访

Section Four：Functional Expression Bank

A. Welcome the guests（迎客）

Host welcomes the guests（主人迎接客人）

1. Come in，Mr. Zhang. It's good to see you. 张先生，请进，见到你真好。

2. Welcome. It's so nice of you to come. 欢迎，你能来真好。

3. Come on in. Let me take your coat. 请进来，让我帮你把外衣挂起来。

Invite the guests to take their seats（请客人落座）

1. Sit down and make yourself comfortable. I'll be with you in a minute.

   请坐，别客气，我马上就来陪你。

2. Please take a seat. Help yourself to the things on the table.

   请坐，桌上的食品，请随便吃。

3. Here. Have a seat. Make yourself at home. Can I get you something to drink? Tea，coffee，or something cold?

   请坐，请别拘束。我给你拿些饮料好吗？是喝茶，咖啡，还是什么冷饮？

The guests' reply（客人答话）

1. I'm very glad I could come and be with you today. 今天能到你这儿来，我非常高兴。

2. Thank you for inviting me/asking me over. 谢谢你请我来。

3. I'm glad to be here. You have a very nice place. 我很高兴来这里，你的房子很不错。

4. A cup of tea would be lovely, if it's no trouble. 最好是一杯茶，麻烦你了。

5. No，thanks. I've just had a glass of water. 谢谢，不用了，我刚喝了一杯水。

6. I'd like something cool. A glass of apple juice，please.

   我想喝点凉的东西，一杯苹果汁吧。

B. Seat the guests at the table（请客人入席）

Request the guests to sit at the table（请客人入座）

1. Please take a seat，everybody. 大家请坐。

2. The table is set. Let's go to the dining-room. 桌子已经摆好了，咱们去餐厅吧。

3. Dinner is ready. Please be seated and make yourselves comfortable.

   饭菜已经做好了，请坐，别客气。

4. Come on to the dining-room. Let's begin before it gets cold. 去餐厅吧，咱们趁热吃。

Arrange a seat（安排座位）

1. Where do you want me to sit? 你要我坐在哪儿？

2. Down here，beside Bill. OK? 这里，坐比尔旁边，怎么样？

3. Bob，you sit next to your uncle. 鲍勃，你坐在你叔叔旁边。

4. Will you please take this seat? 你坐在这儿，好吗？

5. I'll put Jim on my right so he could help me serve.
   我让吉姆坐我右边，这样他能帮我招呼大家。

【注意】在西方，请客吃饭的方式除了让大家围坐在餐桌旁吃饭外，还经常采用比较随意的自助餐（buffet）形式。将食物准备好摆在桌子上，客人们自己动手去取，然后各自找地方坐下来吃。在这种情形下，主人只需宣布"开饭"即可。例如：Dinner is on the table. Everyone，help yourself!（饭菜已经在桌子上了，大家用餐吧!）

C. During the dinner（就餐中）

Invite the guests to drink（请客人喝酒）

1. Would you try our rice wine?［委婉］尝尝我们的米酒怎么样？

2. Would you like some whisky soda?［委婉］来点威士忌苏打水怎么样？

3. Wouldn't you care for something a little stronger?
   ［委婉］喝点稍微烈一点儿的酒，你不反对吧？

4. How about a little port? 来点波特酒怎么样？

5. Which do you prefer, sherry or brandy? 雪利酒和白兰地，你更喜欢哪一种？

6. May I fill your glass again?［委婉］再给你把杯子满上可以吗？

7. You can rest assured you won't get drunk. 你可以放心，你不会喝醉的。

8. Come on，be a sport. A little drink is good for your health.
   来吧，爽快点儿，适量喝点对身体有好处。

【注意】在西方，过分劝酒被认为是不礼貌的行为。

Reaction of the guests（对劝酒的反应）

1. I'll just try a drop then. 那我就尝一点点吧。

2. Just a glass of beer，please. 只要一杯啤酒。

3. It's quite strong, isn't it? 这酒劲很大，是吧？

4. Brandy is too strong for me，I'm afraid. 恐怕白兰地对我来说有点劲太大了。

5. I'm not used to strong drinks. It'll go to my head. 我喝烈酒不行，会头晕。

6. I know very little about drinking. Maybe you could select something for me.
   我对喝酒是外行，也许你可以给我选一些适合我的。

7. I think I'll try the famed Moutai. I hear it's the best liquor in the world.
   我想尝尝有名的茅台，听说那是世界上最好的白酒。

8. I'm trying to stay away from drinking. Doctor's prescription，as a matter of fact.
   我正在戒酒。事实上，这是医生的嘱咐。

Propose a toast（提出祝酒）

1. Cheers! /Toast! 干杯!
   Bottoms up!［非正式］干杯!

2. To you! 为你干杯!

3. Your health! /To your health! /Here's to your health. 祝你健康!

4. Here's to your safe journey home! 祝你回程一路平安!

5. I propose a toast to… 我提议为……干杯!

6. May I propose a toast to our friendship and cooperation?

  ［正式］我能提议为我们的友谊和合作干杯吗？

7. Well，here's to you，—in appreciation of all you have done to promote the friendship between our two colleges. 敬你一杯，感谢你为增进我们两校之间的友谊而做的一切。

8. In conclusion, I wish to propose a toast to the success of our negotiation.

  ［正式］最后，我提议为我们谈判的成功干杯。

9. In closing, I would like to invite you to join me in a toast to the trade and friendship between us! ［正式］最后，请各位举杯，为我们之间的贸易和友谊而干杯！

Reply to the toast（祝酒应答）

1. Cheers! 干杯！

  Bottoms up! ［非正式］干杯！

2. To you! 为你干杯！

  And to you, cheers. 也为你干杯。

  And to yours, cheers. 也为你的（成功、健康等）干杯！

3. I'll drink to that, cheers. 我同意，干杯！

  I'll go along with that, cheers. 我同意，干杯！

4. To friendship and cooperation. 为友谊与合作干杯。

5. To the success of … 为……的成功干杯。

Ask the guest to eat（请客人吃菜）

1. I hope you like Chinese food. I've cooked some typical Chinese dishes today.

  我希望你们喜欢中国菜，今天我为你们做了几道地道的中国菜。

2. Just help yourself to whatever you like. I hope the dishes are to your taste.

  请随便吃，我希望这些菜合你的胃口。

3. Let me help you to some of this sea cucumber. 我来给你夹一点海参。

4. Shall I help you to some pieces of sweet and sour pork chop?

  我给你夹几块糖醋排骨怎么样？

5. How about some prawns? 来点对虾怎么样？

6. Try some cold dishes. This is tuna salad. 尝尝冷盘，这是金枪鱼沙拉。

7. Would you like some mashed potatoes? ［委婉］要点土豆泥吗？

8. Here，have some fruit. ［随便］来，吃点水果。

【注意】若客人不喜欢某样食物，可以坦率说明，如：I'm afraid it doesn't agree with me. （恐怕这东西我吃了不舒服。）或者是：No, thanks, I just don't feel like it. I'll take some… （不了，谢谢你，我只是不喜欢。我想吃点……）在西方，主人请客人用菜，一般情况下只请一次，因为他们认为给别人强塞食物是不礼貌的行为。这一点与中国人截然相反，在中国，一般请客人用菜的次数越多表示主人越热情好客。所以，与西方人吃饭不必客气，因为他们不理解中国人客气的思维习惯，如果请你用菜一次你不吃，对方便不会再让了。

Praise from the guest（客人边吃边赞扬）

1. I like it. It's done just to my taste. 我很喜欢，这正适合我的口味。

2. How appetizing it looks! I'd love some…They are really lovely.

看起来真开胃。我很想来点……太好吃了。

3. What a feast you are giving us! 你的招待太丰盛了！

4. It's such a rich dinner. I've never had anything better.
宴席这么丰盛，我从来没吃过这么好吃的菜。

5. The dishes are absolutely delicious，especially the roast duck and fried shrimps.
味道太好了，尤其是烤鸭和炸虾。

6. Mmm，excellent! What a wonderful cook you are!
绝了！你真是个了不起的厨师！（你做菜的手艺真棒！）

7. All the dishes this evening are well cooked. You take care of color, flavor and taste all at the same time. 今晚的菜烧得都很好，色、香、味俱佳。

Ask the guests to eat a little more（请客人再多吃一点）

1. How about a little more turkey? 再吃点火鸡好吗？

2. Please have some more fish. 请再吃点鱼。

3. Do have another piece of chicken. 一定得再吃块鸡。

4. How about seconds on the barbecue? 再添点烤肉怎么样？

5. May I help you to some more beef? 再给你来点牛肉好吗？

6. Your plate is almost empty. Help yourself to seconds. 你的盘子差不多空了，再来添点吧。

7. Are you sure you won't have any more? 你真的一点也不要了吗？

8. Won't you have some more bread? 你不再要点面包了？

（seconds *n*. 再来一份食物。）

The guest agrees to eat a little more（客人表示再吃一点）

1. I'd like some more beef, please.［委婉］我想再吃点牛肉。

2. I'll have a little more mushroom soup. It tastes wonderful.
我想再来点蘑菇汤，味道不错。

3. I think I'll have seconds on the fried fish. 我想再添点炸鱼。

The guest couldn't eat any more（客人表示实在吃不下）

1. It's very good but I'm almost stuffed. 真不错，不过我已经饱了。

2. No more for me，I'm really filled up. 我一点也不要了，真的吃饱了。

3. I don't think I could eat another bite. 我想我是一口也吃不下了。

4. I'm afraid I've had more than enough. 我想我已经吃得太多了。

5. I've had three helpings. I just couldn't eat any more.
我已经吃了三份了，现在一点也吃不下去了。

6. You need a good appetite to enjoy Chinese hospitality.
要享受中国人的热情好客没有很好胃口是不行的。

7. My appetite is no problem，but my figure is. 我的胃口没有问题，只是我的体型要成问题了。

8. I see another course coming up. I must leave space for it.
又一道菜上来了，我（肚子里）得留点地方（吃那道菜）。

Use chopsticks（使用筷子）

1. Chopsticks or knife and fork? 用筷子还是用刀叉？

2. Do you want knife and fork or chopsticks? 你是要刀叉还是筷子？

3. Can you manage to eat with chopsticks? 你能用筷子吃吗？

4. You place both sticks between the thumb and the forefinger，like this.

你把筷子夹在拇指和食指之间，像这样。

5. The point is to keep one still and move the other so as to make them work like pincers.

要点是让其中一根不动，活动另一根，像钳子那样。

6. You'll soon get used to using chopsticks, I'm sure. 我确信你会很快适应用筷子的。

7. I see you are quite expert with chopsticks. 我看你筷子用得很好。

Help to pass something.（请帮助递一下）

1. Pass the mustard，please. 请把芥末递过来。

2. Please pass the salt around. 请把盐传一下。

3. Can you pass me the…能把……递给我吗？

4. May I trouble you for the butter? ［委婉］能请你把黄油递过来吗？

5. Could you pass me the pepper? ［委婉］请把胡椒粉递过来好吗？

6. Could I have the vegetable salad? ［委婉］能给我来点蔬菜沙拉吗？

D. After dinner（餐后活动）

Ask the guests leave for a rest（请客人离席休息）

1. Let's move to the sitting room and make ourselves comfortable. 让我们到起居室去歇歇。

2. Why don't you make yourselves comfortable in the lounge while I get the coffee?

你们为何不到前厅去休息一会儿，我去准备咖啡好吗？

3. It seems as if everyone's finished. Why don't all of you go and sit and relax in the other room while I take care of the table?

看样子你们都吃好了。我来收拾桌子，你们到那个房间去坐坐，休息一下，好吗？

4. Would you like to go into the living room now? It's more comfortable.

［委婉］现在请到起居室去坐坐好吗？那儿更舒服一些。

Have dessert（餐后甜点）

1. Would everyone like dessert now or later? ［委婉］你们现在吃甜点还是过一会儿再吃？

2. Try some of our home-made biscuits. 请尝尝我们自己做的饼干。

3. My wife has made a cake just for you. 我妻子特意为你们准备了蛋糕。

Coffee and tea（咖啡和茶）

Host：

1. We're making coffee for you folks. You'll have some，won't you?

我们在给大伙煮咖啡，你们都要喝一些，是不是？

2. But first，who would like coffee or tea? 先看看谁喝咖啡，谁喝茶？

3. How do you take your coffee，black or white? 你们的咖啡加不加牛奶？

4. Would you like yours with milk and sugar? ［委婉］你的是不是加牛奶和糖？

Guests：

1. Half and half. 一半咖啡一半牛奶。

2. I'll take mine black. 我想喝点清咖啡。

3. I'll have tea, if it's no trouble. 如果方便的话，我想喝茶。

4. I'd rather have tea, if you don't mind. 如果方便的话我想喝点茶。

5. Tea for me. 给我来点茶。

   Tea, please. 来杯茶。

Praise from the guest after dinner and reply of the host (客人的餐后赞扬以及主人的回答)

Guests：

1. That was a great meal. Everything was delicious. 这顿饭真丰盛，每道菜都很可口。

2. Thank you. This has been a delicious meal. 谢谢你，这顿饭味道很好。

3. You must have spent a lot of time preparing it. 准备这顿饭一定花了你很长时间。

Host：

1. I'm glad you enjoy it. 你吃得满意，我很高兴。

2. It's nothing but a home-cooked Chinese meal. 没什么，只是一顿中式的家常便饭。

E. Take a leave（告辞）

Speech before leave（告辞铺垫）

1. Thank you very much. I had a nice evening. 非常感谢，我今晚过得很愉快。

2. Thank you for asking me over. I had a very enjoyable/nice/pleasant time.
   谢谢你邀请我，我过得非常愉快。

3. Thank you for the lovely afternoon/evening/meal.
   感谢你使我们度过了愉快的下午/晚上/享受了可口的菜肴。

4. I enjoyed our talk and the lovely dinner. Thank you very much.
   我们谈得愉快，吃得也开心。非常谢谢你。

【注意】在告辞前，西方国家的人一般先说些表示自己玩得很高兴，谈话很有启发或者表示感谢邀请之类的话，用来暗示即将提出告辞，以避免让主人感到唐突。

Put forward to leave（提出告辞）

1. I'd better be off, I think. 我想我该走了。

2. I'm sorry to have to rush off like this. 对不起，我得赶紧走了。

3. Well, I'm afraid I must be off/go now. 恐怕我该走了。

4. Actually, we'll have to be thinking of going. 说真的，我们该准备走了。

5. I have an appointment at six, so I'm afraid I'd better hurry along.
   6 点钟我有个约会，恐怕我得赶紧走。

6. It's really time I was leaving. I have a long way to go. 我真该走了，我还要走很长的路。

【注意】在西方国家，一般在别人家中做客，饭后至少要待上半小时再告辞才不失礼。告辞的话通常是由主客（guest of honor）或客人中年长的已婚妇女提出，等她或他起身走的时候，别人才可告辞。如果你有事不得不先走，最好先悄悄地和女主人打个招呼，离开时尽量不要惊动别人。

Persuade the guest to stay longer（主人挽留）

1. But it's still early. 但是时间还早呢。

2. Must you really be going? 你真的要走啦？

3. Surely you can stay a little longer，can't you? 你肯定还能再待一会儿，对吗？

4. Why are you in such a hurry? Stay a little longer. 你为什么这么匆忙？再待一会儿吧。

5. Please stay a little longer for a second cup of tea. 请再待一会儿，再来一杯茶。

6. Are you quite sure you can't stay for a little while? 你真的不能再待一会儿了？

7. Oh，can't you stay a bit longer? We so seldom have a chance to get together.

你不能再待一会儿了吗？我们真的难得有机会相聚。

Consent to the departure of the guests（同意客人离去）

1. Thanks for dropping in. 感谢你来拜访。

2. Drop in again when you're free. 有空再来玩。

3. I hope we can get together again. 我希望我们能再次相聚。

4. Must you go right now? I hope I shall see you soon again.

你非得马上走吗？我希望不久能再见到你。

5. We're sorry you have to leave. It's been so nice seeing you.

真遗憾你要走了，见到你真高兴。

6. If that is the case，I shall not keep you any longer. 如果是那样的话，我就不挽留你了。

7. Well，I won't keep you then. It was very nice of you to come to see me.

好吧，那我就不留你了。感谢你来看望我。

【注意】按照西方人的习惯，主人送客人出家门或来到他的车旁，客人一般不必加以劝阻。为了表示客气，客人可再次说些感谢的话。如：It was a nice evening. I enjoyed talking with you. 真是个美好的夜晚，我喜欢和你聊天。

Section Five：Culture Tips

做客携礼

去外国朋友家做客，出于礼貌尽量带些小礼物。当然，对方请吃饭主要是想请你出席，而不是在意礼物，所以即使未带，对方也不会太在意。

送礼物要看对象，针对不同年龄的人我们应选择不同的礼物。如果对方比较年轻的话，那可能在选礼物方面就比较灵活，啤酒相对来说是比较保守的选择，你可以直接问你的朋友他喜欢喝哪个牌子的，若对方回答随意，你就根据自己的喜好任意选择就好。不建议买伏特加、朗姆杜松子或白兰地，因为这些酒还要混合其他材料，比较麻烦。

如果是去中年人家里做客，那就带一瓶葡萄酒，一般外国人都很喜欢喝葡萄酒。至于葡萄酒种类的选择，可以上网搜索搭配不同食物的建议，更重要的是还有不同场合、不同对象可以送的葡萄酒推荐。如果实在不想花时间想，那就买香槟吧，也是不错的选择。

如果拜访老年人，建议带巧克力或者鲜花。巧克力建议买那种大包装的。至于鲜花，可以上网搜索一下花语再进行选择。只要不是送恋人就别买玫瑰花，即使是拜访恋人父母家也不要带玫瑰。

去别人家做客空手去的确不好，在送礼上花点小心思会让主人很开心。但是礼物的选择并不仅限于上述内容，如果是好朋友，那送什么应该都不会太介意，就算不送也不会抱怨，如果是年长且关系不是很熟的，也可以送本国的特产（吃的就尽量不要带了，怕主人吃不惯），比如工艺品，一般是外国人很喜欢的礼物，即使是很便宜的中国结，可能都会让他们感到很开心。

译　文

第二部分：相关信息

如何成为一个有礼貌的客人

　　一些英国人和美国人喜欢邀请朋友在家吃饭。晚餐聚会通常在晚上 7 点到 8 点之间开始，晚上 11 点左右结束。问问主人你应该什么时候到达。带鲜花、巧克力或一瓶葡萄酒作为礼物是有礼貌的。

　　晚上通常先喝饮料和吃小吃。如果你想要表现得特别有礼貌，可以说你有多喜欢这个房间，或者墙上的画。但是记住，问东西多少钱是不礼貌的。

　　在许多家庭中，丈夫坐在桌子的一端，妻子坐在另一端。他们和客人一起吃饭。

　　这顿饭可能会从喝汤开始，接下来是肉或鱼配蔬菜，然后是甜点，紧随其后的是咖啡或茶。礼貌的做法是吃完盘子里的所有东西，如果需要，可以多吃些。

　　那个晚上你过得开心吗？第二天给主人打个电话，或者给他们写一封简短的感谢信。英国人和美国人总是喜欢说"谢谢你，谢谢，非常感谢"。

第三部分：情境任务范例

情境：上周五晚上，李欣和他的妻子刘倩邀请他们的美国朋友简和山姆在他们家吃晚饭。
（A：李欣；B：简；C：山姆；D：刘倩）

欢迎客人

A：进来，简。很高兴见到你。哦，山姆，谢谢你的波特酒！

B：嗨，李欣。

C：你的房子真漂亮！

A：谢谢。请进来，让我帮你们把外衣挂起来。请坐，随便吃点儿水果。

B：谢谢你。

给客人安排座位

A：简，山姆，桌子已经摆好了，咱们去餐厅吧。

C：好的。

B：倩，让我来帮帮你吧。

D：哦，不用，谢谢，亲爱的。我差不多已经做完饭了。我马上就去。你先去坐吧。

A：简，这里，坐山姆旁边。

B：好的，谢谢。

用餐中

D：简，来尝尝我们的米酒好吗？

B：不用，谢谢啦。我喝烈酒不习惯，会头晕。

D：你可以放心，你不会喝醉的。

B：那我就尝一点点吧。

A：山姆，你喜欢白兰地还是茅台？

C：我正在戒酒，事实上，这是医生的嘱咐。

A：来吧，爽快点儿，适量喝点儿对身体有好处。

C：那我就喝一点儿茅台，我听说那是世界上最好的白酒。

A：好啊。让我把你的杯子倒满。我提议为我们的友谊干杯。

B/C：为了友谊！

D：干杯！……我希望你们喜欢中国菜，今天我为你们做了几道地道的中国菜。

A：请随便吃，我希望这些菜合你们的胃口。

B：我很喜欢，它们正适合我的口味。

D：我来给你夹点儿宫保鸡丁。

B：谢谢，真是太美味了。你做菜的手艺真棒！

A：简，尝尝凉菜，这是皮蛋。

B：不，谢谢，我只是不喜欢这道菜。我想吃点儿酸豆角。

D：你的盘子差不多空了，再来添点儿鱼吧。

C：恐怕我已经吃得太多了。今晚的菜烧得都很好。要享受中国人的热情好客要有很好胃口啊！

D：你喜欢吃，我很高兴。

餐后

D：你们为何不到前厅去休息一会儿，我去准备些喝的好吗？

A：好的，我们走吧……来尝尝我们自制的蛋糕。

B：谢谢，味道好极了。

D：谁喝咖啡，谁喝茶？

C：咖啡，给我一杯清咖啡。

B：请给我来杯茶。

D：给你。

B：谢谢。这顿饭真丰盛，为准备这顿饭一定花了你很长时间吧。

D：没什么，只是一顿中式的家常便饭。你们吃得愉快，我很高兴。

告辞（晚餐后半小时）

B：我们度过了一个愉快的夜晚。但是已经晚了，我们现在得走了。

D：你们能再待一会儿吗？

B：明天上午九点我要参加一个开幕式。我必须早起。

D：好吧，很遗憾你们不能再待一会儿了。谢谢来拜访我们。

C：今晚和你们在一起很开心。

A：有空再来玩儿。随时欢迎你们。

C：非常感谢，我会来的。晚安。

D：保重，晚安。

8.4.2 Have Dinner in a Restaurant

Section One: Tasks

Situation 1: Tom and his girlfriend Alice want to eat outside. They are discussing which restaurant to go. Make a dialogue according to the situation with your partner.

Situation 2: They come to the chosen restaurant, order dishes and eat there. Make a dialogue according to the situation with your partner.

Situation 3: After dinner, Tom checks out. Make a dialogue according to the situation with your partner.

Section Two: Related Information

How to Act at a Dinner Party

In the business world, you always need to attend various kinds of dinner parties. Here are some instructions regarding good table manners that will help you through any formal or semi-formal lunch or dinner party. [1]

1. Unfold your napkin and place it on your knees. Use it for occasionally wiping your lips or fingers once seated. [2] At the end of the dinner, leave the napkin tidily where it used to be. [3]

2. Wait your turn for food. It is traditional to serve the most senior lady at the table first, then the other ladies, and lastly the gentlemen. Never start to eat until the hostess begins to eat. [4]

3. Use the cutlery. If there are lots of different sets of cutlery beside the plate, start at the outside and work in. If in doubt, have a look at what the other guests are doing. Hold the knife and fork with the handles in the palm of the hand, forefinger on top, and thumb underneath. While eating, rest the knife and fork on either side of the plate between mouthfuls. When you have finished eating, place them side by side in the center of the plate.

4. Try your food. In the event of being presented with a dish you dislike, it is polite to at least make some attempt to eat it. [5] Or at the very least, cut it up a little, and move it around the plate. It is quite acceptable to leave some food to one side of your plate if you are full. On the other hand, don't attempt to leave your plate so clean that it looks as though you haven't eaten in days!

5. Make polite conversation with those guests around you. Dinner parties are not just about the food; they are intended to be a sociable occasion.

6. Express gratitude. Thank the host and hostess for their hospitality before leaving.

7. Written thanks. Send a personal note to the host and hostess shortly afterwards thanking them for the pleasurable evening.

Vocabulary

instruction [ɪnˈstrʌkʃ(ə)n] *n.* 教导；指示

regarding [rɪˈgɑːdɪŋ] *prep.* 关于，至于

formal ['fɔːm(ə)l] *adj.* 正式的

semi-formal ['semifɔːməl] *adj.* 半正式的

unfold [ʌn'fəuld] *vt.* 打开；呈现　*vi.* 展开；显露

napkin ['næpkɪn] *n.* 餐巾；餐巾纸

occasionally [ə'keɪʒnəli] *adv.* 偶尔；间或

wipe [waɪp] *vi.* 擦；*vt.* 擦；涂上

senior ['siːnɪə] *adj.* 高级的；年长的；地位较高的；年资较深的

cutlery ['kʌtlərɪ] *n.* 餐具

handle ['hændl] *n.* 把手；柄

palm [pɑːm] *n.* 手掌

forefinger ['fɔːfɪŋgə] *n.* 食指

underneath [ˌʌndə'niːθ] *prep.* 在……的下面 *adj.* 下面的，底层的 *adv.* 在下面，在底下

mouthful ['mauθful] *n.* 一口，满口

sociable ['səuʃəb(ə)l] *adj.* 社交的；好交际的

gratitude ['grætɪtjuːd] *n.* 感谢（的心情）；感激

at the very least　最起码

on the other hand　另一方面

side by side　并排；并肩；一起

as though　好像；仿佛

Notes

1. Here are some instructions regarding good table manners that will help you through any formal or semi-formal lunch or dinner party. 这里有一些关于餐桌礼仪的指导，将帮助你在任何正式或半正式的午餐或晚宴场合下用餐。regarding good table manners 为介词短语作后置定语的用法；that 在句中引导定语从句，先行词为 table manners。

2. Use it for occasionally wiping your lips or fingers once seated. 落座后，不时用餐巾擦一下你的嘴唇或手指。"once＋分词" 常表示 "一旦做某事"，如：Once seen, it will never be forgotten. 一旦见过，就再也不会忘记它。

3. At the end of the dinner, leave the napkin tidily where it used to be. 晚餐结束时，把餐巾整齐地放在之前摆放的地方。

4. Never start to eat until the hostess begins to eat. 直到女主人开始吃东西，你才开始吃。until 用于否定句中，表示动作直到 until 短语所表示的时间才开始发生，即表示动作的起点。一般译为 "直到……才" 或 "直到……之前（……还不）"。

5. In the event of being presented with a dish you dislike, it is polite to at least make some attempt to do so. 如果有你不喜欢吃的菜，那么礼貌的做法是至少尝一下。in the event of doing sth. 万一，如果，倘若……；being presented with 为被动语态用法，本句中意为 "给你上……菜"；at least 至少；make some attempt to do sth. 尝试做某事

Section Three：Situational Task Samples

Situation：*One day, Li Xin and his wife Liu Qian plan to have dinner in a restaurant.*

(*A*: *Li Xin*; *B*: *Liu Qian*; *C*: *Waiter* ; *D*: *Waitress*)

Choose a restaurant

A: I feel like eating out today.

B: Where do you suggest we go?

A: Let's go and eat some western food.

B: How about Milo Sun Restaurant? Their pizzas are pretty good.

A: OK. Let's go.

In the restaurant

Wait for seats

C: Good evening, do you have a reservation?

A: We haven't got a reservation. Well, do you have any table available[1]?

C: I'm sorry we're filled up right now. Would you mind waiting?

B: Will that be long?

C: It won't be long, maybe five to ten minutes.

B: OK.

...

C: Sorry to have kept you waiting. I'll show you to your table. Here's the menu. Your waitress will be with you in a minute.

B: Thank you.

Order dishes[2]

D: May I take your order?

A: Could you suggest something?

D: Today's special is baked shrimps. It's always been a favorite with our customers.

B: OK, we'll try the shrimps.

D: What would you like to start with?[3]

A: Parma ham with melon[4].

D: What's next?

B: Black pepper beef pizza[5].

A: A steak for me, please.

D: Would you like any drinks?

B: Watermelon juice.

A: I'd like red wine.

D: And dessert?

A: I think we'll have strawberry ice-cream[6].

D: OK.

During the dinner

D: I'm sorry, madam, but we have no watermelon juice left. Would you like to change it for[7] something else?

B: Then orange juice for me, please.

A: There's been a mistake. I asked for red wine, not Corona[8].

D: I'm sorry I must have confused the orders. Let me take this back and bring you red wine.

A: That's OK.

After the dinner

A: May I have the bill, please?

D: Here you are, sir. It's $85 in all.

A: Do I pay you or the cashier?

D: Either is OK.

A: Here is $100, and keep the change.

D: Thank you very much!

Notes

1. available 有空的，可获得的
2. order dishes 点菜
3. start with 从……开始
4. parma ham with melon 帕尔玛蜜瓜火腿，一种凉菜
5. black pepper beef pizza 黑胡椒牛肉披萨
6. strawberry ice-cream 草莓冰激凌
7. change A for B 把 A 换成 B
8. Corona 科罗娜，一种常见的啤酒。

Section Four: Functional Expression Bank

Choose a restaurant（选择餐馆）

Suggest eating out（建议去外面吃饭）

1. I feel like eating out today. 我想今天到外面吃饭。
2. Where do you suggest we go? 你说我们去哪儿呢？
3. Let's go and eat some Japanese food. 我们去吃日本料理吧。
4. Which is the best restaurant round here? 这里最好的餐馆是哪家？
5. I'm really not familiar with restaurants here. I was hoping you could suggest some places.［委婉］这里的餐厅我一点儿也不熟悉，我希望你能说说去哪里。

Choose the restaurant（选择餐厅）

1. What about the one in the next block, close to the shopping mall?
   隔壁街区购物中心旁边那家餐馆怎么样？
2. There are thousands of restaurants in London. It depends on what kind of food you want to eat. 伦敦有几千家餐馆，这要看你想吃哪种风味的菜。
3. I've heard so much about the famous Roast Peking Duck and I've been expecting to

taste it for a long time. 我多次听人谈起北京烤鸭很有名，早就想一饱口福了。

4. The restaurant we're going to is quite well-known. The cooking's always good there.
我们要去的那家餐馆很有名气，菜总是烧得不错。

5. That is my favorite place. Their prawns are excellent. 那是我特别喜欢去的地方。他们的虾做得很棒。

6. I have especially chosen this restaurant. It's noted for its quiet surroundings and very good Chinese cuisine. 我特意选了这家餐馆。此处因环境清幽和美味的中式菜肴而闻名。

Make a reservation（联系预订）

Reserve a table（预订餐桌）

1. I want to make a reservation for dinner tonight. 我要预订今晚的正餐。

2. I'd like to make a reservation for next Sunday night.
〔委婉〕我想预订下周日晚上去吃饭。

3. I'd like to book a table for tomorrow lunchtime.
〔委婉〕我要预订一张明天中午的餐桌。

4. Reserve me a table for a party of 6 at 7:00 p. m. this/next Thursday. 给我留一张本/下周四晚上 7 点钟的 6 人餐桌。

5. I want a private dining-room for 4 at 7:30 this evening. 我要预订一个今晚 7 点半 4 个人用的小包房。

Inquire about the dinner time and the number of people（询问就餐时间、人数）

1. How many are there in your party? 你们一行几个人？

2. What time? 订什么时间？

What time do you want your reservation for? 您想预订什么时间？

What time would you like to come? 〔委婉〕您几点来？

Cancel the reservation（取消预订）

I ordered a table for 10 for dinner tomorrow，but I'm afraid I'll have to cancel it.
我预订了明晚 10 个人的餐桌，但恐怕我得取消了。

Explain to/Inform the waiter the reserved table（说明/告知服务员已预订的餐桌）

1. I have made a reservation. A table for six. My name is Anna.
我预订了一张六个人的餐桌，我叫安娜。

2. I have a table booked for eight under the name of Susan.
我预订了一张八个人的餐桌，名字是苏珊。

3. I phoned myself this morning and I was promised a window table.
今天上午我自己打电话过来的，你们答应给我留一张靠窗的餐桌。

Arrange seats for the customers（安排顾客入座）

Arrange seats for the customers with reservation（安排已预订的顾客入座）

1. Please come this way. How would you like this one?
〔委婉〕请这边走，这张桌子怎么样？

2. We have a table by the stage for you. 我们给您留了一张靠近舞台的餐桌。

3. Yes，we have a window table reserved for you. Would you like to come this way?

［委婉］是的，我们给您留了个靠窗的餐桌。请这边走好吗？

4. Can I take your coat，sir/madam? 要我给您挂外衣吗，先生/女士？

Customers without reservation require to be seated（没有预订的客人要求安排入座）

1. Do you have a table for three? 有三人桌子吗？

2. We'd like a table near a window.［委婉］我们想要个靠窗的桌子。

3. We haven't got a reservation. Is there still a place vacant? 我们没有预订，还有空位置吗？

4. We're expecting three more in a few minutes，so there'll be five of us.

还等三位，几分钟内就到，所以我们一共五个人。

Ask the customers to wait（请顾客稍等）

1. I'm afraid there'll be a short wait. 恐怕要稍等片刻。

2. I'm afraid it'll be about five minutes before I can seat you.

恐怕要等五分钟才能给您安排座位。

3. Could you wait a moment to be seated? It won't be long.

［委婉］稍等一会儿再给您安排座位好吗？要不了多久。

4. Would you like to have a cocktail in our lounge while you're waiting? I'll let you know when your table is ready.

［委婉］您一边在我们的休息室喝杯鸡尾酒一边等好吗？有空桌我就来叫您。

Lead the customers to the seats（领顾客入座）

1. We are ready now. Please follow me. 现在可以了，请跟我来。

2. There is a table free now. Come with me，please. 现在有张空桌，请跟我来。

Order dishes（点菜）

Ask the customers to order（请顾客点菜）

1. Are you ready to order now? 现在可以点菜了吗？

2. Would you like to order now，sir/madam?［委婉］先生/女士，现在点菜吗？

3. Would you like any drinks?［委婉］想喝点什么吗？

Ask the waiter to recommend dishes（请服务员推荐菜品）

1. What's good today? 今天有什么好吃的？

2. What would you recommend?［委婉］你推荐什么菜？

3. Could you recommend something light?［委婉］还能推荐点清淡些的菜吗？

4. What vegetables do you recommend to go with it? 你建议我们配上什么蔬菜一起吃？

The waiter introduces the dishes（服务员介绍菜品）

1. Today's special is steak. It's the best here. 今天的特色菜是牛排，这里最好的菜。

2. For dessert，we have cream cakes and apple pie.

至于甜点，我们有奶油蛋糕和苹果馅饼。

3. There is a soup to start with，a choice of thick soup or clear soup.

先上汤，有浓汤和清汤两种可供选择。

4. Would you try our shrimps? They are delicious and not too spicy.

［委婉］您尝尝我们的虾好吗？味道鲜美，也不太辣。

5. Can I persuade you to try our …? It's always been a favorite with our guests.
我能劝您尝尝我们的……吗？我们的客人一直很喜欢它。

The customers inquire about the order（顾客询问点菜事宜）

1. There is no ginger in it, right? 里面没有姜吧？

2. Could I substitute potatoes for radishes?［委婉］我能把萝卜换成土豆吗？

3. Would it be possible to have fish instead of prawns?［委婉］能不能把虾换成鱼？

4. Could you please describe the Veal Marsala?［委婉］能介绍一下玛沙拉小牛肉吗？

Discussion between customers（顾客间讨论点什么菜）

1. Let's have a look at the menu. 让我们看看菜单。

2. What do you feel like? 你想来点什么？

3. What shall we order? Have you made up your mind? 点什么？你决定了吗？

4. I'm starving. I could eat anything. 我饿极了，我什么都能吃。

5. Well, I think I'll have veal cutlet. Who could resist it? 嗯，我想要小牛肉片，谁不爱吃？

6. I'm not keen on … I'm on a diet/I'm trying to lose weight, you know.
我不想要……，你知道我正在试着减肥。

Order for dinner（正餐点菜）

1. The braised mutton dinner for me, please. 请给我来一份香焖羊肉饭。

2. —How would you like your steak done? 您的牛排想要几分熟？
—Medium rare, please. 请给我做四分熟。

【注意】在描述牛排的生熟程度时，以五分熟为标尺，medium 意为"中等的"，所以五分熟的表达就是 medium。五分熟再熟一点 medium well，即七分熟；五分熟再生一点 medium rare，即四分熟；四分熟再生一点 rare，即三分熟；如果彻底熟了就是 well done，即全熟。

3. —With or without garlic? 要不要大蒜？
—A little bit, please. But make sure there's no MSG in it. It's important that you do because I'm allergic to MSG.
请少来一点。但一定不要放味精。你千万别忘了，因为我对味精过敏。

4. —What would you like to start with? 您先来点什么？
—Mushroom soup/Borsch. 蘑菇汤/罗宋汤。

5. —And for your main course? 主菜您想吃什么？
—I think I'll try the shrimps. 我想要尝尝虾。

6. —Would you like something to drink with your meal? 你想配点什么喝的吗？
—A dark beer, please. 来一杯黑啤吧。

7. —And dessert? 甜点呢？
—I'll have an ice-cream, vanilla. 我来份冰激凌，香草味的。

8. I'd like to start with shrimp cocktail, then an onion soup. For the main course, I'd like a veal cutlet with creamed potatoes and beans. No sweet for me, I'd have biscuits and cheese instead, with some black coffee afterwards. 我想先来个虾仁杯，再来一个洋葱汤，

主菜我要小牛肉片加奶油土豆和豆子。我不要甜食，改为饼干和奶酪，最后来点清咖啡。

Order for breakfast（早餐点菜）

1. I'd like to order a full breakfast, please.［委婉］我要一份全套早餐。

2. —What kind of juice would you like, sir? 先生，您要哪种果汁？

   —French orange juice. 法国橙汁。

3. —Bacon, sausage or ham? 培根、香肠还是火腿？

   —An order of Ham, please. 请给我一份火腿。

4. —How would you like your eggs done? 您的蛋要怎么做？

   —Two fried eggs, sunny side up. 两个煎鸡蛋，单煎一面。

（注意：鸡蛋的做法有以下几种，over 指煎两面蛋；sunny side up 煎一面的蛋；poached egg 荷包蛋，poached ［pəutʃ］ adj. 水煮的；over easy 煎半熟蛋；over hard 煎全熟蛋；scramble egg 炒蛋；boiled egg 煮蛋）

5. I'll start with tomato juice, and then two boiled eggs, a buttered toast and a cup of black tea. 我先要番茄汁，再要两个煮鸡蛋，一份黄油烤面包和一杯红茶。

6. Just a pancake, please. 只要一个烙饼。

7. Just a bowl of oatmeal for me. 我只要一碗燕麦粥。

8. Tea and muffins for me. 我要茶和松饼。

Repast（就餐）

Advice to waiter（对服务员提出意见）

1. The steak is overdone, and it is practically cold. 这牛排煎得太老了，而且也差不多凉了。

2. These carrots are not cooked enough. 这些胡萝卜煮得不够熟。

3. I like my coffee real hot, but this is only lukewarm. 我喜欢喝热咖啡，可这只有点温。

4. The soup is much too thick/clear for me. 我觉得这汤太稠/稀了。

5. There's been a mistake. I asked for beef, not pork.

   菜送错了，我要的是牛肉，不是猪肉。

6. I think you've made a mistake. This isn't what I ordered. 我想你们弄错了，这不是我点的菜。

7. We've been waiting for half an hour. What has happened to our order?

   我们已经等了半个小时。我们点的菜怎么样了？

8. We're in a hurry. Please rush our orders. 我们时间很紧，请催一下我们的菜。

9. I must tell you I'm disappointed with your service. 我必须告诉你，我对你们的服务很失望。

10. Can I see the manager? 我能见见经理吗？

The waiter informs that certain dish is out of stock（服务员告知某菜品缺货）

1. I'm very sorry, sir, but we have no more herring left.

   先生，很抱歉，可是我们的鲱鱼已经卖完了。

2. I'm very sorry, madam. The Romany Beef is not being served any longer.

   很抱歉，女士，罗曼尼牛肉不再供应了。

3. Would you like to change it for something else?［委婉］您是否愿意换个别的什么？

The waiter acknowledges the mistake（服务员认错）

1. I'm really sorry indeed that this has happened. 发生了这样的事，我非常抱歉。

2. I'm sorry I must have confused the orders. What did you want?
   对不起，我一定是把菜单搞混了。您点的是什么？

3. I'm sorry. Let me take this back and bring you another one.
   对不起，让我把这个拿走，再给您上一份。

4. I'm terribly sorry. Do you wish to try something else? That would be on the house，of course.［委婉］我非常抱歉。您愿意尝尝别的什么吗？当然，那将是免费的。

Apologies from the manager（经理道歉）

1. I do apologize for this inconvenience. 给您造成这种不便，我深表歉意。

2. We'll certainly see what we can do about it. 我们肯定要尽力去想办法。

3. I'll see that it's changed right away. 我一定关照让人马上换掉。

4. I'll attend to it right away. 我马上处理这事。

Leave the table（离席）

1. Excuse me. 对不起。

2. May I be excused? 可以走开一下吗？

3. I'll just go and tidy myself up.［女士用语］我想去收拾一下。

4. I'll just go and powder my nose.［女士用语］我想去打扮一下。

【注意】社交场合，一般客人起身这么说，主人就明白大概是要去洗手间。如询问他人是否去洗手间，可以说 Do you want to wash up?

After dinner（餐后）

Ask the waiter to check out（叫服务员结账）

1. Waiter，let me have the bill. 服务员，给我账单。

2. Will you bring the bill? 你是否能把账单拿来？

3. May I have the check，please? 可以把账单给我吗？

4. Can we have a doggie bag? 能给我们一个食品袋吗？

【注意】吃不完的食物，可以向服务员要一个口袋打好包带回家。尽管叫作 "doggie bag"，但带回的东西还是自己吃的。

Bill problems（账单的问题）

1. Could you explain this to me? What's item 3?
   ［委婉］你能为我解释一下吗？第三项是什么？

2. Is service included in the check/bill? 服务费包括在账单内吗？

3. I think there's a mistake here. You've charged me twice for the same thing.
   我想这里弄错了。同一样东西你们重复收费了。

Tipping（支付小费）

1. Keep the change. 零钱别找了。

2. We enjoy your service. 我们对你的服务很满意。

3. Thanks for your good service. 感谢你的优质服务。

Customers pay the bill 顾客付账

One person pays the bill（一人付账）

1. Here，let me pay. 让我来付账。

2. This will be my treat. 这次我请客。

3. It's on me this time. 这次我付账。

4. No，this is on me. 不行，这次该我付。

5. Next time. This time you're my guest. 下次吧，这次你是我的客人。

6. Let me pay today. You can pay next time. 今天我来付，下次你来。

7. Don't argue about such a small sum of money. Your treat next time，OK?

   这么点钱就别争了。下次你请，好吗？

8. At least let me leave the tip. 至少让我付小费。

Go dutch（各付各的）

1. Let me pay for my share. 让我付自己这份。

2. Better each pay for his own. 最好各付各的。

3. We might just as well go dutch. 我们最好还是各付各的。

4. Let me pay the bill first if you don't mind. I'll settle with you later.

   如果不介意的话，我先付账，之后我和你们算。

【注意】在西方国家，朋友们一起去饭店吃饭是各付各的，还是一人请客都是事先说明的，服务员在顾客点菜时也经常主动询问"是否分开记账？"如：Separate checks? /Do you want that on separate checks? /Shall I make out two checks? /Would you care to have separate bills or one common bill?

Section Five：Culture Tips

西方酒吧文化简介

酒吧间，美国人叫 bar，英国人叫 pub，是人们喝酒、娱乐的场所。营业时间，一般从上午 11:00 到下午 2:30，再从下午 6:00 到晚上 10:30 或 11:00。酒吧间供应啤酒、白酒、果汁、沙拉和肉类等。儿童不允许进店，对不满 18 周岁的青少年不供应含酒精的饮料。饮料供应一般在柜台上进行。顾客每点一次，就得付一次钱，而不是在吃完离开的时候一次付清。到柜台上去买饮料可以不用给小费，如果服务员把饮料送到桌子边，就得付小费。小费的金额一般为餐费的 10%～15%。如果你对服务和食品非常满意，就多给点儿，否则就少给。小费可付给服务员，但一般放在桌上或压在盘子下面。有的酒吧间还提供一些娱乐活动，如音乐节目、电子游戏等。

译　文

第二部分：相关信息

餐桌礼仪

在商界，你经常需要参加各种各样的聚会。这里有一些关于良好的餐桌礼仪的指导，将帮助你在任何正式或半正式的午餐或晚宴场合下用餐。

1. 展开餐巾，放在膝盖上

落座后，不时用它擦一下你的嘴唇或手指。晚餐结束时，把餐巾整齐地放在之前摆放的地方。

2. 按次序等候上餐

在餐桌上，按照传统，先为最年长的女士上餐，然后是其他女士，最后是男士们。直到女主人开始吃东西，你才可以开始用餐。

3. 使用餐具

如果盘子旁边有很多不同的餐具，使用时要按照从外往里的顺序。如果有疑问，可以看看其他客人在做什么。拿着刀叉时，将把手放在掌心，食指放在上面，拇指放在下面。用餐时，在咀嚼过程中，把刀叉放在盘子的两边。当你吃完后，把它们并排放在盘子的中央。

4. 尝一尝食物

如果有你不喜欢吃的菜，那么礼貌的做法是至少尝一下。或者最起码把它切一点，然后在盘子里挪动一下。如果你吃饱了，把食物放在盘子的一边是完全可以让人接受的。从另一方面来讲，不要试图把你的盘子弄得那么干净，看起来就像你好几天没吃东西了！

5. 与周围的客人进行礼貌的交谈

晚宴不仅仅是为了吃，还为了社交。

6. 表达感谢

在离开前要向主人和女主人表示感谢。

7. 书面感谢

稍后给主人和女主人寄一封亲笔信，感谢与他们共度的愉快夜晚。

第三部分：情境任务范例

情境： 一天，李欣和他的妻子刘倩打算去餐厅吃饭。（A：李欣；B：刘倩；C：男服务员；D：女服务员）

选择餐厅

A：我今天想出去吃饭。

B：你说我们去哪儿呢？

A：咱们去吃西餐吧。

B：米罗阳光怎么样，那儿的披萨很不错。

A：好的，走吧。

在餐厅

等候座位

C：晚上好，请问您有预订吗？

A：我们没有预订，还有空桌位吗？

C：很抱歉桌位现在都满了，你们介意等一会儿吗？

B：我们需要等很久吗？

C：要不了多久，大约五到十分钟。

B：好的。

......

C：很抱歉让您久等了，我这就带您入座。这是菜单，服务员马上就来。

B：谢谢你。

点菜

D：我可以听候您点菜了吗？

A：你建议我们吃点儿什么？

D：今天的特色菜是烤虾，我们的顾客们一直很喜欢它。

B：好的，那我们就尝尝烤虾。

D：您先来点什么？

A：帕尔玛蜜瓜火腿。

D：接下来再点什么？

B：黑胡椒牛肉披萨。

A：请给我来一份牛排。

D：您想喝点儿什么吗？

B：西瓜汁。

A：我想要红酒。

D：甜点呢？

A：我想我们要草莓冰激凌吧。

D：好的。

餐中

D：对不起，女士，我们没有西瓜汁了，您能换别的吗？

B：那么请给我来橙汁吧。

A：一定是搞错了，我要的是红酒，不是科罗娜。

D：对不起，我一定是把订单搞混了。让我把这个拿回去再给您拿红酒来。

A：没关系。

餐后

A：请把账单给我好吗？

D：给您，先生。总计85美元。

A：付给你还是到款台结账？

D：都可以。

A：这里是100美元，零钱别找了。

D：非常感谢！

8. 4. 3 Banquet

Section One: Tasks

Situation 1: *Zhang Liang is the executive director of GEK. He is calling the Hilton Hotel to make a reservation for the company's annual meeting. Make a dialogue according to the situation.*

Situation 2: *At the banquet, Zhang Liang is receiving Mr. and Mrs. Wade, the VIP customer of the company. Make a dialogue according to the situation.*

Situation 3: *Imagine you were Mr. Cotton, the president of the company, give a speech at the beginning of the banquet.*

Section Two: Related Information

Banquet

A banquet dinner is usually a formal, sit-down meal for a large group of people (more than 25), for occasions such as corporate events, weddings, dinner rehearsals, retirements, business meetings or conferences, reunions, birthdays or anniversaries, fund raisers, award ceremonies, auctions etc. [1]

Banquets are usually held at restaurants, conference centers or hotels. As well as a lavish meal, a banquet dinner usually also includes a number of speeches and some entertainment such as bands, singers, comedians, DJs or orchestras. Some banquet halls also offer themed dining such as medieval dining and princess dining. [2]

When you book a banquet dinner, the order would contain a rundown of the exact information of what you are paying for. This will include date, place and type of the banquet, number of guests, timeline of guests' arrivals, speeches and presentations, cocktails, appetizers, entrees, desserts, toasts, aperitif services, entertainments, bar services etc. [3]

Banquet meals are usually lavish and sumptuous. Dishes in common banquet usually include appetizers, main courses[4], desserts and drinks. Banquet servers will ensure that food and drinks get to the guest tables promptly. If the dinner is a buffet meal, they will keep the buffet well stocked. If the banquet involves cocktail service, the banquet servers will make sure that the drinks and finger food[5] keep circulating.

Vocabulary

banquet ['bæŋkwɪt] *n*. 宴会；盛宴

rehearsal [rɪ'hɜːs(ə)l] *n*. 排演；预演

retirement [rɪ'taɪəm(ə)nt] *n*. 退休；退役

reunion [riː'juːnjən] *n*. 重聚；（班级或学校的）同学会；同窗会

anniversary [ˌænɪ'vɜːs(ə)rɪ] *n*. 周年纪念日

auction ['ɔːkʃ(ə)n] *n*. 拍卖

lavish ['lævɪʃ] *adj.* 丰富的

band [bænd] *n.* 乐队

comedian [kə'miːdɪən] *n.* 喜剧演员；滑稽人物

orchestra ['ɔːkɪstrə] *n.* 管弦乐队

medieval [ˌmedi'iːvl] *adj.* 中世纪的；原始的

rundown ['rʌndaun] *n.* 纲要

cocktail ['kɒkteɪl] *n.* 鸡尾酒

appetizer ['æpɪtaɪzə] *n.* 开胃物，开胃食品

entree ['ɒntreɪ] *n.* 主菜

dessert [dɪ'zɜːt] *n.* 餐后甜点；甜点心

toast [təust] *n.* 土司；烤面包；

aperitif [ə'perɪtiːf] *n.* 开胃酒

sumptuous ['sʌm(p)tjuəs] *adj.* 豪华的；奢侈的

buffet ['bʌfɪt] *n.* 自助餐

Notes

1. A banquet dinner is usually a formal, sit-down meal for a large group of people (more than 25), for occasions such as corporate events, weddings, dinner rehearsals, retirements, business meetings or conferences, reunions, birthdays or anniversaries, fund raisers, award ceremonies, auctions etc. 宴会通常是为一大群人（超过 25 人）举行的正式聚餐，用于举行公司活动、婚礼、晚宴彩排、退休、商务会议或大型会议、团聚、生日或周年纪念、筹款、颁奖典礼、拍卖等场合。fund raiser 筹款；award ceremony 颁奖典礼

2. Some banquet halls also offer themed dining such as medieval dining and princess dining. 一些宴会厅还提供主题餐饮，如中世纪风格餐会和公主风格餐会。themed dining 主题餐饮；medieval dining 中世纪风格餐会；princess dining 公主风格餐会

3. This will include date, place and type of the banquet; number of guests, timeline of guests' arrivals, speeches and presentations, cocktails, appetizers, entrees, desserts, toasts, aperitif services, entertainments, bar services etc. 这将包括：事件的日期和地点、宴会类型、客人的数量、客人到达的时间、演讲和演示、鸡尾酒、开胃菜、主菜、甜点、面包、开胃酒服务、娱乐、酒吧服务等。

4. main course 主菜

5. finger food 小吃，手抓食物

Section Three: Situational Task Samples

Situation: *ABC Company was going to hold a 10-year anniversary banquet. Li Xin, the administrative assistant, was booking a banquet. Then the banquet was held as scheduled. Mr. and Mrs. Stewart, clients of the company, came to the banquet. Mr. Reed, the president of the ABC Company welcomed them and also gave a short opening speech.（A:*

Hotel reservation receptionist；B：Li Xin；C：Mr. Steward；D：Mr. Reed，the president of ABC Company.）

Reserve a banquet

A：Good morning, banquet reservation. What can I do for you?

B：Yes, I'd like to book a banquet for next Thursday.

A：What would you like, Chinese, Western, French or Japanese cuisine[1]?

B：That would be Western.

A：For how many people?

B：Let me see. About 60 people.

A：When will the banquet begin?

B：At 7 p. m.

A：We happen to have a deluxe hall that can hold 80 people.

B：OK.

A：How much would you like to spend per head?

B：Around $80.

A：OK. May I know your name, please?

B：Oh, yes, Li Xin. L-I Li, X-I-N Xin.

A：Thank you. So the reservation is made by Mr. Li Xin, a western banquet for about 60 at 6 p. m. next Thursday.

B：Thank you.

During the banquet

B：Good evening, Mr. and Mrs. Steward. How nice to see you.

C：Thank you for inviting us.

B：What would you like to drink?

C：Two glasses of wine, please.

B：OK. Come, I want you to meet the others. Gentlemen, I'm very pleased to introduce our Canadian friends Mr. and Mrs. Steward. This is our president, Mr. Reed.

D：I'm so glad you could come.

C：Well, I've been looking forward to getting together.

...

D (To all)：We are very much honored and pleased to give a banquet this evening here in honor of[2] celebrating the 10-year anniversary of our ABC Company. Our company has made great progress[3] in the past ten years. Our trade involves various fields, and has been extended to more than 10 countries abroad. Today, we are gathered here to celebrate the 10th anniversary founding of the company. On behalf of[4] the company, I would like to express my heartfelt thanks to all our customers, staff and shareholders[5].

...

C：Thank you so much, Mr. Reed. It's been a wonderful evening.

D：I'm glad you come to attend our celebration. I hope we can have more cooperation in the future.

C：I'm sure we will. We are full of confidence in your company.

Notes

1. cuisine 菜肴

2. in honor of 为了纪念……；为了向……表示敬意

3. make great progress 取得巨大的进步

4. on behalf of 代表……

5. shareholder 股东

Section Four：Functional Expression Bank

Welcome the guest（迎宾）

1. I'm delighted to see you. Welcome！［正式］见到您很高兴。欢迎！

2. Hello. It's a pleasure to see you again.［正式］您好，真高兴再次见到您。

3. I'm so glad/happy you could come. 您能来我真高兴。

4. Good evening, Mr. and Mrs. Brown. How nice to see you！
   晚上好，布朗先生和夫人。见到你们真高兴。

5. Good evening, Mr. Wang. Come on in！It's nice to see you again.
   晚上好，王先生。快进来，真高兴与您再次相见。

Reply of the guest（客人应答）

1. It's nice to be here. 能来这里真好。

2. Well，I've been looking forward to seeing you/getting together.
   哦，我一直盼望见到你/大家能聚聚。

3. Thank you for inviting me. 谢谢你邀请我。

4. Thank you. I've been looking forward to your party/this evening.
   谢谢，我一直盼望你的这次聚会/今天晚上。

Host the guest（主人应酬）

1. What would you like to drink？［委婉］你想喝什么？

2. Why don't you get something to drink and find a place where we can talk？
   为什么不喝点什么，然后咱们找个地方谈谈？

3. Have a glass of wine，please！Let's go over and meet some of them. This is…
   请拿杯酒，咱们过去见见他们一些人。这位是……

4. Come，I want you to meet the other guests. Gentlemen，I'm very pleased to introduce
   our Australian friends…This is… 请过来，我想让你们见见其他客人。诸位，我很高兴给
   大家介绍我们的澳大利亚朋友。这位是……

5. I'm sorry. I have to take Mr. Carter away. Here's another important man，Mr. Reed,
   the CEO of the ABC company.
   对不起，我得把卡特先生请走，又来了位大人物，ABC公司的首席执行官里德先生。

6. There's the Chairman of 6M Company，Mr. Clinton，coming this way. The woman

behind him is his assistant, Miss Miller. I'll introduce you. 向这边走来的是 6M 公司的董事长克林顿先生，后面的是他的助理，米勒小姐。我来给你引见。

The opening words of the host（主人致辞）

1. We are very much honored and pleased to give a banquet this evening in honor of…

［正式］今天晚上我们在这里为……设宴，感到十分荣幸和愉快。

2. We are honored by the presence of so many old and new friends at the reception.

［正式］有这么多新老朋友出席此次招待会，我们感到很荣幸。

3. It's a great pleasure for me to preside at this dinner in honor of Mr. …

［正式］我非常高兴能够在这里主持为……先生举行的这次宴会。

4. At this happy juncture of bidding farewell to the year and ushering in the new, I am honored to host this dinner in honor of …

［正式］能在这辞旧迎新的时刻为……举行宴会，我感到十分荣幸。

5. Today we are especially glad and happy to receive the delegation from…

今天我们能够接待来自……的代表团，感到格外的高兴。

6. Allow me, first of all, to express my warm welcome and fraternal greetings to our distinguished guests from Germany.［正式］首先，请允许我向来自德国的贵宾表示热烈的欢迎和友好的敬意。

The opening words of the guest（宾客致辞）

1. It's great pleasure to be invited to the reception hosted by…

［正式］能应邀参加由……主办的招待会，我感到万分荣幸。

2. Please allow me to express my thanks to the host of tonight's reception.

［正式］请允许我向今晚招待会的主人表示我的感谢。

3. I'd like to extend my heartfelt thanks to Mr. Brook for his enthusiastic and friendly words.

［正式］对布鲁克先生的热情、友好的发言，我表示衷心的感谢。

4. We feel very pleased to attend your reception and have the opportunity to talk with Ms. Green about our cooperation.

［正式］我们很高兴能参加你们的招待会，并能借此机会就合作事宜和格林女士进行交谈。

5. On behalf of all the members of our mission, I would like to express our sincere thanks to Mr. Liu for inviting us to such a marvelous dinner tonight.

［正式］我谨代表我们代表团的所有成员对今晚刘先生为我们举行如此丰盛的晚宴，表示衷心的感谢。

6. Thank you for your kind words, Mr. Sharp, to which I would like to offer a few words of my own on behalf of…

［正式］夏普先生，感谢您这番亲切的话语。现在，我想代表……说几句话。

Guests thank the host after the banquet（客人散席致谢）

1. Thank you for a most pleasant evening. 谢谢你，今晚过得非常愉快。

2. It was a great party. Thank you for inviting me. 聚会很成功，谢谢你的邀请。

3. Thank you so much, Mr. Fox. It's been a wonderful evening.

十分感谢，福克斯先生，今晚过得真愉快。

Section Five: Culture Tips

宴会礼仪

生活中，我们可能需要参加各种各样的宴会，在宴会中表现得体是每一个人的必修课程。

要准时赴宴，并在赴宴前注意搭配合适的着装并修整仪容。在安排座位时，客人要听从主人的安排。坐下后，要等主人招呼大家，并且主人开始取餐时才开始进餐。取餐时不宜一次性取太多，可多次取餐。如主人为你夹菜，要表示感谢。吃东西时要注意礼貌，闭嘴并细嚼慢咽；嘴里有食物时不宜说话。取餐和用餐过程中，尽量避免餐具碰撞发出声音。当口腔或齿间留有食物残渣需要清理时，可以离席或用手、餐巾等遮住口。当有人祝酒时，应停止进餐并注意倾听。与人碰杯时，如遇主人、长辈或上级，那么杯口高度应略低于对方杯口高度。当就餐人数众多时，可同时举杯，不一定要碰杯。饮酒要适量，不能贪杯；可敬酒，但不能强行劝酒。宴会结束前应再次向主人表示感谢。

译 文

第二部分：相关信息

宴 会

宴会通常是为一大群人（超过 25 人）举行的正式聚餐，用于举行公司活动、婚礼、晚宴彩排、退休、商务会议或大型会议、团聚、生日或周年纪念、筹款、颁奖典礼、拍卖等场合。

宴会通常在餐厅、会议中心或酒店举行。除了丰盛的饭菜外，宴会通常还包括一些演讲和娱乐活动，如乐队、歌手、喜剧演员、DJ 或管弦乐队。一些宴会厅还提供主题餐饮，如中世纪风格餐会和公主风格餐会。

当你预订宴会晚餐时，订单将包含你所要支付的确切信息的纲要。这将包括：事件的日期、地点、宴会类型、客人的数量、客人到达的时间、演讲和演示、鸡尾酒、开胃菜、主菜、甜点、面包、开胃酒服务、娱乐、酒吧服务等。

宴会菜品通常是丰盛的。一般宴会的菜肴通常包括开胃菜、主菜、甜点和饮料。宴会服务员要确保食物和饮料迅速送到客人桌上。如果晚宴是自助餐，他们要确保自助餐食物的充足。如果宴会涉及鸡尾酒服务，宴会服务员要确保饮料和零食的供应。

第三部分：情境任务范例

ABC 公司准备举行十周年庆祝宴会。行政助理李欣正在预订宴会。宴会如期举行，公司的客户斯图尔特夫妇前来参加。ABC 公司总裁里德先生欢迎他们的到来，并致简短的开幕词。（A：酒店预订接待员；B：李欣；C：斯图尔特先生；D：ABC 公司总裁里德先生）

预订宴会

A：早上好，宴会预订。能为您做点什么？

B：是的，我想订一个下星期四的宴会。

A：您想订什么菜系，中式，西式，法式还是日式？

B：西式的。

A：有多少人？

B：让我想想。大约 60 人。

A：宴会几点开始？

B：晚上七点。

A：我们恰好有一间豪华厅，可以容纳 80 人。

B：好的。

A：您想每个人花多少钱？

B：大约 80 美元。

A：好的。请问您叫什么名字？

B：李欣，L-I 李，X-I-N 欣。

A：谢谢。所以李欣先生的预订为下星期四下午 6 点，约 60 个人的西餐宴会。

B：谢谢你。

宴会期间

B：晚上好，斯图尔特先生和夫人。见到你们真高兴。

C：谢谢你邀请我们。

B：你们想喝什么？

C：请来两杯酒。

B：好的。请过来，我想让您见见其他人。诸位，我很高兴给大家介绍我们的加拿大朋友斯图尔特先生和夫人。这位是我们公司的总裁，里德先生。

D：你们能来我很高兴。

C：哦，我一直盼望大家能聚聚。

……

D（致所有人）：今天晚上我们在这里设宴庆祝我们 ABC 公司成立十周年，感到十分荣幸和愉快。我们公司在这十年里已经有了长足的发展。我们的贸易涉及多个领域，范围已经拓展到海外十多个国家。今天，我们在这里欢聚一堂，庆祝公司成立十周年。在此我谨代表公司，向所有客户、全体员工以及各位股东表示衷心的感谢！

……

C：十分感谢，里德先生，今天晚上过得真开心。

D：很高兴您能来参加我们此次庆典。希望我们能够在未来有更进一步的合作。

C：一定会的，我对贵公司的前景充满了希望。

References

[1] 房玉靖，刘晓春，马峥.实用英语口语.第3版.北京：清华大学出版社，2018.

[2] Amanda Crandell J.商务英语情景口语100主题.许卉艳译.北京：外文出版社，2014.

[3] 约翰·兰甘，佐伊·奥尔布赖特.美国大学英语写作.北京：世界图书出版公司，2017.

[4] 创想外语研发团队.酒店英语口语实例大全.北京：中国纺织出版社，2016.

[5] 徐广联.当代高级英语语法.第2版.上海：华东理工大学出版社，2017.

[6] 张心，陈沫.面试英语口语大全字词句段.北京：机械工业出版社，2013.

[7] Ben Riggs.旅游英语口语.北京：中国对外翻译出版有限公司，2014.

[8] 梅仁毅等.英语国家社会与文化.北京：外语教学与研究出版社，2010.

[9] 耿静先.商务英语翻译教程（笔译）.第2版.北京：中国水利水电出版社，2010.

[10] 蒋秉章，老青.新航标职业英语.北京：北京语言大学出版社，2017.

[11] 许德金.实操商务英语教程.北京：首都经济贸易大学出版社，2009.

[12] 翟象俊，余建中，陈永捷，姜荷梅.21世纪实用英语.上海：复旦大学出版社，2014.

[13] 宿荣江，曹丽珊，周媛.会展实用英语.北京：中国人民大学出版社，2008.

[14] 孙万彪，王恩铭.高级翻译教程.上海：上海外语教育出版社，2003.

[15] 梅德明.高级口译教程.上海：上海外语教育出版社，2003.

[16] 徐小贞，赵敏懿，刘建珠.商务现场口译.北京：外语教学与研究出版社，2009.

[17] 范革新.英语教学策略与方法.北京：知识出版社，2004.

[18] 熊建衡，赵织雯.当代英语交际指南.上海：上海译文出版社，1994.

[19] Mary Ellen Guffey, Richard Almonte. Essentials of Business Communication, Fifth Canadian Edition. Canada：Southwestern Educational Publishing，2004.